car
February 1967 2s 6d
£9130? p25!
(You may prefer
our £669 Ford,
test-matched
with the Viva: p39)
car
heart-throb duet
Marcos v
Elan
VPO 321F
C000100880
car
MAY 1972 20P
SCOOP!
VW's SECRET
BEETLE-
CRUSHER
the engine's
in the middle
& the line
falls on the right
car
SEPTEMBER 1973 30P AUS75c NZ80c SA77c
RACING:
THE £MILLION
YAWN
Shell
17
CIBIE
CIBIE

THE BEST OF car THE '60s & '70s

First published in the United Kingdom in 2007 by
Portico
10 Southcombe Street
London
W14 0RA

An imprint of Anova Books Company Ltd

The publishers would like to thank all the models who participated in the photo-shoots contained within this book.

ISBN 10: 1 90603 220 3
ISBN 13: 9781906032203

A CIP catalogue record for this book is available from the British Library.

10 9 8 7 6 5 4 3 2 1

Reproduction by Rival Colour Ltd., London
Printed and bound by Artes Graficas, Toledo, Spain

This book can be ordered direct from the publisher.
Contact the marketing department, but try your bookshop first.

www.anovabooks.com

CONTENTS

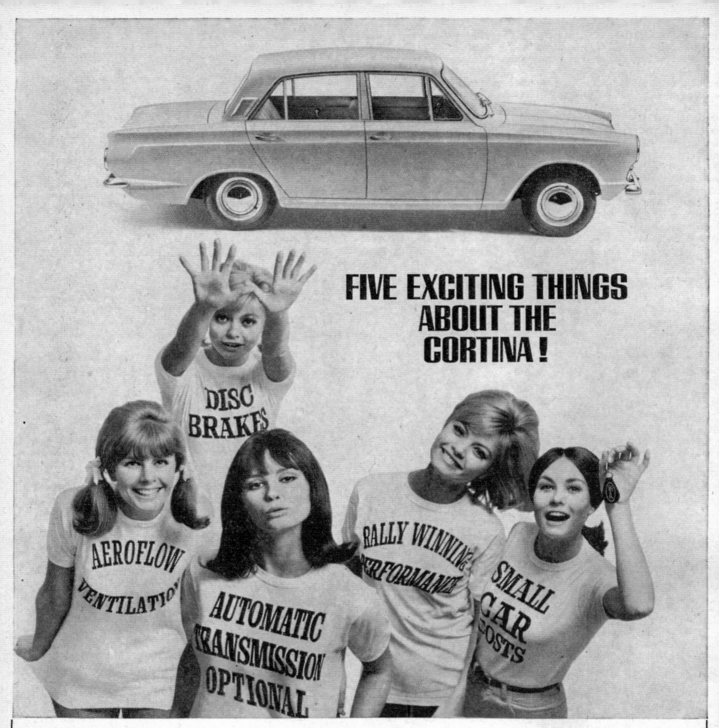

FIVE EXCITING THINGS ABOUT THE CORTINA!

The Cortina is full of exciting new ideas. 'AEROFLOW' VENTILATION an inspired new way to ventilate and heat the whole car with the windows closed. An AUTOMATIC TRANSMISSION option which gives you the lowest-priced family car with this feature. A RALLY WINNING PERFORMANCE that's the toast of race and rally drivers the world over and, to match this performance, fade-free DISC BRAKES. All of these, plus big car comfort for five lively teenagers—or their dads—at SMALL CAR COSTS.

Low first price, low running costs, low-cost service (5,000 miles or twice a year), no greasing, 12 months/12,000 miles warranty and Ford's traditional high resale value. 1,200 cc engine (1,500 cc option), all synchro gearbox, floor or column change (automatic transmission available on 1500 cc versions). Over 20 cubic feet of boot. Windscreen washers and safety belt anchorages fitted. De luxe, Super, Estate Car and high performance versions available.

Test-drive a Ford Automatic today!

INTRODUCTION

When the first issue of *Car* magazine burst onto the scene in 1965 it was into a world where the men drove Minis and the girls wore them. It was a world in which small was beautiful and Sixties' style-bible *Queen* magazine actually declared the Mini Moke more desirable than an Aston Martin DB5. For a brief period even *Car* magazine couldn't resist it, launching itself onto the unsuspecting motoring public as *Small Car* magazine. But as love affairs go, it was short-lived.

After all, there's a limit to how long you can write about nothing but Minis, Imps and Minxes, let alone want to read about them. And that limit was six months. By the July issue the prefix had been dropped, the magazine had gone through puberty and emerged as the newly invigorated hairy-chested *Car* magazine, extolling American muscle cars, and all manner of exotic, expensive Italian erotica.

Did someone mention erotica? The tone had also changed. Perhaps the editorial voice had broken or, just as likely, it was a reflection of those more innocent pre-PC days of when gay still meant 'brightly coloured' and you could be a swinger without swapping your wife. Whatever the reason, the serious motoring writers of *Car* magazine were not the least embarrassed to declare a favourite car as a 'tart trap' or 'crumpet-catcher'. And from here it was only a matter of time before glamour models first made their appearance on the cover and inside pages, draped incongruously and uncomfortably over bonnet and bootlid, once more perpetuating the male myth that cars really are 'girl-magnets'.

Advertisers were just as guilty, with long-legged, luscious lovelies used to promote everything from rust-proofing lubricants to MG Midgets, art-directed with all the finesse of a sixties' porn flick and with copy lines straight from the script of a Carry On film. Take for instance the advert for Pirelli Cinturatos. The copy line: 'Of all the hazards facing Italian drivers, two in particular stick out' is innocent enough, until you cut to the well-endowed lady cyclist with a tight fitting top. Lest we miss the pun, the photo is cropped below the neck and above the waist. If they could have done a pop-up, they would have.

The fact is sexy girls and fast cars are one of motoring's greatest clichés, and as such plenty of examples are included in this book. Well, it would have been churlish not to, wouldn't it?!

It is all the more surprising then, looking back, how, for a while at any rate, the girlie content could sit happily astride motoring journalism that was second to none. Setting the world to rights were serious writers like LJK Setright, Douglas Blain and Stirling Moss. If these chaps thought a new car was crap, they said so. They berated Ford for introducing three new Cortinas in eight years, while Volvo's latest offering was likened to a domestic appliance. No pandering to advertisers here.

At times the tone was even, dare I say it, reactionary. Regular columnist Moss was so bitterly opposed to the concept of a 70mph speed limit he produced a tear-out coupon for more apathetic readers to send off to lobby the Transport Minister Barbara Castle. Elsewhere there was much harrumphing about the affront to an Englishman's liberty when the wearing of seat belts became compulsory.

For nearly a decade *Car* magazine was a remarkably accurate barometer of its time, charting the gradual decline of British manufacturing and the rise of super powers like Germany and Japan. There's the early appearance of the BMW. In 1965 you could buy into the dream for as little as £679. Much, too, was made of the revolutionary but unfortunately named Wankel engine and the fully automatic DAF. But not all imports received a warm welcome. Who wouldn't want to own a Wartburg, for instance? Well, everyone, as it turned out.

However, perhaps the most prescient piece of journalism is the profile on the relatively young Japanese company Honda, then making a name for itself in motor racing. It is Peter Miller's introduction to '12-Year Wonder: The Honda Story' which is both unwittingly and chillingly prophetic: 'If hard-won racing victories can lead to world-wide sales domination, it's lucky 59 year-old Soichori doesn't build saloons.' Ah, well, as we now know, that's exactly what he went on to do, and the rest is history.

What now might seem like a serious case of xenophobia, was in fact a reaction to a British car industry in free fall, crippled with pay disputes and strikes and a dearth of new ideas. We even had to go to Italian design houses to try to rescue cars like the Allegro, and unashamedly named one disastrous collaboration the Morris Ital.

But in the February 1974 'Crisis Issue', *Car* tackled the biggest question of all, and one that has come back to haunt us today: 'Would you go to war to keep your car?' In an apocalyptic feature the magazine addressed the green issues that we are only now coming to terms with, forecasting when natural resources like oil would finally be depleted and at what cost to the planet. The feature concludes with the lines: 'The question should not be "How long can we last?" but "When should we change?" And the answer is ... now'.

Thirty years on that question is more relevant than ever. And so is the answer.

Roy Kent

For the Largest and Finest Selection of Speedy Motor Carriages for Sporting Gentlemen

How does she do it? We asked Laya Raki, and we'll tell you what she said when you pop out and see us on Stand 57

WHAT MAKES THE RACING CAR Show so different from the Earls Court one is that people don't necessarily go to see *new* cars. Let's be absolutely honest, the only thing that can lift the October picnic at Earls Court out of the rut for us is a luscious and varied display of revolutionary new cars with exciting styling, scintillating performance and roadholding that's a dynamic miracle. Anything less just doesn't tempt our jaded motor-noters' palates any more. We've seen it all before.

But as we said, the Racing Car Show is different. Many of the cars are the successful heroes of last year's competition. Many of the new ones are new only in a few well-tried details – a tidied up body here, a rethought-out suspension there, nothing startling: just quiet, careful development. And for the last few years the centrepiece of the exhibition has been a paddock-full of colourful racing cars from all stages of motor racing history. Glorious old dicers like Bugattis and Maseratis, Aston Martins and Sunbeams, all there to be seen and gloated over by the enthusiasts. The point is that for anyone interested in racing cars it's enough to be able to wander through an exhibition stuffed to the roof with what Bill Boddy would call accelerative sporting machinery. As somebody once said of Everest, the important thing is that they're *there*. They don't have to be new as well – we'd still go.

So imagine our surprise when the BRSCC calmly told us it won't be showing *any* of the older cars this year. Not one. Seems there's going to be less paddock space than before, since the stands are going to take up a larger proportion of the hall. Not only that, the club feels the emphasis of this year's show should rest exclusively on new cars.

Now this may well be a good idea, but we can't help feeling those old cars had something. The paddock was a splendid place to show off cars that had actually proved their worth conclusively as a contrast to the new cars on show on the stands. Quite a lot of the people who go to the show don't actually *buy* any cars, they only go to look. So what better attraction than cars whose names have been household words for a long time – cars you can't see at a race meeting? To the public a racing car is more interesting when it's got some good solid wins behind it that when it's promising but still new and unproven.

But so much for the paddock. Space is (as always) short and we must get on with telling you what's going to be on the stands this year. Let's take new cars to start with. Lola is showing two new ones: a sports-racer and the new Formula Two monocoque racing car. The sports car is designed by Eric Broadley for 200mph-plus and is based on a lighter version of the chassis used for the Lola and Ford GT cars, made from aluminium alloy and steel. Two engine options are available: the 4.7litre Ford V8 as used in the Cobra, pushing out 350bhp at 5600rpm and running up to a limit of 6700rpm, and the 90lb lighter Traco-tuned Oldsmobile which Bruce McLaren favours for his mighty McLaren banger.

The Lola racing car will be used in F2 next season by the Midland Racing Partnership works team, using the new BRM twin ohc four-cylinder Formula Two engine. The monocoque chassis holds a glass-fibre body on the track through double wishbones and coaxial coil springs front and rear. Provision is also made for the Cosworth single-overhead-cam engine as an alternative. Both engines work through a Hewland six-speed box, with different sets of ratios to order.

Jack Brabham will be showing the '65 version of his highly successful Tauranac-designed F2 racer, and his people told us they hope to have their GT Vauxhall Viva keeping it company on the stand. Jack's one-time sponsors will be there too, showing the new Type 76 1965 model Cooper-BMC F3 car. The rear suspension has been re-designed and the geometry altered to improve roadholding. Tests at Silverstone lopped 1½sec off the times of Jackie Stewart's '64 Formula Three car and Jackie himself won last September's F3 event at Oulton Park in the '65 prototype. John Cooper says he's 'quietly confident' about this year's Formula Three prospects. Time will tell, John; time will tell.

One of the interesting things about this year's show is that many firms are beginning to show the same interest in the Imp as they have for so long in the Mini. Paul Emery has done his own little bit of body surgery to the Imp, lowering its roof by six inches (screams of 'headroom' all round) and fitting two better, lower bucket seats to match. We tried the road version for a few quick circuits of Brands and there seems to be plenty of potential there (but more details next month). This version is being offered provisionally at £660, new, tax paid, which seems reasonable enough. We also saw the racing version circulating at Brands and we await its debut with interest. Demonstration cars will be available during the show, and one of Enery's bored-out Imp engines will be on the stand. This one's a 998cc model, but his organisation will supply them as big as 1148cc.

Tunex Conversions is another firm making use of Hillman's baby. The new Imp-engined Tunex car should be on show, together with the current production Diva GT.

Colchester Racing Developments has upgraded last year's Mark Seven Merlyn F2/3 racing car to the 1965 Mark Nine version, and it'll be on show in forms to suit both kinds of racing. Alfa will be there too in the guise of Halsales Motors. Halsales told us it would have a Ruddspeed Sprint GT or a Giulia TZ in full racing trim for our diversion and delight.

We can't really do more than scratch the surface of the bolt-on offerings on view – there's just space to mention that Taurus, Nerus and Viking (among others) are starting off with conversions for the Austin 1800, SAH is hoping to introduce Tecalemit-Jackson fuel injection kits for Triumph 2000 and Stage Two Spitfires, and Paddy Hopkirk is showing the latest thing in racing cuff-links.

So there we are. We've tried to rush through the enormous amount of machinery on show to give you some idea what to look for. Apart from cars and engines, there's the BP cinema showing something called 'The Time Between' that takes you behind the scenes in GP racing. There isn't a model race-track this year, but relax children – there's a model hillclimb instead. Four classes (sports, racing, GT or saloon) with a prize for ftd in each class and a cup for overall ftw.

See you on the starting line! ✱

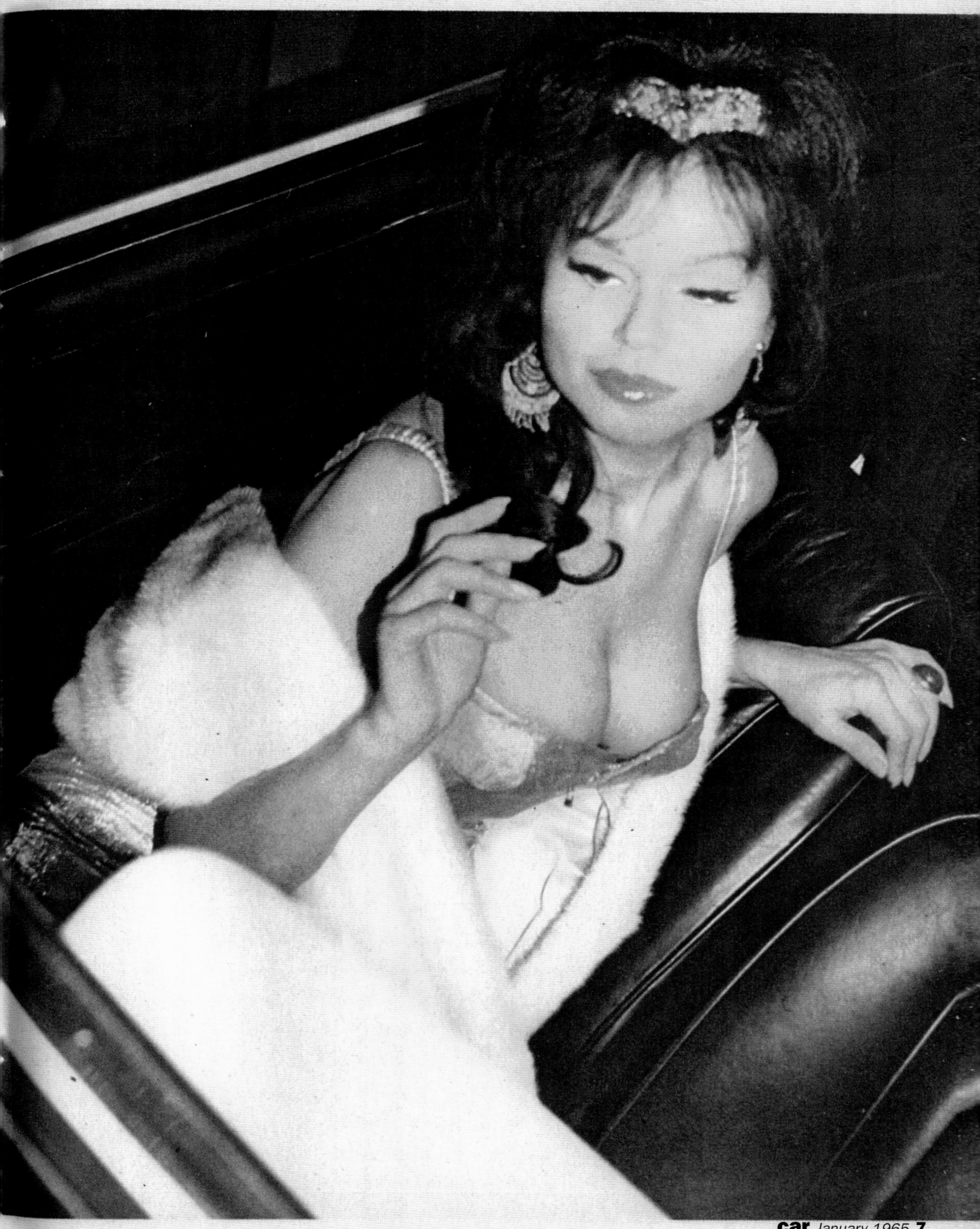

If hard-won racing victories can lead to worldwide sales domination, it's lucky 59year-old Soichiro doesn't build saloons

12-YEAR WONDER: THE HONDA STORY

Geoff Goddard

発進前点検項目

1. スパーキングプラグ
2. ブレーキオイル
3. ブレーキ及びクラッチペダル
4. フューエルポンプ
5. フューエルレベル
6. フューエルインジェクター
7. タイヤープレッシャー
8. サスペンション
9. オイル
10. オイルキャッチタンク
11. 点検完了の旨 JACK BRABHAM に告げること。

1. *Check sparking plugs*
2. *Check brake fluid*
3. *Check brake and clutch pedals*
4. *Check fuel pump*
5. *Check fuel levels*
6. *Check fuel injectors*
7. *Check tyre pressures*
8. *Suspension check*
9. *Oil*
10. *Oil catch tank*
11. *Speak Jack Brabham*
12. *Wipe foot pedals*

Blasting into action at Nurburgring early last year (top), the V8 transverse-engined Honda GP car showed Japan's intentions despite countless minor bugs. Engine for '65 (top left) is largely unchanged. Note flexible injector gear

Above left is one of Honda's three main motorcycle plants. At right is the man himself, ageless and inscrutable, scanning intricately machined bike crank. Left: all the Honda F2 mechanics are Japanese, so there's no security problem

PETER MILLER DELVES INTO JAPAN'S BIGGEST SUCCESS STORY

Geoff Goddard

ON SUNDAY, JUNE 13, THE motor racing world might well receive a staggering oriental face-slap from the Land of the Rising Sun. On that day a sleek ivory-painted Honda Formula One car driven by Californian Richie Ginther is *actually likely* to win the Belgian Grand Prix on the ultra-fast Francorchamps circuit through the wooded Ardennes near Spa.

But even if the Japanese challenge fails at Spa, I predict that before the 1965 European season is out we shall witness a Honda victory in one of the world championship events. And when it happens, it will be the finest thing for the future of racing since Mercedes-Benz flung down the grand prix gauntlet at Rheims on July 4, 1954. Then, after a 15year break, the German team swept to a determined one-two victory in the French GP and went on to win eight out of the 11 remaining races in the 1954 and 1955 seasons.

Honda's much-rumoured entry into Formula One came to fruition, you'll recall, in last year's German GP at the Nurburgring, when a comparatively unknown American called Ronnie Bucknum was given the chance of writing a page in motor racing history. Bucknum had never raced a single-seater before, was making his debut on the tortuous 14.1mile circuit weaving round the Eifel mountains and had to face the harsh glare of publicity surrounding the V12 transverse-engined Honda. Critics smiled scornfully when an empty Coca-Cola can was lashed onto the car's tail in practice to catch oil drips from the gearbox, but that temporary expedient didn't fool the experts. Although Bucknum crashed in the closing stages of the race, he proved there and later at Monza and Watkins Glen that Honda was a serious threat. As in the world of family car sales (page 26) the smiles had turned to nervous twitches.

High-pressure work

During the winter of 1964/1965, little news leaked out of Japan about the Honda Formula One car – although it was certain a great deal of high-pressure development was going on behind closed doors at the ultra-modern £1.5m Technical Research and Development centre at Yamato, outside Tokyo. This new research institute (it was opened in 1961 and now employs 700 people) is the scene of all new Honda development work, including that on the grand prix car. In April this year it was announced that a two-car Honda F1 team would take part in all the European events of world championship status driven by Ginther and Bucknum, with motorcycle champion Jim Redman probably getting a single drive.

Industrially, the Japanese are among the quickest learners in the world. Accordingly it was obvious even before Monaco that the 1965 version of the Honda F1 car would be radically different from last year's model. As you may have seen, the 1965 cars have modified front and rear suspension, and the rather bulbous bodywork has been tidied up considerably. Although the original superb V12 transverse engine is of course retained, the new power units have overcome their earlier overheating problems and the cars should be much quicker and more reliable than before.

Before looking into the amazing rise to power of the Honda Motor Company, which since its establishment in 1948 has grown into one of Japan's major industries, it's as well to know something of its brilliant founder. Soichiro Honda, affectionately called Oyaji (Pop) by his employees, was born in a small rural village near the city of Hamamatsu in 1906. His father was a blacksmith and he grew up amid the smoke of the forge.

Honda's love of machinery goes back to his early childhood, when he first became fascinated by a diesel engine which operated a rice-milling plant near his home. He didn't enjoy school much apart from science and chemistry – but he did manage to become an excellent craftsman and metalworker by helping his father on every possible occasion in the smithy. By the time Soichiro left school at 16, his father had switched to the bicycle business and so his son became apprenticed to the Art Trading Centre – one of the few car (*sic*) repair shops in Tokyo. About 18 months after his arrival the city was levelled by the great earthquake of September 1, 1923. With the flames from the shattered buildings roaring into the air, the young mechanic was ordered to drive away one of the customers' cars by his foreman. Although he had never driven before he managed to get it out to safety without hitting any of the thousands of homeless fleeing from the catastrophe.

After the city had burned out, razing Art Trading with it, young Honda was one of the three people who stayed on rebuilding cars which had been damaged in the fire. It was then that Soichiro rode a motorbike for the first time, through the rubble-strewn streets of the devastated capital. His foreman was so confident of Honda's ability by the time he was 22 that he allowed him to use the name Art Trading when he returned home to Hamamatsu to set up his own garage business.

Meanwhile, soon after he'd arrived in Tokyo his patron had asked Honda to build him a racing car, using first a Daimler-Benz and then a Curtis aircraft engine in an American Oakland car chassis. The result was fairly successful. Back at Hamamatsu he started constructing his own racing motorbike and cars, winning a number of races himself. But his racing career came to a dramatic stop when he was 31, during the all-Japan automobile speed championships. Soichiro and his brother, who was a passenger, had a narrow escape when their supercharged Ford special somersaulted end over end after avoiding another car which pulled out of the pits.

Salvage operation

Before the start of World War Two, Honda switched over to manufacturing piston rings. But his business faltered and he had 50 employees on the payroll. To salvage the firm, he enrolled in a technical school at night studying casting while he continued to run the business by day. After two years of intense study he got the little company on its feet . . . and throughout the war he was making piston rings for cars, ships and aeroplanes until the US Air Force flattened the lot.

The remnants of the piston ring company were sold after the war and Honda tried a variety of jobs: processing salt out of sea water, developing a rotary type of weaving machine and finally picking up 500 surplus lightweight generator power plants on the cheap. The generators had been designed for portable communications equipment used by the defeated Imperial army, and Honda adapted them to power ordinary pedal cycles.

On the strength of the bicycle boom, Honda set up the Honda Motor Company with a capital of £1000 in 1948. When the war surplus stock ran out he turned to building engines himself. Five years later the company began making motorcycles; today it is the biggest producer in the world. Paid-up capital stands at well over £10 million, with the Honda family controlling 15percent of the total stock and the firm's employees holding another 30percent. The remaining 55percent is public.

Ever since the start of Honda Motor, the man behind the company's meteoric rise has devoted his life to its expansion and the welfare of its 15,000 employees. Now aged 59, Pop Honda – the balding, energetic little founder – spends a lot of his time in the research laboratories and factories, testing most of the new models at the company's proving grounds and getting into frequent technical discussions with his engineers and workers on the bench. He is often to be seen at any of the company's three plants on Japan's main island of Honshu, at Suzuka, 280 miles west of Tokyo, at Hamamatsu, or at Saitama, the nearest to Tokyo. He invariably wears a white cotton coat and striped Honda jockey cap, the standard works uniform. He could easily be mistaken for a mechanic.

Honda is obviously a firm believer in the international publicity and prestige to be gained from racing. It was in 1959 that his high-revving motorcycles with two and four-cylinder engines first entered in the Isle of Man TT races. They weren't particularly fast, but they won the manufacturers' team prize and returned the following year for a second attempt without too much success. Then in 1961 Honda machines swept to victory in two of the four world championships, dominating the 125cc and 250cc classes and starting a sensational string of victories. In the four seasons between 1961 and 1964 Honda bikes scored 80 firsts, 71 seconds and 62 third places in Grand Prix events in the 50cc, 125cc, 250cc and 350cc categories, establishing an unshakeable reputation for original design, workmanship and tenacity.

With Honda fast emerging as a major world producer of sports and passenger cars and commercial vehicles and about to embark on a full-scale UK sales operation, it's obvious that Soichiro Honda must look even more to motor racing and particularly the Grand Prix field to publicize his products. But his interest is not entirely rooted in commerce. The patron retains a very genuine interest in the sport, dating from his own racing days, and he has already entirely financed the superb new racing circuit at Suzuka. Like Enzo Ferrari, he rarely attends race meetings. Instead he expects racing director Nakamura or his assistants to send back minutely-detailed technical information immediately after each practice and the race itself. In 1964, the company spent £1.5 million on research and development into racing, including both motorbike and car programmes.

Already in the 1965 racing season it has been easy to see how the Honda challenge can sharpen in the course of a few weeks. Knowing the tremendous struggle at present being waged in Formula Two racing for single-seater cars of four cylinders with a maximum engine capacity of 1000cc (*small CAR* April), Honda has produced three engines for Jack Brabham's team. This twin overhead camshaft power plant with four valves per cylinder and fuel injection arrived with the actual engine designer, Tadashi Kume, and two mechanics, Ito and Kishi.

During the new engine's early circuit troubles, full technical details of every modification were telephoned back to Tokyo where Honda engineers had an identical engine to Brabham's running on a test rig. At Snetterton during its third race the Brabham–Honda was seventh fastest in practice, and Brabham came storming in third in the first heat. Then in the second heat he shot into the lead for the first two laps, dropped back to second for the next two and led again for the next 12 laps – astonishing the opposition with the Honda's tremendous speed. Then he was slowed by throttle linkage trouble and broken exhaust pipes and dropped out three laps from the end in third place. Before his retirement, Brabham had set a new Formula Two lap record at 103.13mph and left Honda writing on the F2 wall.

Will others follow?

The fascinating question about Honda's onslaught into the realms of motor racing is whether it will force other Japanese car and motorcyle producers to follow suit. The Isuzu Motor Company has of course already introduced saloon cars into Great Britain for production car racing under the banner of Nippon Racing and it is probable that Toyota, Suzuki and Mazda will all one day go into grand prix racing. All these are known to be waiting, though, for the change of Formula One regulations from January 1, 1966, to cater for cars with a maximum capacity of 3000cc unsupercharged or 1500cc supercharged. Honda is apparently ready and waiting for the big formula. So is Toyota. This might well throw Mercedes-Benz and some of the wealthy Americans into the battle.

In fact 1966 could see the start of one of the most exciting eras in the history of motor racing – and behind it all will be the wiry little blacksmith's son from Hamamatsu. ❋

GRAND PRIX VIEW '65

Honest Stirling Moss's guide to the British GP

THIS YEAR THE BRITISH GP see-saw swings down at its Silverstone end for the last time in the present Formula One. But even though the formula is in its last year of existence, things certainly haven't been standing still. More changes and improvements have happened since the end of last season than in the previous three years – or so it seems at the moment. There's been a big shuffle of drivers with more promising newcomers promoted from F2 racing, there's been a big increase of new machinery, and wild speculation about who's going to do well and who's going to be disappointed is all the rage just now. Certainly it's going to be very difficult to give any firm predictions on form until we've seen a few more of this year's important races – last year's events may as well have been raced under a different formula for all the use they're going to be in forecasting this year's results.

Let's start with what we *know* about the British GP. First of all, it's at Silverstone. Now Silverstone is a difficult course, because it's fast. There aren't any really vicious corners, it's a kind circuit, a good circuit from the driver's point of view. There's enough variety in the corners to make it interesting, and it's difficult enough to make you work quite hard to get round as fast as your car will let you. It's got the edge over Brands in that it *does* have high-speed corners, and you can get round at 110 mph-plus. Also five of the corners are right-angles or near right-angles. Now I like right-angles on a circuit, I think the big drawback of this new Le Mans GP circuit (even though it's beautifully engineered) is that it hasn't enough of them. After all, you get plenty of right-angles on ordinary roads, and I think a circuit should be as much like a road as possible. But I'd really like to see the British GP held on a course like Dundrod, with so much variety in its bends that it would be a proper test of top-class drivers. In fact the ideal course would be one that only had world-class drivers competing on it – no weekend club racing at all.

There are other trends you can spot to help you see the way things are developing – for instance, the F1 cars are getting much more reliable now than they were. This means that the top drivers are going to be evenly matched and they're going to have to try harder to force a convincing lead over their rivals, and this should give the more promising second-string men their chance.

The tyre war is going to be terribly, terribly important. Tyres matter so much to a racing car's performance. The difference between Dunlop green spot and Dunlop yellow spot can be as much as two or more seconds a lap for the same driver in the same car, and when you introduce unknown quantities like Goodyear and Firestone . . . well! And for my money, I think Goodyear are certainly not standing still and they may well be competitive in time.

Ferrari, as for so long, still has reliability for his long suit. While his British competitors may switch over to the new and untried Flat-16 Climax engine (though personally I think they won't – they've got too much to lose and it may well not show its full promise till the end of the season, when it'll vanish with the start of the new F1) he still has two very competitive power-plants to choose from.

Silverstone's a good circuit from the spectators' point of view too. Its flat surfaces give you a good chance to stand in just the right spot to size up the line each driver takes through the corner. And don't be fooled by what people say about each driver taking the same line through a given bend, about there being only one correct line. Each driver has to find the line that's correct for *him* and stick to it, lap after lap after lap. What's the fastest line for Fangio may not be the fastest line for you, me or Joe Soap. Watch and you'll see people like Graham Hill taking a fairly wide line through most bends. Myself, I used to take a narrow line – this let me brake slightly later. After all, cars are so alike on performance and handling that most races are won on braking these days – and it also gave more room for error in case of too much oversteer. But other people disagree, and you'll get plenty of chance to see the different theories put into practice. Don't miss it!

drawn specially for CAR magazine by Lewis Allard

LOTUS

Clark

If I was putting any money on the result, it would still go on Jimmy and Lotus as odds-on favourites. The combination of the fast and pretty reliable 33B with Jimmy's fantastic ability should prove a winner as it has so often before, although in racing, of course, nothing's certain. That's the fascination of the sport for me

Spence

Every driver, however good, likes a good team-mate to back him up – and Clark's got a good one in Spence. In a way he's doubly lucky, after Arundell's tragic crash and illness, to find such a good man so soon

BRABHAM

Brabham

Jack's big problem is reliability. However good a car is (and this one is potentially one of the very best) it won't live up to its promise until you can iron out those inevitable stupid little nagging troubles, especially in the engine and transmission. Tyres (Goodyear) could be vital here too

Gurney

I rate Dan as one of the top men in GP racing today. If he can repeat the wonderful performance he gave in the Race of the Champions at Brands a few months ago, when he was really *trying, then it's well worth the journey even if the car doesn't hold together. If it does, then he's definitely a first-place contender*

FERRARI

Surtees

John's as reliable as the cars he drives – steady, dedicated and very, very professional. If he can persuade the others to overreach themselves by trying too hard, then this could be his race. Certainly he'll try his hardest, and if his team backs him up he may yet outrun the opposition – but pit management is Ferrari's weak point

Bandini

Not what I'd call one of the top flight – but he proved me wrong in Austria last year and he may well do it again. Certainly a very competent driver, and if anyone gives him his chance he'll take it without stopping to worry about consequences

COOPER

McLaren

Bruce seems to have been off form lately – but maybe if his luck and his car had backed up his ability properly he would have done a lot better. He's always been a good place-man, but without up-to-the-minute form-pointers like Monaco I wouldn't like to tip him for a win yet. Maybe a place in the top half-dozen

Rindt

Another of those fast, tough drivers coming up from Formula Two who are making this season so interesting. He's new to GP racing, but we all saw how fast he went in the wet at Pau. If it rains it should suit Rindt down to the ground

BRM

Hill

Graham seems to have the knack of always appearing relaxed – even when he's really fighting for his position. But under the deadpan exterior, he's a fast and very smooth driver. Consistency is his strong point, though competition from Jackie Stewart may be forcing him to try almost over-hard these days

Stewart

Definitely one of the names to watch in future – though I think expecting him to walk away with a full-scale grande epreuve *in his first big-time season is asking too much. But he's fast, and if the more experienced men run into trouble Stewart'll be up among the leaders. It looks as though the car in its new form suits him well – and he had a convincing win at the May Silverstone meeting*

HONDA

Ginther

With the Honda team, everybody's talking about the car rather than the drivers. But Richie Ginther proved himself to be an excellent number two from the days when he backed Phil Hill in his world championship season. He certainly deserves his number one spot. The big question-mark is not with him

Bucknum

I wouldn't bet on Bucknum this time. He and the car and the team haven't really got the experience you have to have in GP racing to do well. But with Japanese backing, it's impossible to be sure . . .

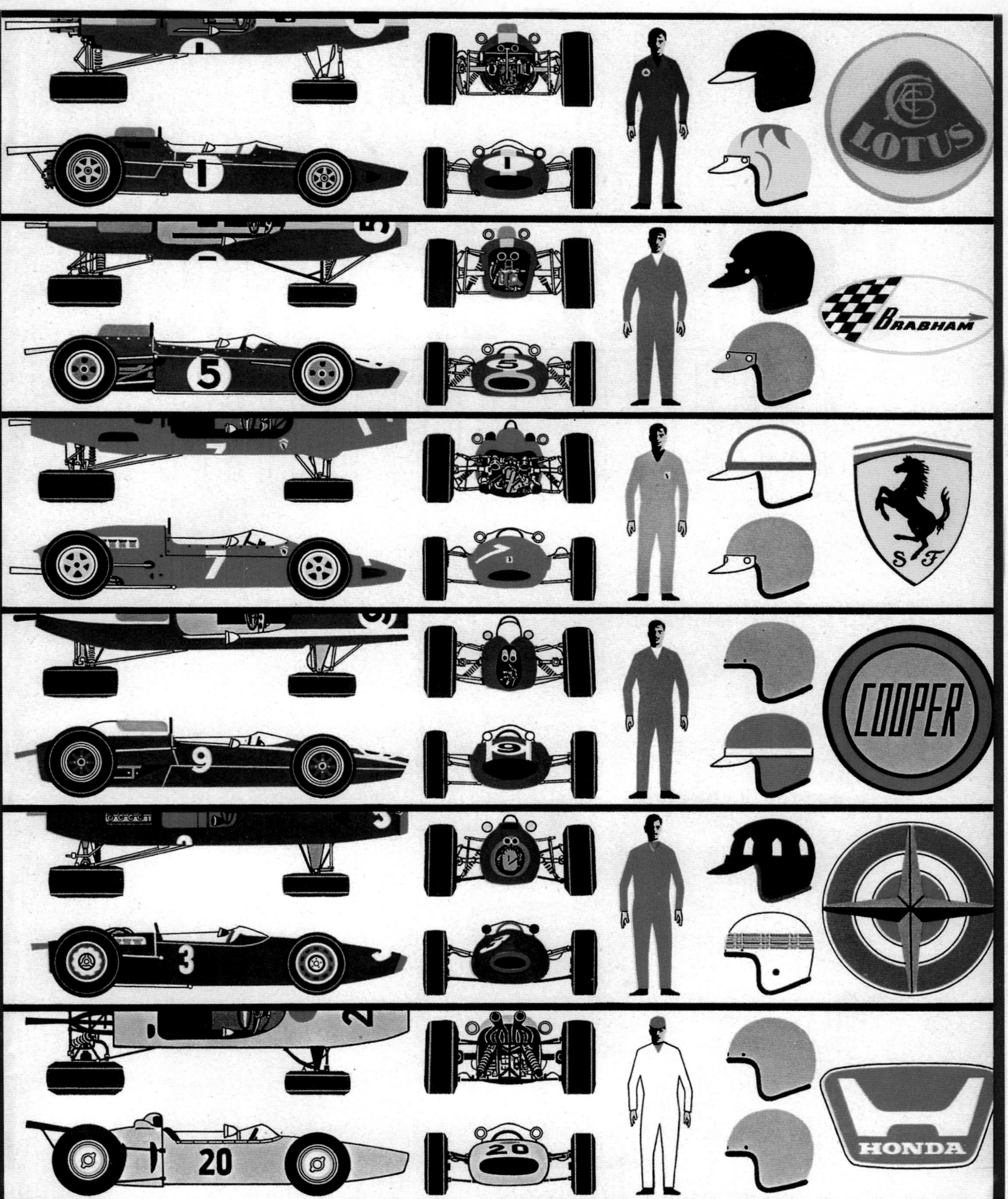
LOTUS
BRABHAM
SF
COOPER
HONDA

FOR A LONG TIME IT HAS been a closely guarded secret that most European cars are gutless. To get performance of even a reasonable level the customer has to buy one of several cad's cars with their penchants for petty troubles or else expensive and fragile sports machinery. Of course all this is the fault of the Government (cries of 'Poujade was right!') which has been exerting financial pressure practically since Boadicea invented the Coupe Saxonne to keep the English motorist trundling safely down the middle of the road at 30mph. By government diktat acceleration is minimal to keep everyone in line, horns are weak so as not to startle sleeping drivers, and until just recently only the Upper Crust in their Royces were allowed to pass. I remember testing a Flying Standard or something like that after the war and we all laughed till the tears ran down our faces at *Motocar*'s report that the acceleration was 'sparkling.' Such carriages as the Bristol and Bentley, although fearfully expensive, could be seen off by any good 1939 splash-and-dip six cylinder Chevy and the excuse of European workmanship came to naught when we saw primer showing through the paint on a new Ferrari's bootlid, the rubber parts rotting within three months on Fiats, those back-to-front cut glass Hillman gearboxes, rapidly inversible 4 CVs, and the unforgettable Goggomobil with its M Maus designed gearbox. Even the Austin A90 Atlantic didn't turn the export tide.

Okay, so the Americans built some heaps too but they were big heaps. At least they went quickly enough – sometimes too quickly if it comes to that – but I have known slow cars that handled worse. The main trouble was that they were subject to a different set of politicians who limited speed to 55mph at best and often 45mph at night but kept the price of petrol relatively cheap. The tax on it actually went into motorways, unlike some other countries I could mention. As most of the US is laid out in accordance with surveying section lines drawn straight after the Cherokees were chased off, the roads tend to be straight as well. So who needs cornering? And why not have a big engine with big bits so that Mum could sneer at the neighbours and Dad need only pay an annual visit to the garage for a set of plugs and points?

A very good idea, but Mum wanting something flashier than the neighbours caused Detroit to nigger the design up and they all got too big. Seven litres for 60mph! So certain people started driving those funny little furrin cars and Detroit Struck Back with compacts. All very well, but then we saw ads for the longest lowest compact and then compacts got as big as Fairlanes. About this time somebody in Ford Motor Company decided to take notice of a performance image (ugh), which led to Fords on the stock car tracks (where they happily motor in tight groups at 150mph), Fords at Le Mans, Fords in the Monte Carlo and Fords at the drag strips. Everyone seemed to want a slightly smaller car that looked really interesting and – voila! the Mustang. Notwithstanding its slightly nauseating name with overtones of Madison Avenue consumer manipulation, the Mustang sold well from the start in spite of (so a learned informant tells me) being really no better than any other compact in performance or handling. They could be *made* to handle, as their touring class victory in the Tour de France showed, they looked sportive, and that's what cuts the mustard as Jaguar long ago found out.

We were curious about this phenomenon, not knowing much about American cars any more, as it looked to be the answer to a motorist's prayer. Since big bits can be made stronger than little bits, there should be less of the pk screw and bent tin, mentality. Since there would be power to spare, overhauls should come a lot less often and the delicate question of passing in dense traffic would be eased. Since it was made by a big company, it should be fairly cheap. And if it wasn't as big as most American cars it should share the advantages of both camps. So we got onto George Trainor of Ford International in Brussels, suggesting that a trip to the Targa Florio would be a fair trial, and were pleased to hear that we could have his

Henry Manney in Quality Street, 2

MUSTANG RAMBLE

Our man in Paris herds Ford's 200bhp V8 to Sicily and back

289cu in (4.7litre) V8 hardtop with front disc brakes and four-speed floor-change gearbox for the voyage. Spares? Well, we'll put in a fan-belt if you must. Preparation? It'll be greased. Bring it back when you like.

I took it from Ford's Mr Kuhn in densest Paris and the Muskrat looked pretty large. Inside, it looked even larger with two theatrical bucket seats separated by a flat tray on the driveshaft tunnel plus a reasonable bench for two adults in the back. Trying to work it through traffic was a bit off-putting at first as the visibility is not too good . . . the bonnet is long, the car rises up towards the front, there are too many thick pillars . . . and the ridged edges of the wings seemed awfully far away. Soon I found that the thing could be aimed by using the central bonnet ridge as a parallax substitute for the right front wheel (lhd, remember) and this seemed to work pretty well. Having 200 horse on tap with maximum torque at 2500rpm was also a trifle unusual; applying full noise in first as is normal in the Paris GP resulted in going faster than was really necessary but it was lovely to give the chop in a definitive fashion to the pesky taxis which always try to pull their bullying act. Furthermore, the bumpers look really substantial and since most French cars dent rather easily our progress became much less nervewracking than is customary. In all this traffic, including being stopped for long periods of time, the V8 (which was the most cooking one in any case) didn't show any sign that it was even thinking of getting hot nor did it fluff once or alter its even idle. At all speeds the gearbox was likewise a pure delight to use but the clutch took a bit of learning as it is apparently a centrifugal type that grips like grim death at higher revs and needs to be pushed right down, otherwise you go rumblerumble rumbleRumbleRumbleRUMBLE RUMBLEblaaaaah as you can't get it out of gear.

Once I'd picked up photographer Geoff Goddard at Orly and got on the open road to Tournous, Bourg en Bresse, Chambery, the Mont Cenis and Turin we could use the performance a little and the car didn't seem so huge. There was a strong wind blowing that day and, frankly, we wandered all over the road as the front was hunting round in the air like an anteater and the steering was a trifle vague. More pressure in the tyres helped considerably (about 32lb) and the handbook said that up to 40lb was permissible for what it called 'precision driving'. Good grief. We whispered along using 3500 to 3700rpm (130 to 140km/h on the speedo) as we had no idea what the rev limit was in spite of a small tach being fitted and Sicily was a long way away, keeping up our speed all right through the smoother sort of main road curve but bounding about on the bumpy ones. Mechanical quietness was really exemplary at these speeds although the fan commenced to make a bit of row at 4000 (just under 100mph); wind noise was another matter and anything open produced a good deal of whistle or roar. There were handy fresh air feeds under the facia that produced a good volume of air, but there was nowhere for it to go with the windows shut . . . eventually we opened one of the rear quarter lights a bit which at least meant that the roar was behind us.

In spite of our modest pace, we were covering a lot of kilometers by virtue of mounting such ranges of hills as the Morvan after Saulieu without even noticing. The bigger Citroens or a Peugeot 404 would occasionally come thrashing up behind on their high top gears and pass triumphantly, but the slightest traffic holdup from one of the enormous lorries would bring us up on their tail again. Staggering out from behind the *poid lourd* with them, we would sit on their bootlid until they moved over and then majestically ploop by in top gear while they furiously massaged gears and pushed the champignon through the floorboard to no avail. It ➞

didn't need full throttle to manage this, nor peak revs – in fact we didn't try either until we did the acceleration figures–as it simply wasn't necessary. Weep, peasant, weep. The same sort of thing happened on the autostrade even when we had more confidence in the car and were cruising at 150–160 km/h and did our benighted souls good.

We hit a powerful rainstorm near Chambery and this continued over the Mont Cenis, unfortunately illustrating a less glamorous side of the vehicle. In twisty mountainous country the front end seems to rise up in the air on corners like a surfboard, probably from being set up front-light to further the young-America dragster image, and due to the lack of proper front adhesion we quickly felt the need to develop a method of getting the car pointed straight and then squirting it. This worked very well until the rains came and we almost went off the road three times in rapid succession. As we really weren't going fast in this section we eventually decided it was the Goodyear tyres fitted, which were not of the latest model but looked all right with plenty of sipes and tread depth. If the car were mine I would present these tyres to a canal barge for fenders; they offered less adhesion than bald Michelin Xs. At one point a mere touch of the brakes locked up the front wheels at 60mph on a dead straight highway and only the presence of an escape road meant that we didn't go straight into the ditch. Really.

The front brakes also needed a bit of sorting out as, even though they were discs, they had a combination of too-fierce servo pressure and soft pads. Incautious application in the dry would lock one or the other front wheel and this was especially noticeable at lower speeds. When we were really tramping we didn't experience any fade (even round the Targa course), but then we were consciously driving ahead of ourselves as they didn't feel as if they really gave enough straight line retardation. Again, if it were mine I would get some Cinturatos on it with wide-base wheels if possible, lop a coil out of the front springs, change the shockers to Konis (ours were very weak from the beginning, tap-dancing us all over the road on anything even remotely bumpy), put a distance piece under the top suspension pivot point to get the roll centre up, and install hard pads. Shelby puts rear axle radius arms on as well which undoubtedly are lovely but require serious carving.

While we are having our complaint section, we also thought that the door handles were poorly situated as they presented themselves for grab handles and also fouled the clutch leg while changing gears. The facia lip over the glovebox intimidated my passenger's nose, the controls are good but need a column-mounted light flasher, there are no shelves or pockets to keep odds and ends apart from a moderate-sized glovebox, and lap straps with freely folding seat backs are a menace. We should also request higher edges and perhaps partitions on the flat tunnel to keep glasses, cigs, maps etc from sliding about.

We took just a few performance figures in view of the fact that we didn't want to spend the week in Calabria, discovering in the process why there was no redline. Max power is delivered at 4400rpm and at 4500 the V8 dries up as completely as if someone had turned off the juice. Perhaps there is a governor on company cars, perhaps there are hydraulic cam followers that pump up, or perhaps the valve springs are purposely weak. The hot 289s rev to 7000 so 4500 shouldn't hurt it. Anyway, the speeds in gears were: first, 36mph; second, 54mph; third, 72mph; and fourth, flat out, 108mph. There was a funny cam effect, the only one noticeable, at about 4100rpm; it really gave an extra boot over the last 20mph or so. The speedo was quite accurate for a change, and we got 0–60mph in 11sec (in spite of axle hop) and 0–100 in 30.7. An incidental flexibility test of 40 to 80mph in top took 23sec. The two standing start times could have been improved if we had changed at 4200, I feel, but we lacked courage.

Martingale, anyone? Galloping through a fast curve, Mustang lifts its muzzle characteristically

In the saddle. Controls (below) are garishly styled but all there. Engine looks more modest

photographed by Geoff Goddard at Mont Cenis, France

Summing up, in spite of the few sordid comments above we really liked the car and felt we could live with it. The Mustang's main advantages to me are the effortless horsepower, smooth engine and gearbox, good looks, and feeling of being anything but flimsy. I am *so* tired of buzzing little tin cans worn out in a couple of years. Its main drawbacks are the uncertain suspension in rough country and the brakes which haven't been well thought out yet . . . It is also far too big still for crowded cities and English-type lanes. The suspension can be sorted out, but until somebody brings out a glassfibre bonnet dropping sharply toward the front the Mustang will still be too big.

Nevertheless, in present form it is as sporting as a few so-called Grand Touring cars I could mention and could be made better than most. Luggage space, while small by American standards, is pretty fair by European ones (not up to my Lancia, though), the driving position is as untiring as any I have tried, the rather hard seats give first class support and the fuel consumption isn't outrageous. With all sorts of running including 1500 miles on the autostrade, trips round the Targa course, getting lost in the back streets of Palermo, commuting among the race garages and winding through the mountains my shaky arithmetic shows approximately 18.6mpg. This is a little over 1·5 times the consumption of my Lancia Flavia (a quite economical car) over the same distance.

The point I am trying to make is not that the Mustang is a first class GT but that it could be. At present it gives roughly Ferrari performance up to 100mph without the expense of a Ferrari or having to resort to expensive Ferrari servicing methods. The iniquitous taxes foisted on you make the Mustang cost as much as a racing car (which it isn't); just remember that in the States they are turned out like Lyons' fruit pies to be the US equivalent of a Morris 1100. Viewed as such, the true value of the car becomes apparent. Wait for the other tests in this exotic series (last month's Lamborghini was the first) and do your own comparison.

OVER A MILLION MINIS SOLD

—BECAUSE THEY'RE MADE FOR THE TIMES YOU DRIVE IN!

You can't put the clock back. So have a Mini instead. Minis are realists in the too-little-space age. They're compact yet roomy. Fantastically lively and manoeuvrable. Easy as pie to park. Cheap to buy and run. Minis belong to the new generation of BMC cars brilliantly engineered* to preserve the pleasure of motoring in today's conditions . . . Wouldn't you feel happier — *more contemporary* — in a car like this?

AUSTIN MORRIS MINIS

BMC

*** FRONT-WHEEL POWER: TRANSVERSE ENGINE: HYDROLASTIC ® SUSPENSION**

Prices from £469.15.10 inc. tax. Backed by 12 months' Warranty and BMC Service—Express, Expert, Everywhere.

The British Motor Corporation Limited, Birmingham and Oxford Overseas Business: BMC Export Sales Limited, Birmingham and 41-46 Piccadilly, London, W.1.

photographed by Jerry Sloniger at Stresa, Italy

We join Fangio on a lighthearted exercise with the world's most luxurious limousine

REMEMBER: YOU READ IT here first. It is simply not (repeat – *not*) true that the Mercedes Benz 600 is entirely automatic. 99.44 percent power-operated perhaps, but CAR has found one feature you actually have to operate manually. Read on!

Now, isn't it a good thing we dropped the *small* in time to bring you this scoop? With the old 1800cc top limit for coverage we'd have been faced with spreading the information over four issues. Of course you can't shake all the effects of brain-washing so quickly. Here is Daimler making a proper CAR and we only test the short-chassis model – the compact as it were, leaving the Pullman to big-big big-car testers when and if they can beat us to it. In point of fact we didn't 'test' even the mini-600, all 5400lb of it. Didn't even take a Tapley to Stresa, though we did make good use of a stop watch.

This is quite understandable; makes sense for Daimler-Benz's press people to keep a wary eye on the mad types they turn loose with nearly £9000 worth of limousine, so the test consisted of some rather clogged Maggiore lakefront road and a belt down the Turin autostrada which caused no little bug-eyed wonder among the natives. On the other hand we once tried a 600 round a mickey mouse go-kart track for a couple of laps and found it handled as well as the works rally car – a fact which has since been substantiated by our man Moss, who has been seen to hurl the gentle giant fully laden round Brands within a mere few seconds of the outright saloon-car record. Even more recently, however, we have discovered that the wily D-B people were not above fitting even the 600 with track mods such as an extra 3mm front, 4mm rear on the anti-roll bars.

In a motor carriage capable of 125mph, hour in and hour out, San Marino and its used car market is not all that far from the tip of Lake Maggiore by autostrada. Hence the eagle-eyed man with bulging briefcase who rode shotgun in each of the four big Mercs as we proceeded to wring them out along the chosen route. Mind you, there is something impressive about an air-conditioned (almost) all-power boosted limousine doing a true 125 at a whisper, four up, all day long. So maybe he was just there to fill the empty seat.

In one case, though, the passenger spent most of the four hours or so holding fast to the two hand grips available with a look of stark terror on his plump, swarthy visage. He was the paunchy, balding type they brought in who during his driving spells kept using the automatic lever to change down instead of the kickdown. He relaxed noticeably when not being shown by some journalist how much faster the scribbler was than Fangio. Why? He was Fangio. As for the rest of us – well if you're going to have a chauffeur, have a Fangio.

Using Juan Manuel as outrider in one of the mighty 600s underlined the double-think among Mercedes press people. Here they make a car with front seats you can run up and down, back and forth and to any degree of tilt by waggling a small lever, back seats with an adjustable back rake/cushion tilt relationship (help! – *Ed*) power to burn, a limited slip diff and all the mods – then they call it a limousine and tell you to employ a chauffeur to enjoy it all. Seemingly, only a Fangio will do. We can see the ad now:

CHAUFFEUR WANTED
Competition licence desirable - Master's degree in hydraulics and dynamics essential. Ideal seating conditions; separate cool air outlets (must be willing to lift bonnet).

You could hardly miss getting your man with that come-on, assuming that the nasty fact about the bonnet were set in four-point Times roman and blurred a little in the printing. Because this – *this* is the big let-down. It's a sad fact that in a machine where you don't even have to push down those little buttons which lock the door – using the one by the driver's seat causes all four to sink silently from sight and we can vouch for the silence, having applied our standard decibel test as always in your service – you still have to open the bonnet in the old-fashioned, energy - consuming way. In fact the D-B 600's is trickier than most. There is the usual under-dash handle which you can't distinguish from two similar and unmarked ones, but in typical damn-the-expense style they've fitted not one but *two* safety second releases, one at each side. Perhaps we'd do well to insert another line in that advert: minimum armspan of applicants must exceed six feet. You have to unhook both catches at once, you see, and then lift most mightily.

At the other end, a simple pressure on the boot lid button and stand clear. It goes up all alone, hydraulically. Shove the button the other way and get your fingers out quick; the guillotine is descending. This sudden result when toying with the buttons appears with the side window glasses as well.

With our usual thoroughness we timed not one side window but several, averaging the runs in both directions to report that a Mercedes 600 driver's drop pane descends from zero to full open in precisely one second. Due to atmospheric conditions the return trip takes 1.5sec, with a best single recorded run of 1.4. It will also clip a cigarette (king size, mostly virginia, micro-meteorite filter) in two equal parts with no measurable delay – but only on the return run, needless to say. We couldn't find a volunteer for the finger-caught - waving - to - the - crowds experiment. In any case smokes are expensive in Italy and tobacco grains were clogging the mechanism already.

Incidentally, this was far from idle play – or at least if it was we were in good company. On a recent important visit of a certain royal personage to Germany an unnamed but reliable source caught a certain prince who shall be nameless running the seats up and down when his wife wasn't expecting it. This may explain (a whole new theory of protocol is being unfolded here) why the two rode in different cars most of the time. Anyway it might interest you to know that, although D-B had a hydraulics engineer in constant attendance, the press department claims it was *not* the new 600 which suffered full stoppage during the tour but a much older and more heavily used 300. And anyway, it was only a battery cable short, not a mechanical failure – again according to the authorised version. This doesn't explain that embarrassing *Daily Express* picture showing, unmistakably, the back end of a new Pullman being pushed away.

But back to these push-buttons. You can't have your state limousine being unreliable. One coup in the wilds and the choice of the people gets his head stuck through the window and the button pushed because he couldn't get underway and out in time. Yet have no fear, you selfless toilers for the social good. D-B has thought of everything. A recess in the boot wall is filled with a tailored kit of parts for the hydraulic system which you'll probably never use anyway. Certainly we would far rather change some of these connections than replace a fan belt in the underbonnet maze. Somewhere under there lies a 6329cc V8 putting out 300 SAE hp at a quiet 4100rpm, but it takes a keen eye and a well-trained →

truffle bound to find it beneath the pumps, compressors and finned extras.

The other end is well filled with nearly 25 gallons of the super fuel this super motorway cruiser consumes at about 12 mpg if you flog it. But with a massive 900 by 15 Super Sport Firestone tucked in the tail as well, luggage capacity isn't all that impressive. No doubt the theory accords with the previous Duke of Bedford's: that any man who can afford a 600 can buy a Rolls to follow with the golf sticks. Or maybe they had a shrewd idea where the cars would sell. One choice field of opportunity is apparently Hong Kong where you don't need much luggage for any trip you might possibly make as owner of the largest newspaper in town. He bought one, anyway, and, face being what it is out there, the owner of the other biggest paper bought one too. There is no confirmation but good reason to believe that proletarian toiler Mao has even ordered one under a pen name. In any case a good chunk of his cash did purchase a 600 indirectly – for the North Korean Ambassador to Algeria. After that, three for the Rumanian government hardly seems worth mentioning.

If you care, over 300 people had one 600 (or more) by June, with most going overseas and only five to seven percent of them Pullmans. One short-term owner was Cecil King, proprietor of *Motocar,* who sent it back with a rude message about reliability – a fact which went unrecorded, we notice, in any of his journals. Nearly 200 more are ordered, but it isn't true that as soon as the homologation papers go through D-B returns to racing in the open GT class – even though they claim to lap Nurburgring faster in a 600 than the works rally car, a hot 300 SE.

Line forms to the right, friends. Any colour you want, even white: we detected a distinct shudder when we inquired if ours could be heather rose with primrose side panels and a metallic flake bronze roof, but they would do it. 'Wouldn't we rather have a special cocktail bar instead – not just any bar but a special just like Tito's? And remember it does 0–60 in 9.3 seconds'. The car, presumably. Frankly we're more impressed by the real round rev counter on the dash, and by back seats you can lay out one-quarter flat at the flick of a button. As a friend once said, it's getting so a gal ain't safe nowhere these days.

Things like air suspension, dual-circuit all-wheel discs (they work so smoothly) a rather jerky four-speed automatic box that you can operate like a racing driver (Fangio maybe?), total comfort, quiet and GT speeds are fine, too – but windows that go down in one second flat. Can the men of Crewe match that?

Mercedes 600's lines (top) are surprisingly restrained; in crowded city traffic, car looks much like any other Merc. It's only when you climb in through those wide, wide doors and ensconce yourself in some of the most comfortable seats ever built that you realise what a truly remarkable piece of engineering this is

One of the most astonishing things about the 600 is its (literally) sports-car handling characteristics. Brisk workout shows how stable it is in a situation which would have any other car its size lurching towards the outside verge. However, Mercedes is inclined to mar demonstrations by fitting 'competition' extras

Giant 600's front door is as crowded with complicated electrical equipment as most cars' dashboards. In an exclusive 'road test' by our man Sloniger the Super-Merc's electric windows accelerated from zero to fully open in exactly a second. Return run takes only 1.5sec and will chop a cigarette in half on the line

"I like your new **LOD**..."

. . . so will you!

***LOD** and **LODI** worn normally. An instant hit!*

***LOD** with peak down in what we call the "Green Label Bentley" position!*

A SMALL CAR PRIVILEGE PRICE OFFER TO READERS BRINGS YOU THESE FABULOUS NORWEGIAN MOTORING HATS AT LOW COST

The *LOD* (for men)

Ideal for open-car types, vintage enthusiasts, rallymen, and drivers with a difference! Made of quality leather, with quilted lining. Trimmed all round with real beaver lamb fur to include "neck and ear" flaps and peak. The warmest winter driving headgear we've found. Available in sizes $6\frac{7}{8}$ to $7\frac{1}{4}$.

NORMAL PRICE	SMALL CAR-TO-YOU PRICE
£4 4s. 0d.	£2 14s. 0d.

***LOD** with flaps away. The "Scandinavian Rallyman" look!*

The *LODI* (for the girls)

Not so much a driving hat—more a touch of glamour! Again quality leather fully lined, and trimmed all round with real beaver lamb fur. An elasticised knitted wool insert pulls down to keep the ears snug. You'll keep warm *and* look good! Elasticised, fits any size head.

NORMAL PRICE	SMALL CAR-TO-YOU PRICE
£3 3s. 0d.	£2 0s. 0d.

SEND YOUR ORDER FORM NOW (Offer applies to U.K. and N. Ireland only)

COUPON 1: FOR RECORDS
Small CAR "LOD" OFFER, Belgrave Library, 22 Armoury Way, Wandsworth, London, S.W.18.
Please send me a LOD/LODI for which I enclose Cheque/P.O. for £2–14–0/£2–0–0.

SIZE REQUIRED (LOD ONLY) [ ]

NAME.............................

ADDRESS.............................

....

....

Cheques/P.O.'s payable to Belgrave Library.

COUPON 2: LABEL FOR RETURN
Small CAR "LOD" OFFER (Use Block Letters)

NAME.............................

ADDRESS.............................

....

....

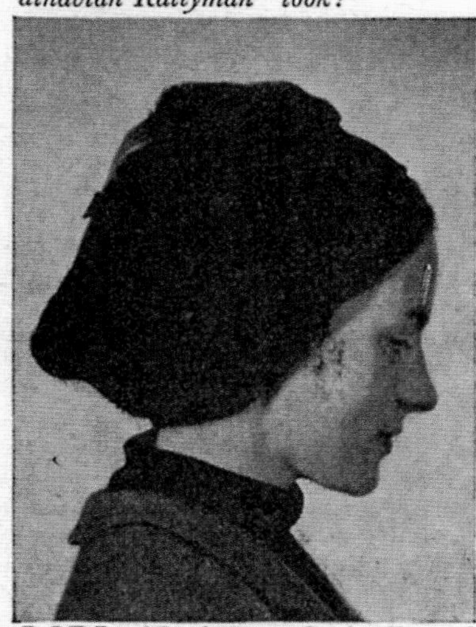

***LODI** with the cute back tilt and wool insert down. Nice?*

Ever fancied yourself behind the wheel of one of these?

How many times, while at a motor race as a spectator, has the unspoken question crossed your mind: How would I make out in the hot seat? Have I got what it takes to drive a real racing car, at speed, around a real circuit? Now you can find out for as little as eight guineas. For this modest outlay, an experienced tester of Motor Racing Stables will sit beside you in a Lotus Cortina and analyse your driving technique in three laps around Brands Hatch. He will offer critical advice, and then you are on your own—for five further laps in a formula F.3. Lotus. Think of it. Now you can discover just how good a driver you really are—or could become. Sessions for new members commence 9.30, 11.30, 2.30 every Friday.

Write for further details of this, and the advanced course, to Motor Racing Stables, Brands Hatch Circuit, Fawkham, Kent, or Telephone West Ash 404

MOTOR RACING STABLES BRANDS HATCH

LOOK-one hand!
SNACNIC
have a drink—have a bite
have a SNAC-NIC
Motoring, picnics, parties, buffets, TV breaks, canteens
Light strong plastic in colours blue, yellow, turquoise, ivory
Trade Enquiries Invited
2/11 each
SNAC-NIC
SNAC-NIC
SNAC-NIC
COMPONENTS & ACCESSORIES LTD
Station Road - Radlett - Herts Tel: Radlett 4822

Now priced at **£679.8.9,** the BMW 700 Coupé is the ideal car for those who value genuine "Grand Touring" performance from a power-packed, 2–4 seater model unequalled in its class and for those who require a compact town car for efficient operation in heavily trafficked streets. What makes the 700 Coupé so outstanding? To begin with, such significant features as full independent suspension, high compression sports engine developing 46 b.h.p. at 5,900 r.p.m., hemispherical cylinder heads, twin carburettors and 4-speed close ratio gear box. But the real answer lies in the thrill you get from handling such a spirited thoroughbred on the open road. Alternatively, for family use, there is the 700 L.S., a wonderful performer with de luxe specification, seating four or five in comfort. At its new price of **£598.9.7** it is so well worth the little extra that real quality always costs. **Other models include the 1500 (£1350.10.0), 1800 (£1481.6.1) and 1800 T.I. (£1615.15.0). All prices include P.T.**

B.M.W. CONCESSIONAIRES ENGLAND LIMITED
VICTORIA ROAD, PORTSLADE, BRIGHTON, SUSSEX (BRIGHTON 47814)

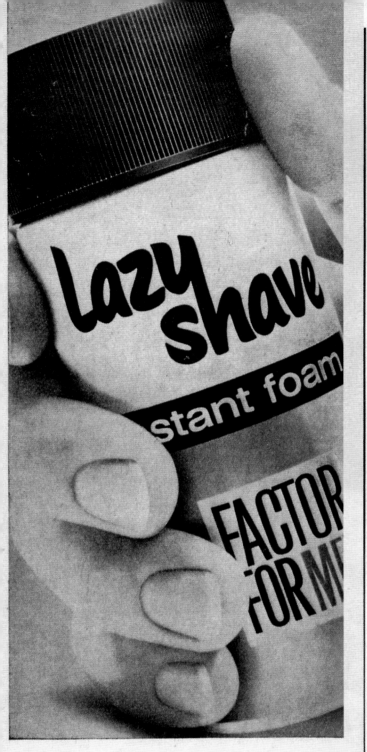

Grrrmph! said the serpent, and . . .

Henry Manney and Alan and Eve went down to the strip to play. But there came a great Cobra (a Tiger inside 'er?) and frightened the lady away

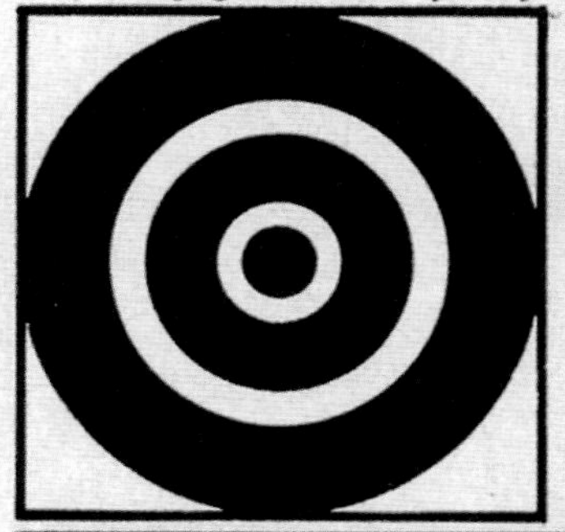

FROM TIME IMMEMORIAL, it seems, the Ferraris have been the kingpins of big GT racing. Consequently it was with some amusement that the world watched Carroll Shelby's attempts to stuff a huge Ford V8 into the antique AC Ace and, better still, to make it work. To be perfectly frank, it didn't – for a while. Eventually, though, a plunge into the deep bath of international competition was decreed, whereupon it early became obvious that the roadster Cobras were pushing too much of a built-in headwind. Shelby's Pete Brock therefore designed the more streamlined and stiffer Daytona coupe, the requisite number of races were won (although Le Mans was sort of a debacle), and lo and behold the GT title was Cobra's. To be sure, Ferrari didn't make any great efforts to defend his crown after the homologation of the 250LM blew up in his face and that of the GTB was delayed; but for a rocker-arm hotrod to win the Championship of Constructors isn't too bad.

We had two brief bashes at this particular Daytona, once when it was nice and fresh and once after Bob Bondurant had won the GT class in the 500 km of Enna. In either case Alan Mann Racing Ltd of Byfleet, who prepare and race the car as an extension of Ford's comp programme, were not terribly concerned about what harm might come to it as before (1) it would obviously be too quick for me before I got to redline and after (2) . . . well, the engine had to come apart anyway. The Cobra gives you that sort of feeling, as if it is made of indestructible iron even when the body is mostly alloy. The academic question of performance figures suffered, though, as on the first occasion the problems of light and a girl model used up all of the time while on the second, problems of traffic, navigation, a too-inquisitive noddy on his noddy-bike, and too much oil passing upwards through the bores ensured that the plugs became irrevocably sooted. Just as well since I'm ➞

→ not sure I have the guts to drive it full bore anyway.

I must say that the Daytona coupe is not everyone's idea of a GT car. The passenger's seat is on the floor, there doesn't seem to be much trim or sound deadening about barring a thinnish coat of black paint, the baggage accommodation is confined to what space is available round the spare tyre, and the noise is UNBELIEVABLE. What about those silencers GT cars are supposed to have? However, from the driver's point of view, especially if he is stone deaf, it *is* a GT car and quite a comfortable one too. The padded bucket seat reclines at a cosy rake that gives a modified straigntarm position, the fat leather-padded wheel is at a good angle, and visibility is excellent forward and rearwards. As befits such a businesslike machine, all controls fall readily to hand (to coin a phrase) and there are enough instruments to suit even the most finicky Bentley Boy. To the driver's right are laid out two rows of dials including a smallish tachometer redlined at six, oil pressure (usually at 65), water temp (between 140 and 150) and a big 160mph speedo. Down below there were the ammeter, oil temp (around 140) and the fuel pressure gauge at about 5lb. As in old VWs, there

was no visible fuel level gauge but perhaps one of the others was doing double duty. Anyway, below the instruments on a panel built onto the gearbox tunnel were two rows of those phosphorescent-ended aircraft toggle switches so dear to the Californian builder, reading Ign Start Fuel Head Drive Tail (second row) Horn button Main pump Res pump Washer, with handbrake, a fuse box, dashlight rheostat and winki winki switch more to the right. As the night races of Le Mans and Reims were planned at the model's outset, a generous lip shields the screen from reflections and every switch plus the enormous fire extinguisher ('just point it at any hole you see fire coming out') on the passenger's side are easily reached.

As *Motocar* says, starting the Cobra is simplicity itself. One first opens the generous filler and peers down in the cavern (taking care not to disturb the bats) to see if there is any fuel. That curiosity satisfied, one flicks on the Fuel, Main pump, and Ign switches, waits till the castanet dance subsides a bit, and then presses the spring-loaded Start switch upwards. The Cobra-ized 4.7litre Ford, somewhat improved by Ted Woodley and his Mann men, almost always springs silently into life with little more effect than a mortar shell going off, asking only that it be kept idling at 1000rpm or so to keep from drowning in its own juice. One enormous Weber throat for each inlet port, after all, is a bit much when the mill is designed to run between 5000 and 6000rpm. That done, it remains only to look carefully around for the coppers and move off.

In spite of the God-awful row emanating from under each door, the big V8 runs very smoothly and it is just as well to remember that the days of the racing engine vibrating like all b——y are over. If it shakes about, as for instance the big Offies do to an extent that the steering wheel is some six feet round at 3500rpm, everything not wired is liable to fall off and for that matter may fall off anyway. Also surprisingly, the clutch pedal is very light and so are the gear-changing pressures in the admirable Ford box even if it was a bit grotchy after Enna. The brakes are a different matter, requiring that the driver be young and strong to apply them hard, and attention must be paid that the feet do not slip off the bare metal pedals at some crucial point. Those used to typically vague Ford steering should try the Cobra, as all the bungy bits have been removed, roller bearings inserted at critical points, and the final result is a dead accurate and light mechanism under normal directions of travel that is as good as any car anywhere. Due to the enormous gummy Goodyears, though, quite a bit of heaviness creeps in when negotiating slow corners at full lock and also there is considerable kickback on rough stuff at moderate velocity.

To say the least, the Cobra attracts a bit of attention on the road. The squat blue and white figure with its hulking lines and fat ass doesn't much resemble the herds of Minxes that inhabit that region of Surrey and furthermore there is the Noise. To be perfectly fair, it is a good deal louder inside the car than out, but at the Cobra's softly muttering approach passers-by would start scanning the sky for flights of Gothas or perhaps inspect the manholes in search of Underground trains. Meanwhile the conductor is tiptoeing along gently in second or even first (the gearing is a bit high) owing to the dirty thirties until a sharp corner or some other hazard is reached, at which time a muttered *harruumph* is called for with the changedown.

Actually, as long as headway is kept up the Cobra will potter along quite happily in third at low speeds (before Enna) without sooting plugs or giving more than an occasional pop or belch; if acceleration or any sort of a rise becomes necessary, though, a changedown is essential as there is so little power available off the cam. As the Cobra is geared to do about 152mph at 5800 in top, the cam is rigged to start operating properly at around 4000 and most of the poop is above that figure. Up to 4000 there's a good deal of unused overlap which really doesn't make for a smooth idle and also renders it a bit difficult to get acceleration figures. We sort of made a pass at winding it up gently and then jabbing away (keeping in mind the wear and tear at Enna) but the combination of no torque low down, uneven running and the extreme stickiness of the big Goodyears gave us a series of times that varied too widely to be worth printing. The only proper way would be to wind it up and drop in the clutch, but it's so embarrassing to telephone Alan to come and get us. . . .

Blubbering along

Frankly, it was tremendous fun blubbering along at about 1500rpm (the tach was on the blink, I fear, as it never showed more than 3000) in second and then coming to a clear space. Having a crafty look round we could then push more firmly on the treadle accelerator and wait for the action. There would be a definite increase in resonance, a fairish push in the back, a before-the-storm gathering of forces, and then all hell let loose with all sorts of fiendish acceleration. The poor wight we were passing would dart affrighted on to his side as he was bombarded with concentrated sound waves and we would rocket past him, going far too fast for the approaching corner and feeling just like Fangio, only to realise that we still had another two gears to go.

Funnily enough, it wasn't much of a problem getting round the corner itself as the coupe sticks like glue and the steering is quite light; we never got near to the moment of truth on the road but research on the skid pan shows that the Cobra will understeer in a determined fashion up until the time that it plows off at a tangent. The celebrated Jack Sears, who has considerable Cobra time, informs me that the way to deal with the beastie is to give it a mighty bootful and kick the back end out, whereupon everything floats about nicely. We also tried this at relatively slow speeds in first and second gears on the skid pan (see pictures).

As Alan Mann is going to campaign something else next year, I imagine that these coupes (he has three) could be persuaded to come on to the market. They could make great road cars with proper silencers plus a few less carburettors and a good air cleaner, as the rest of the car seemed to be fairly taut and not too rattly. The Enna engine, which could only be described as completely clapped and leaking oil fumes from every pore, would naturally be replaced with a more sanitary unit. The main components would thus be big and long-lived, the ride is a bit stiff at low speeds, but smooths out amazingly further up, and directional stability seems outstanding as far as we took it. The main drawback, applicable only in hot weather, is that precious little air gets in but perhaps the old bits of lace curtain could be unstoppered from the cockpit air vents. Lovely fun, and you wouldn't be about to meet yourself coming down the road. Wonder what the Dorchester doorman would make of that?

Just park it, please!

MACH 1

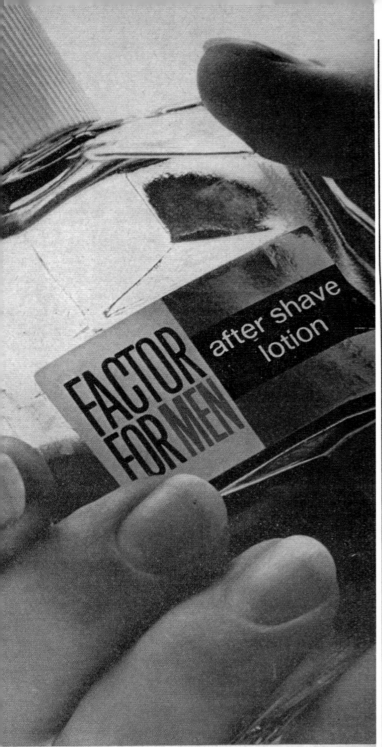

Donald CAMPBELL, accused of spending too fast and driving too slowly, talks 800mph with DENNIS MAY

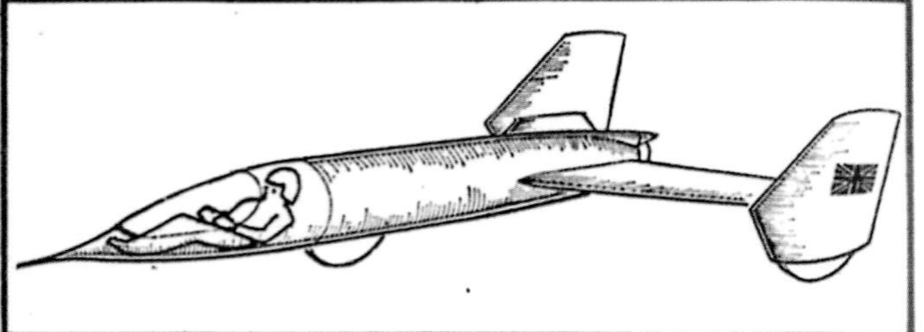

FORTY YEARS AND THE ODD months ago, at Pendine beach, Carmarthenshire, a chair-high Donald Campbell was blending his alto geewhizzes with gruffer adult plaudits in honour of a notable feat of speed. His father, Capt Malcolm Campbell, had just driven his 350bhp Sunbeam over the flying kilometre at 150.869mph to notch up the world's first century-and-a-half on wheels. The veils of the future are lifted one by one, we're told, so it's fair to assume that the Campbells, Sr and Jr, could have been CKD with a feather if some Welsh visionary had popped out from behind a dune and told them that four decades thence Jr would have a supersonic project on the easel...

Forty yearsworth of veils having been duly lifted, Sir Malcolm (as he became in 1931) is seen in history's perspective as a nine-time breaker of the Land Speed Record as well as the first man to exceed two and a half centuries, four miles a minute and finally *three* centuries. Donald subsequently turned four centuries ahead of anyone else, and his 403.1mph at Lake Eyre, South Australia, in July of last year remains the highest speed ever reached by a car powered through the wheels.

Meanwhile, following the FIA's famous decision to legitimise jet and rocket propulsion for LSR cars, *the* record has soared to its present 576.5 mph level (Art Arfons *mit* Green Monster, November 1965). Up in this stratosphere the whole scale of values alters and mere century accretions hardly turn a head. In the '60s the only target worth shooting at is Mach One, the speed of sound, 840mph. And that indeed is the goal for the elite of speed – Campbell in Britain (if he can raise the cash) and Bobby Tratoe in the US.

Key figure on the American side of the LSR fence is actually Art Arfons's brother Walt, not Tratoe who fills the postillion role in Arfons's latest project, a second edition of his Wingfoot Express. Both the prospective Machbusters, Campbell's embryo Bluebird and this new Arfons job, are needlenose trikes with the bachelor wheel in front and two at the back. Where these cars differ basically is in their power sources: Campbell turns to jet propulsion for the first time (he knows which gas turbine he wants but when this was written it remained to be seen whether the government would make it available), whereas rockets will lend Tratoe's feet their wings. Fifteen rockets to be exact. They are said to be able to push the car to 750mph in 21sec . . .

Comparing Campbell *père*'s 150 per hour dice in 1925 with his son's quadruple century last year, about the only common factors were the drivers' surnames and the lack of interest shown in either enterprise by the British press. *Autocar*'s 1925 story, for instance, which doesn't read like an eye-witness account anyway, occupied less than half a page and was unillustrated. About all the detail it gave on the Sunbeam was that it used 24 Lodge plugs and two double Claudel carburetters. Forty years later, in an aside to answers to some questions popped on CAR's behalf, Donald Campbell remarked bitterly that the Lake Eyre record 'was not covered by a single British pressman'.

Costwise, the contrast could hardly have been greater. Nobody knows what Malcolm Campbell paid the old Sunbeam company for his six-year-old car but it could probably be reckoned in hundreds. Secondhand in the sense that it had had one previous owner, it had been raced and used for records by at least four drivers (René Thomas, Lee Guinness, Hornsted and Chassagne) before Campbell acquired it in 1923. Donald's backers in the latterday Bluebird project, on the other hand, didn't see much change out of £2m. This would include the cost of the expensive modification and rebuild job following the 1960 Bonneville crash which nearly cost Campbell his life.

Now consider these facts. Nearly a quarter of a century after John Cobb set his 394.2mph record in 1939 Campbell, with two millions' worth of motorcar, raised it by nine per hour. By five stages in the same year, 1964, American rivals piled on a further 141mph . . . and the Arfons car which put the record where it now stands, cost less than £4000 to build, exclusive of its special Firestone wheels and tyres. On the face of it these statistics make absolute nonsense, if that, and there are those who point the finger at Campbell (when he's out of sight) saying 'Verily, if this man motored as fast as he spends money we would have nothing to fear'.

This interpretation, of course, ignores certain relevancies of which the following are samples. One: US government policy (unlike ours) permits the public sale of such delicacies as the General Electric J79 jet engine that Arfons used to set his current record; although obsolete as far as its original fighter aircraft role was concerned, it delivers 17,500 pounds of thrust and cost a laughable £1700 at auction. Two: Designed and developed long before the FIA decision to recognise jet and rocket propulsion, Campbell's four-wheel-drive Bluebird carried the colossal financial handicap of a transmission system.

This gigantic V12-cylinder overhead camshaft engine with its 24 spark plugs and twin Claudel carburettors powered Donald Campbell's father Malcolm to the first 150mph run ever made on land. That was 40 years ago. Today the same car still races regularly in its original livery. Beside it in the picture (right) are Campbell Jnr, his Bluebird (first of the ground-traction cars to top 400mph both ways) and Leo Villa.

That new trike

His new trike, as we've seen, is to be a pure jet vehicle and thus devoid of transmission. 'The cost of the new supersonic car will be fractional compared to the Proteus Bluebird, due to the lack of mechanical complexity' he tells us in a written reply to a whole series of questions.

'The FIA's decision regarding jet propulsion was inevitable and should have been taken in 1946' he goes on. 'At that time the Union of International Motorboating, which controls the Water Speed Record, immediately realised the potential of the turbojet and admitted its use.

'There is considerable popular misconception on this question of propulsion, particularly in relation to constant thrust versus ground horsepower. A natural phenomenon limits a propellor-propelled aircraft to an approximate maximum speed of 475mph, a wheel-propelled land vehicle to 500mph, a screw-propelled boat to 200mph. This situation was as well known in 1946 as it is today. If you wish to go fast in any of the mediums mentioned the use of the jet or rocket is mandatory.

'Last October, having for years steadfastly refused to recognise the inevitability of the jet on land, the FIA suddenly altered its regulations overnight, making them retrospective to admit this medium. The FIA is currently in discussion with the FIM (motorcycling's international governing body) to frame rules to cover the Land Speed Record in future. It seems they now contemplate recognising any manned vehicle supported by the ground.

'This means that it is now entirely feasible to contemplate speeds in excess of sound. The critical problem of adhesion is almost eliminated and, at this stage, it is difficult even to say whether or not the pneumatic tyre would provide the best medium of ground support. Inflation pressure would have to be so high that any tyre would be virtually solid.'

Yet more than 20 years after John Cobb closely crowded four centuries it wouldn't have made sense, surely, for the designers of the Proteus-engined Bluebird to set their sights for the mere whisker over 400 mph that in fact was achieved?

No, indeed. 'On a hard, dry track there is absolutely no doubt the machine would have reached the 500mph for which she was designed' says Campbell. 'This is the considered opinion of her designers, Norris Brothers Ltd, in consultation with Bristol Siddeley, who designed the Proteus engine.

'When related to the appalling track conditions under which the car was running at Lake Eyre, its performance was little short of fantastic. The surface was wet and soggy from continual rain and at 400plus mph the tyres were wearing two-inch ruts in the surface – ruts which ran for the best part of six miles.' If you doubt any of this, make a point of seeing *How Long a Mile*, the new Bluebird film. Wow!

(Parenthetically, in racing over terrain that nature had temporarily reduced to a gigantic squish area, Donald was repeating 40-year-old family history.

At Pendine in 1924, during the first of the two Land Speed Records he set with the 350hp Sunbeam, his father too had gone in inches deep. 'The car was slowed badly by running in its own tracks' reported *Autocar*. What was that line of Tennyson's . . . 'In deep and awful channel runs, the sympathy 'twixt sires and sons'. In fact, though, the sympathy 'twixt this sire and this son was a one-way thing as far as the dangerous trade of record-breaking went. 'My father did everything in his power to dissuade me from following in his footsteps' Donald recalls.)

If record-breaking at LSR level improves the breed at all (here's where Alec Issigonis, if he reads this, will reach for the vomitorium), does it do so more or less today than when Campbell *père* was traversing those deep and awful channels at Pendine in the '20s?

Breed-improvement

Sir Malcolm was always faithful to that breed-improvement line, vide this quote from *My Thirty Years of Speed*: 'The very great amount of research necessary to create the machine obliges scientists to make detailed investigations in metallurgy and streamlining, and to overcome problems of transmission and braking . . .' Meaning, obviously, problems of transmission, braking and all that Brahms which have an actual application to roadfaring vehicles. But it's sometimes argued that the Land Speed Record car of today – and tomorrow even more so – has so tenuous an affinity with even the starkest and hairiest roadster that it's sheer sophistry to pretend it can affect The Breed. What does Campbell think?

Boxes of gears

Apart from the fact that they were both powered by reciprocating engines driving their back wheels through boxes of gears, he points out, there was practically nothing in common between the LSR cars of his father's day and any passenger vehicle. The former, moreover, were 'intractable and had an appalling low-speed performance. The greatest advance that ever took place was with Proteus Bluebird. Immediately following last year's world record, this car demonstrated its amazing flexibility by safely driving through the main street of Adelaide *at a sustained speed of 5mph* – something which never could have been achieved by any of her predecessors.

'Attaining the speed of sound will be a major technological and human achievement, and in promotional terms something which could have significance throughout the world.

'By the same token it can well be argued that the entire endeavour is totally absurd and will have no meaning whatever. The same argument can equally be applied to the climbing of Mount Everest or the Olympic Games, which cost so many millions to organise, where men and women are striving to run a little faster or jump a little higher. In terms of productivity, such activity has no meaning. The subject was concisely summed up by the late John Rhodes Cobb, who said "When man ceases to try to do better he will have reached a time of decadence".'

H'mm.

GRAN TURISMO WHEELS & ACCESSORIES LIMITED

World Champions!

JOHN SURTEES Driving Gloves

*Strong touch-thin leather. *Ventilated fingers. *Knuckle pad. *Chamois leather. *Dye-fast. Washable. *Elasticated wrist. Black, Black/White, Black/Red, Tan.

49/11
Per Pair
Plus 1/- P.P.

59/6
Per Pair
Plus 1/- P.P.

JIM CLARK Driving Gloves

As specified and worn by him in the 'Indy 500'. Made from touch-thin Kangaroo skin. Washable Dyefast. Black, Tan, Red or White. Medium and large sizes, also ladies.

JOHN SURTEES Elegant Driving Shoes

Hand-made by craftsmen in finest leather. Cutaway heel. Perforated inner sole for maximum comfort. Black or brown. All sizes.

89/6 Per Pair
Plus 3/6 P.P.

MOSTILE Driving Shoes

The trend-setters worn by leading continental drivers for safety and comfort. Super quality, soft chrome leather with non-slip studded soles.

89/6 Per Pair
Plus 3/6 P.P.

JOHN SURTEES Competition Boots

Made exactly to the World Champion's specification for Racing and Rally driving. Black or 2-tone Brown all sizes.

★Special 3-layer chrome leather sole giving greater heat resistance than other boot of its kind. ★Heel to toe anti-heat and scuffing strip. ★Super - soft leather uppers. ★Sorbo cushioned heel.

S F

99/6 Per Pair
Plus 3/6 P.P.

Post early for these superb Christmas Gifts.

To G. T. WHEELS LTD., TWO COUNTIES MILLS, EATON BRAY, Beds.

PLEASE SEND .... £ .... enclosed

NAME ....

ADDRESS ....

....

"Isn't it common sense nowadays to have a coat that's actually styled to be worn in the car. These Car Coats are so practical and comfortable you're sure to want to own one. Even when you're not in a car!"

L Jackson

Luxury Wool and Cashmere Car Coat, by Jackson the Tailor, camel shade, side vents, flapped breast pocket. 9 gns.
Double breasted Reefer Coat, inset/raglan style with side vents, two slant pockets and two casual pockets. 7 gns.

Jackson
the tailor

Method of payment:
Cash, credit or subscription to your preference.

Casual wear.
Have a look at our selection of casual, easy-going clothes—they'll complete your wardrobe

Branches at Newcastle upon Tyne and
ABERDEEN ☐ ASHINGTON ☐ BARNSLEY
BALLYMENA ☐ BELFAST ☐ BIRMINGHAM
BIRKENHEAD ☐ BISHOP AUCKLAND
BLACKPOOL ☐ BOLTON ☐ BRADFORD
BRISTOL ☐ BRIXTON ☐ CARDIFF
CARLISLE ☐ CHESTER-LE-STREET
COVENTRY ☐ CROYDON ☐ DARLINGTON
DERBY ☐ DONCASTER ☐ DUNDEE
EAST KILBRIDE ☐ EDINBURGH
ELLESMERE PORT ☐ GATESHEAD
GLASGOW ☐ HULL ☐ KILMARNOCK
KIRKCALDY ☐ LEEDS ☐ LEICESTER
LIVERPOOL ☐ OXFORD STREET, LONDON
MANCHESTER ☐ MIDDLESBROUGH
NOTTINGHAM ☐ OLDHAM ☐ PAISLEY
PECKHAM ☐ PRESTON ☐ PORTSMOUTH
PLYMOUTH ☐ SHEFFIELD ☐ SHREWSBURY
SLOUGH ☐ SOUTHAMPTON
SOUTH SHIELDS ☐ ST. HELENS ☐ STANLEY
STOCKTON ☐ SUNDERLAND ☐ SWANSEA
TOOTING ☐ WIGAN ☐ WARRINGTON
WOLVERHAMPTON ☐ WREXHAM

get out from under

Rebel contributor Joe wrey warns the Government: a Channel tunnel will be the ultimate folly*

**the man who stirred up all that TV fuss about drugs in rallies, remember?*

PAYING SEVEN VISITS TO THE continent during 1965, my slowest cross-channel journey took eight and a half hours in transit, plus another four hours or so of waiting time at Ostend and at Dover. As those eight hours were spent very uncomfortably in seasick company, and were in any case noctural ones such as I prefer to pass asleep, and as my next cross-channel journey was preceded by a two-and-a-half-hour wait for weather which would let car-ferry aeroplanes take off, I have the strongest personal reasons for wanting improved communications between Britain and France.

But a Channel tunnel? I could not be more strongly opposed to this project, which the state-owned railways of Britain and France are so avidly encouraging. Apart from being an unsatisfactory answer to our problems, a Channel tunnel would be so expensive a folly that its construction would almost certainly delay by 20 years the building of a much-needed link between us and Europe's mainland – still the ultimate need.

Let one thing be clearly understood. Nobody is proposing to build a road tunnel beneath the Straits of Dover. Such a 25 mile traffic tube would not merely be claustrophobic in the extreme, it would pose tremendous problems when it came to venting the poisonous exhaust fumes of internal combustion engines – plus some other quite tough problems associated with breakdowns and accidents. What the Channel tunnel enthusiasts propose is a submarine electric railway from Britain to France, with facilities for transporting road vehicles on trains.

How useful would a cross-channel railway tunnel be to car owners? The answer to that question need not be imagined but can be based on observed fact, since a prototype has already been in operation for almost 80 years! It was in 1886 that the railway tunnel under the estuary of the River Severn opened to passenger traffic, and for most of the time since then cars have been carried on trains between the English and Welsh sides of the water. The system works, certainly. But it works in such a tediously cumbersome fashion that relatively few drivers use it, and a very expensive road bridge over the estuary is now approaching completion only about two miles away.

Propagandists for the Channel railway tunnel paint impressive pictures of the facilities which could be provided for taking cars beneath the Straits on trains. As to the reality of how effective a link between Bristol and Monmouth the existing car-carrying trains actually are, the propagandists are strangely silent. Government acceptance of the need for a costly Severn road bridge, despite the fact that the rail tunnel is already in existence at the chosen spot, is surely irrefutable proof that car-carrying trains rate rather below ferryboats as efficient devices for linking roads across water.

There has been an exactly parallel experience in the Alps, where snow blocks through-routes during the winter. Despite the long-established facilities for taking cars on trains through the Mont Cenis, Simplon and St Gotthard tunnels, two new *road* tunnels have just been dug to link France and Switzerland with Italy. More are planned.

Let's face it, the commercial incentive to provide good facilities for car transport through railway tunnels is not exactly strong. Carrying cars on trains between Dover and Calais would be a far less profitable business than carrying their passengers on longer city-to-city hauls between Glasgow or London and Paris or Geneva. The same would be even more true of freight, much of which would have to be diverted from lorries to trains if heavy vehicles were refused or discouraged in the Channel tunnel. Car-carrying trains on such routes as London–Perth or Boulogne–Lyon have to attract customers, but car-carrying trains across the Channel would be able to exploit the motorist unmercifully.

It has been claimed that a Channel tunnel would be the cheapest kind of land link between Britain and France. All my engineering instincts make me doubt this claim. Whilst cost estimates for a Channel tunnel are lower than those for a Channel bridge, I do not believe that the comparison is a fair one. Bridges which need supporting piers at intervals can almost always be built at closely predictable prices. There are few major uncertainties concerning their foundations. Tunnels always have to explore the unknown. No number of test borings from above can ever disclose all the geological faults and springs of water which can delay or divert tunnelling and multiply costs. Even in London, recent work on building the Victoria underground railway apparently met costly and unex-

At left is the Channel Tunnel Study Group's idea of how a bored-out tube line from Calais to Dover might look during construction. Centre core is for service vehicles, machinery and staff. At top is an impression of one of the terminals—looking much like the starting point for an under-Alp train

At right: the staggering Chesapeake Bay combination road bridge and tunnel—17 miles long and (says Joe Lowrey) just the thing for linking us with France. Tunnel part runs between natural shoals in far distance, is of simple immersed-tube type such as engineers have considered for Channel (above)

pected snags which diverted its line – although London's subsoil must be drier and much better known than that under the Channel.

Building a bridge across the Straits of Dover is apparently regarded as a perfectly practicable engineering proposition. Depths of water seldom exceed 100ft, and are far less in many areas. At this moment plans are going ahead to guide the dangerously chaotic and congested shipping of this area into nautical one-way streets. A bridge supported on frequent pillars in the shallower areas but rising to higher and longer spans over the shipping channels, able to mount lights and radar, could actually make navigation safer in these streets–not more hazardous as certain critics so doggedly argue.

On a Channel bridge, too, it would be possible to have both railway tracks *and* a road with eventual flexibility to widen the road by 'doing a Beeching' on the rail tracks. So far from there being a ventilation problem, vehicle stability in side winds would need study – but aerodynamicists know enough already to use shaped panels of expanded metal or similar porous sheeting to divert and slow down gales without turning the bridge into an overhead tunnel.

Besides the Channel bridge or series of bridges, another possible form of road link exists. The 17.5mile road across the mouth of Chesapeake Bay, in the USA, opened to traffic in 1964, could be copied in modified form for the 25mile Straits of Dover. Over shallow water the Chesapeake road is built as a bridge supported on piles, with higher and wider spans over the inshore channels which are used by small vessels. Towards the middle, pairs of artificial islands have been built in shallow water at each side of two main shipping channels. Between each pair of islands the road dives down into an easily-ventilated tunnel slightly more than a mile long. Instead of digging conventional tunnels, the Americans used concrete-weighted steel tubes which they sank into dredged sea-bed trenches at slack tide. Then they coupled up the sections, each nearly 100yd long, in situ on the sea bed.

In the Straits of Dover there are already convenient shoals around one-third and two-thirds distance across. On them, engineers could build artificial islands suitable for linking to England and France by bridges, spanning the gap by a road tunnel of practicable length. This does seem to be a serious alternative to the bridge. And it would leave a wide shipping channel with unrestricted headroom for giant vessels.

That railway tunnel under the Channel, I am certain, will eventually cost at least as much to build as either a rail-and-road bridge or a composite bridge-tunnel-bridge road link. In the motorway age, putting road vehicles on trains will not provide much better communication between Britain and the Continent than should come from improvements in ferry services. Journey times will not be reduced very much, since even with today's fairly slow ferries the journey time from Dover to Boulogne or Calais is less than the total time which an average driver spends awaiting a boat, embarking, disembarking, and passing customs amidst a mass of other cars. Putting cars onto trains instead of boats would still involve long waits for the next departure at times or seasons when traffic was slack. There would still be long waits in queues whenever too few trains or crews were available to cope with a sudden rush of cars, as on a sunny week-end. Customs would still be faced with a complete train-load of cars at intervals, instead of with the flow off a bridge.

If we go ahead with the Victorian idea of building a railway tunnel under the Channel I'm sure we shall soon find that a real drive-across link with France remains necessary. Escape from seasickness will be the only major advantage of car-carrying trains over car-carrying ferry boats. If, however, our Government once wastes its money (correction, OUR money!) on a rail tunnel it will want to see that money recouped as rail fares before spending as much again on a cross-channel road bridge.

Are we to be able to drive cars, coaches and trucks to and from the European mainland at some time within the next quarter-century? Only, I would say, if we can prevent this folly of building a get-out-and-get-under rail tunnel. The Severn Tunnel and the Alpine railway tunnels have proved that car-carrying trains are no effective substitute for a road. Can any sensible person believe that a Channel tunnel would work any better? That it could even face competition from the giant hovercraft which ferrymen are already ordering?

it's the limit

STIRLING MOSS

Don't just stand there. Let's get together and act. Now!

I NOTICED IN THE CORRESPONDENCE columns of one of our competitive magazines, I don't remember which, that some chap had stopped his AA subscription because he felt the 70mph limit was a betrayal – an issue which the Association had dodged. I agree. After all, what's the AA for? One can buy maps and hotel guides from other places. The AA and the RAC do offer a breakdown service which is quite useful at times, and they do give you a key so that you don't need to carry money but can go into one of their boxes and phone for help. But after all you can get a credit card now from the GPO and phone from anywhere in Britain. Whether they like it or not, the most important duty of both associations is more than ever to safeguard the motorist. And that means fighting the 70 limit.

Dennis Poore, an ex-racing driver friend of mine who used to be very fast up a hill (we found out why he was so quick; he couldn't see too well and he just used to drive flat-out until he could focus on whatever he was going to hit; then he stood on the brakes and got out of the way) called me up the other day and said 'Look, Stirling. It's about time we did something to start an organisation that will *really* safeguard the motorist.' If Dennis's organisation does get going – and I shall certainly support it – what sort of case can it make out against this misguided measure?

The standard of driving in this country is on an equally low par with four other places in the world: Switzerland, Belgium, South Africa and possibly Germany. But on British M-roads I do think that, with a few exceptions (there are always exceptions, just as there is always the idiot who will abuse an ordinary limitless road), the standard is the highest anywhere. Certainly it is higher than on the German autobahnen, which are restricted in places, and much higher than on American freeways. I think there is every reason to suppose the explanation for this is that, up to now, motorways have *not* been restricted. People realise that speed is what M-roads are built for. They have always been publicised as express trunk roads without crossroads, intersections and the like, with plenty of warning to get off, with particularly good signposts and adequate space off the carriageway if your vehicle happens to be in trouble. They are respected as such. The realisation that others may be going faster than you are keeps you alert – keeps you out of the fast lane and on the ball. The accidents that occur on M-roads in normal weather are, I believe, a bare minimum caused purely by an irresponsible section of the public which can never be curbed. I mean you can't stop a certain percentage of criminals killing people even though they may know they'll get hanged for it. You can't stop people stealing because it is wrong. You can't even stop people breaking the 30 or 40 limit now and then; I must admit I've done it myself. Equally you will never stop those people who are not only breaking the law but exceeding our idea of what is morally right – in other words driving in a fashion which is dangerous. These are the people who cause the motorway accidents, and all that happens when the government says 70 is the limit is that they spend more time looking in the mirror and even less concentrating on what they are doing.

Pulling out

Without an overall limit, the man who is going slowly is more inclined to keep to the left and let the faster man pass him on the right. This is a lot safer than it sounds, even in an extreme

'One answer is to write to our new Minister, but the trouble is people don't do this. They won't even write in and say who they think should be the Sportsman of the Year, so how can we expect them to make an abstract political protest? I can tell you I haven't written to Barbara Castle and I don't suppose you have.

'But let's reform. I promise here and now that if you will fill in the form on this page saying you agree with me that the 70 limit is a mistake, every voucher you give me will be passed on and will ultimately get to the highest person I can reach. I can't necessarily say it'll go to the Minister herself. I'm not even sure the Minister is the right woman. Her predecessor, I happen to know, drove a vehicle with a leopardskin thing on the steering wheel. This one doesn't drive at all. But I'll do my best to find someone with the right approach and the right influence'

Stirling Moss

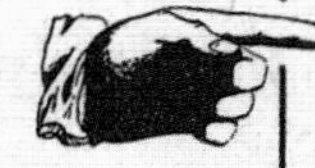

to Mrs Barbara Castle MP, c/o Stirling Moss, 46 Shepherd Street, London W1

Madam

Like Stirling Moss, I am seriously concerned at the incidental effects which the nationwide 70mph speed limit is having on an already impossible traffic situation. As a thinking individual I doubt sincerely that the restriction, in itself, will have any beneficial effect.

With Mr Moss, I urge you to do all in your power to see that the limit is not extended as a sop to 'public opinion'.

Yours sincerely

this letter is sent in response to an appeal by Stirling Moss in CAR

case. Assume there is a man doing 45mph or so on the left and he comes behind a truck that is only doing 40. Naturally he wants to pass. If he looks in his mirror he can usually see 500 or 600 yards back at the very least. If it's reasonably clear he indicates he's pulling out and starts to turn. Now let's assume that at that distance of 600 yards there is in fact a car coming up extraordinarily fast – at 120, say, which was known on the M1 until recently. The faster car will take 14sec before it catches the slower one even if its driver doesn't slow at all. If he does brake, as in 99 cases out of 100 he will, the chances of an accident diminish. They diminish to the point of insignificance so long as the man in the slower car remains alert and ready to pull back in behind the truck in an emergency. Can we be sure he will retain his alertness after the 70 limit has had time to breed in him a false sense of security?

No. I feel that the limit can only lessen the quality of driving, especially on motorways – partly because it will encourage people to drive *up* to 70 (there must be many who used to do 65 who will say 'I'll do 70 now: it's quite safe and it's legal') but primarily because it will make people who are doing 70 feel that they have the right to do it in the fastest lane and to do anything they like at that speed without further thought.

In short, the limit is not only failing to curb this minority, it will in time introduce hazards of its own. Let me show you another. I'm in a 30 zone going along just over the limit. I think to myself 'Well, all right – I'm taking a bit of a risk and the police may nab me and so on, but it's reasonably safe'. I come across a man in front of me on a reasonably wide stretch, maybe wide enough for three or four cars. He's in the outside lane. I toot on the hooter. Is it likely the man will move over? It's a lot more likely he will either shake his fist or put two fingers up. Now why does this happen?

'I am the law'

Well, the man in front at this particular moment feels that he is the law. It says on the side that 30 is the limit and 30 is the same for everybody. This happens all the time in driving; it doesn't happen in golf because if you can go round the golf-course in 70 it doesn't mean I can; it doesn't even mean I ever will. But the reasons for the slow driver's attitude are complex and far from consistent. It frequently happens that somebody is attacked in the street and bystanders will watch the man knocked down and then walk round him. If people don't go to help others, even when they can see that a lawless act has been carried out, why the devil should they suddenly see fit to say 'Boy, I'm the law' when the sign says 30 and their speedometer points to 29? Whatever the reason, the same thing is beginning to happen at 70 – particularly on motorways. And when you find someone trying to do at 70 what is already dangerous and frustrating enough at 30, it's easy for a big accident to develop.

Now I don't need to tell you that if there's an accident at 70mph, when there are going to be more cars driving along in knots with proportionately less braking time available, more than one car is almost certain to be involved. Accordingly I feel that the 70 limit is bound to bring more multiple pileups. There was one in Los Angeles not so long ago on the freeway in which 400 cars were involved. This is something which would be unbelievable if one couldn't see the making of it here already.

Perhaps it will pay to consider how much worse an accident is at, say, 90 than at 70. Of course there are people who point out that a 20mph speed differential means the difference between a 20mph accident and none at all. But I maintain there is a very low point at which the modern car is incapable of withstanding impact, and that above that one's precise speed doesn't matter very much. I can state definitely that in racing, where accidents do happen occasionally, more people have been killed at slower than at higher speeds. It is a fact, too, that in this country – and I think in America, where the accident rate is much higher (even though they have a maximum limit) and where insurance premiums are nearly double ours – there are more accidents below 35mph than above. Of course you can say this is because of the urban areas and to some extent you're quite right. But nevertheless we're never going to cut accidents out altogether. A car is only safe if it's standing still with the engine switched off in a garage: as soon as you start it up you can get asphyxiated by carbon monoxide, and the moment the thing begins to move at even two miles an hour you can run somebody over. The same car does not suddenly become more dangerous as soon as it exceeds 70mph, and in the same way the accident it causes bears much less relation to its *precise* speed than people like ex-minister Fraser seems to think. It depends almost entirely on what you hit and how you hit it – not at what speed, give or take 20mph. It is known by many of us that quite often the trouble is caused by brakes. Uneven braking and too much braking at the wrong time in the wrong place will have a disastrous effect at any speed. Even from 35mph, particularly if it happens to be damp, very few cars are capable of stopping safely without any contribution in skill from the driver. What I am saying is that cars are dangerous by their very nature – no more so at 70mph than at 50 or 100. This leads me to suggest that the sensible thing to do, if one is looking for a single, simple, popularly appealing measure such as the present government has obviously sought in this case, is to concentrate on the people who drive these fundamentally dangerous vehicles rather than on the way the vehicles themselves behave.

I feel that you've got to apply the same reasoning as we do in racing. For a licence, a racing driver has got to have some form of qualification that is better than the current road test – a qualification based on his actual reactions to everyday racing situations. In the civil driving test too much accent is put on whether you know what shape, colour, size or whathaveyou the road signs are going to be, and too little on the proper way to react in a real emergency. As I see it the thing we've got to do long before we bring in a permanent 70 limit or any other blanket restriction is try to say 'Right, instead of issuing 12 million licences we will make the test a lot more difficult and get the number down to exclude incompetents.' Okay, this may mean there are only seven, eight or nine million drivers who can go on the road – but surely this is the obvious way to lessen danger? Accidents are caused by people, sometimes assisted by the car and occasionally, to a slight extent, by the road, but by and large you can say that an incompetent driver at any speed is a far greater menace than an intelligent and experienced one doing 170 in the proper circumstances. Have any of you readers ever seen or met a person who went off the road purely because he was driving too fast? Not very often, I'll bet.

Most of the accidents one hears of are caused by →

it's the limit

LAURENCE POMEROY

The hunters and the hunted. A grim 20th century parable

→thoughtlessness, stupidity or cussedness. The man who comes dashing up to a T-junction and makes a person poodling down the road run into a tree because he thinks the first chap is going to stand on the brakes and go out of control. The man who makes a right turn when everybody thought he was going to go left. The man who failed to use his mirror. These are the sort of people who *really* cause accidents far, far more often than the man going down the M1 or any other adequate road at 90mph. In racing, I think the most dangerous time – and you ask any driver – is when you're either leading or losing by a large margin. In other words when you're not really concentrating on what you're doing. When you're driving at a reasonably high speed you're more than ever conscious of what Freud said, that life is most important to us. You concentrate . . . whereas when you're forced down to a slower, constant speed you're going to start thinking 'Well, I wonder if there's a quicker way to get to so-and-so . . . if I make a turn earlier, or if I go on past this turn . . . let's just see if I can get a quick squint at the map.' Maybe you even do as I used to do in racing if I had the time to spare: start cleaning up the cockpit a bit, get a rag out and polish my goggles, check the gauges time and time again when they didn't really need to be checked. All of these things take one's mind off the job. I don't care how much ability you give a man – he can be Jim Clark and Fangio rolled into one – if you take away his concentration and then let him loose even at low speeds he will still go off the road in time.

The 70 limit, whether or not it works, is a guaranteed popular success because so few people do 70 anyway – and all of them are looking for someone else to blame. There's been a lot of press given to the idea that speed kills. 'We'll stop these young hoodlums from dashing around . . .' Well, let's get one thing quite straight right now. It doesn't take a young idiot to do 70 in a car, just as it doesn't take a ton-up boy to do 100mph on a motorcycle – not that I'd think of it myself, but what the devil? I draw my own limits. My speed varies according to my ability. After I'd had my big crash four years ago I started driving again at 25 or 30mph and even then I felt I was hardly competent. I certainly didn't say 'Well, I'm allowed to get on the M1, so I'll go and take a Jag and see if I can beat up 150 and get this out of my system.'

Doing something

Another reason so many people have thought the limit a good thing is that they feel at last the Minister is *doing something.* But what a very bad way to do something! What a negative way to go about it. To stop something is negative; it's time this country progressed, got better roads and better communications. Britain has an income of over £800m from the motorist and the government sees fit to put back only £180m into the roads. This is wrong. What we want from any government, even a Communist government, is progress – in road safety just as in construction.

We know there is a connection between speed and death. But I don't think it's as big a relationship as people make out. When people go around saying 'I've had so many years without an accident' it doesn't necessarily mean they're good drivers – it just means they've been lucky enough to keep out of the accidents they've caused. This is a negative attitude in just the same way. It's up to us to convince the government that we can see through it. ✲

THESE QUOTATIONS (ABOVE right) underline the contention that speed limits are a symptom of a human struggle which has gone on not just between carriage-owners and others since the 18th century but for at least 7000 years between two different types of humanity. The most primitive of primitive men lived by hunting. Survival depended upon physical skill, strength and endurance. Even these would not get any man very far without bravery and contempt of danger as well. Fearlessness and sheer strength were less needed by those who were able to live in lakeside settlements and hunt fish. Indeed around 5000 years ago, on the banks of the Euphrates, Tigris and Nile, settled communities learned to till the fields and live a peaceful, orderly life which led to the great cities of antiquity and the birth of civilization as we know it.

But the agrarian and city dwellers in the plains always lived under the threat of the hunters in the hills and were periodically destroyed by them. 'The Assyrian came down like a wolf on the fold . . .' and the hunters, after some centuries themselves civilized, gave way to new invasions.

It became plain that for any society to remain viable it needed a vigorous but disciplined official and military caste in parallel with the craftsmen, traders, jurors and scholars whose minds were more peaceably inclined. For example, there were two different educational systems among the Aztecs. Soustelle writes: 'One set had to get up in the darkness to go solitary into the mountains and draw blood from their ears and legs with thorns. They were obliged to undergo frequent and rigorous tasks. They had to work hard and were severely punished for the least fault . . .' (Floreat Etona.) 'How very different was the life of the ordinary people. It is true that the boy went with others to take part in public works such as repairing ditches and canals, but the day ended and all the youths went singing and dancing until after midnight, when those who had mistresses went off to sleep with them . . .'

At this stage I can hear readers muttering to themselves 'Has Pom gone mad? What on earth has all this ancient history to do with the M of T and speed limits on the M1?' The answer is: everything.

As I understand it, in November the last Minister and his advisors were much troubled with the outcry in the press about multiple pile-ups in fog on the motorway. It is ironical that one of the biggest of these was, we now learn, caused by a police car dashing along in misty conditions at well over a mile a minute and attracting to it a comet-like tail of other vehicles. When the policeman (who says he had been forewarned of where dense fog patches would be) slammed on his brakes, a multiple shunt immediately followed. However, under the pressure of 'public opinion' (really headlines in the daily press), it was decided that some action must be taken and that this should be a crash programme for fog warning lights which, when switched on, would render any motorist liable to a charge of dangerous driving if he were found to be going over 30mph.

Doing the ton

It appears someone then said that if a car were moving at say 100mph immediately before the lights were switched on it would be a considerable time before it could reduce speed to 30, and for this reason alone it would be necessary to impose a maximum limit of 70mph on the motorways in England. And if on them, on other roads also since it would be absurd to permit a higher speed on ordinary roads than on

MAGIC IN A NEW SHAPE

MGB MG GT

Safety fast!

If a new shape was all it took to make a Grand Touring car, we'd have done it sooner. But shape alone is not enough. You need function as well. Our formula was this: we took the best features of the MGB—performance, handling qualities, durability—and added the requirements of a *real* GT car. Our GT had to be comfortable, roomy. It had to have elegance and sophistication, restful and fatigue-free control for the driver, the ability to cover many hundreds of miles in a day. We got the MGB magic into the new shape. And we put in some more magic as well. Come and see for yourself.
MGB GT £998.8.9 (inc. £173.8.9 P.T.).

Backed by BMC Service—Express, Expert, Everywhere

The **BRITISH** Motor Corporation Limited

THE BRITISH MOTOR CORPORATION LTD · BMC

THE M.G. CAR COMPANY LIMITED · SALES DIVISION LONGBRIDGE BIRMINGHAM · OVERSEAS BUSINESS: B.M.C. EXPORT SALES LIMITED · BIRMINGHAM & PICCADILLY W.1.

E-TYPE EX

If you're going to ignore the limit, why not take the kids along? asks our Manney

TENDED

IT HAD TO HAPPEN. THE WIMmen are going to take over (if the birds or the ants or the archeopteryx or somebody else doesn't) the last bastions of malehood. Next thing you know they'll be wearing jockstraps and Purdey will be doing his fowling pieces with dayglo sequin inserts in the stocks. Practically the last place a man can go by himself to prove he is a man (by frightening himself half to death) or with some young crumpet to prove he is a man (by frightening her half to death) has been encroached upon by the female-oriented Practical Approach. The Jaguar E has now got four seats, the better to hold those noisome children, two bridesmaids, the Vicar and old Mrs Betise who does so much good work, or else the (shudder) groceries for the entire week so she won't have to drive the Mini you especially bought her to get the groceries. It's the thin edge of the wedge, mates, that's what it is. To the barri . . .

Seriously, there are plenty of 2+2s around, 2+2 being slang among the makers for two proper seats and two dwarf ones, their company including such august marques as Ferrari, Lamborghini (to come), Alfa Romeo, Lancia, Fiat, Porsche (laughter), Jensen, and Motosacoche I think. Most of these extra 'seats' are really to put luggage or crates of beer on as a semi-sporting body configuration plus space for the rear suspension to operate means that such places were designed around Quasimodo or Toulouse Lautrec. Just the same they are a sound commercial proposition and no doubt Sir William has not been slow to notice that the Ford Thunderbird didn't sell worth a damn in America until it got two extra seats. Okay, so it isn't a sports car. But then neither are a couple of those mentioned above.

Lumbered

With their customary acumen in marketing matters, the Jaguar people have ascertained that there are really a number of people who either would like Jaguar Es but are lumbered with children or already have Jaguar Es but are going to be lumbered with children. A market exists as well for those gregarious types who always seem to have their car full of friends, and for them it is even handier as spare blondes can be stowed on the flat luggage space behind. A side thought occurs that, since the buyers of 2+2s are presumably God-fearing family men, will the insurance go down?

After all, it is more or less the same car with 4.2 engine and bags of poke but with nine →

photographed by David Phipps near Dartford, Kent

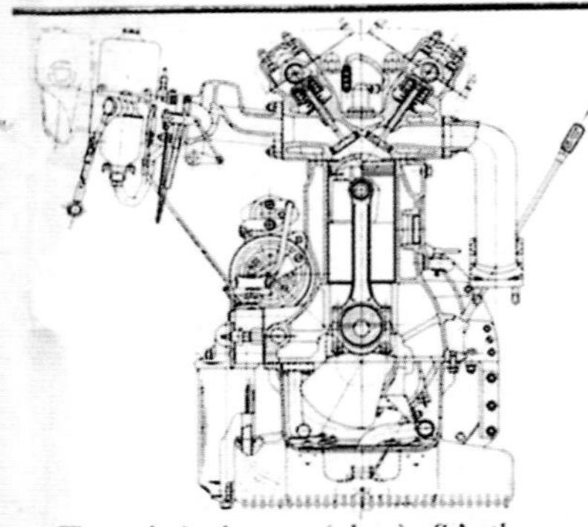

The engine's the same (above). So's the suspension. Differences include dashboard, altered to incorporate extra safety features, plus rear seat with top half which slides forward to boost baggage capacity

→ inches more in the wheelbase behind the front seats and a slight two-inch increase in height. Lovers of the Jaguar's slippery shape will find that the body is a trifle more bulbous but this isn't really noticed unless it is standing alongside a two-seater. Other added attractions to fit it for its new role include a deeper screen to get rid of that armoured car feeling, longer outside wiper blades to match, stiffer rear springs and shock absorbers to take the expected load, and a host of creature comforts like a lockable glove bin, parcel shelf, burstproof locks, more asbestos on the scuttle, and other things like that which will eventually show up on the normal E. There is also the option of the three-speed Borg-Warner (thank *you,* George) Model 8 automatic transmission. In breaking the news of this gently to the customers the lead of Mercedes is followed (on the 230SL) by having a great long lever with progressive gate sticking out of the driveshaft tunnel. In ektual fect this is a crafty move as very many Es spend a lot of their life in town, and who enjoys swopping gears in town? The rear end ratio for the automatic, incidentally, is 3.31 to one and the normal one is 3.54.

I WAS THE FIRST PARIS-BASED AMERICAN JOURNALIST WITH A RED BEARD TO DRIVE THIS NEW CAR AND MY VERDICT IS THAT IT WILL SELL. That it will. AND THAT IT REMAINS A REAL JAGUAR. So it does, and not surprising either as it has the same engine, suspension, wheels, brakes, gearbox, and so forth. Getting in, a job made slightly easier because of the longer doors, it feels like one and sounds like one and rumbles like one and drives off like one. All very comfortable with good seats finally achieved by the organisation and even improved visibility. As far as I could tell in the midst of the sappy 70s, rain, and far too much traffic for my liking, the 2+2 has lost very little performance if any (0–60 in 9.2) from its increase in weight – nobody seemed to know how much – nor did the chassis twist even on bumpy roads from having a lump grafted into it. I had a look at this operation later on the assembly line and it seemed to be done neatly with due regard for bracing, mostly by continuing the front-seat footwells and flattening out the bulkhead behind. As a bonus, you can now recline the front seats!! Anyway, besides being able to get the squab to a comfortable angle there was little to tell that this was in fact the 2+2 although I think that the ride was a bit smoother owing to the longer wheelbase. This should also have the effect of making the car run a bit straighter at speed (or so Jenatzy said) but it still seemed to me to haver about in the normal Jag IRS fashion.

In the interests of Science I even got into the back seats while Andrew Whyte drove, and really they are quite reasonable. The squab is split longitudinally so that half of the seat back can slide forward on rails to make more baggage room when just two are aboard. This has the unusual advantage of forming a convex shape when joined up to the bottom half in the four-place position. Thus it gives very good support to the small of the back. Your shoulders still wave about in the air, but that is infinitely preferable to a flat squab giving torture after 10 miles. Legroom for a six footer (me) was pretty good, considering. I sat at first behind the passenger's place which was quite far back and had given me more than enough legroom to the scuttle. Now in the back I had to sit with my legs apart but wasn't too cramped, nor did I have my feet trapped. Thus it would be no hardship for anybody but one of the Harlem Globetrotters to slide his seat up a bit to provide the back seat passenger with more comfort. In any case the runners have two sets of holes for mounting near or far.

Behind the driver's seat was more difficult, as Andrew is one of these blokes who slams it right back. If the car was mine that would be no problem as I sit fairly close up, but there you are. Headroom was also ample even with my hat on; I would suggest, though, that Jaguar change that fuzzy cloth headliner for a padded plastic one to avoid hairoil marks and also provide panic grips on each side, both for passenger support on corners (the back seats don't give much) and also for weaseling in and out. One wouldn't need them for bouncing up and down as the stiffer rear end works very well indeed, only bottoming once on a farm track in the Cotswolds. In fact if it were up to me I would have the front stiffened up to match as it bobs and weaves about a bit.

All in all the 2+2 is a very practical proposition. If Sir W Lyons devoted half of his E type production to it he wouldn't be sorry. The man with a family who doesn't quite want a saloon yet will applaud it, the sports car man with friends will applaud it, and no doubt Sir William's bank manager will applaud it too. Amazing how he keeps coming up with something useful. ❄

The frustrations of the long-distance road-tester

THERE CAN BE FEW THINGS more frustrating than driving a really good GT car on a deserted motorway at 70mph. Before last December I drove regularly along M2 in complete safety at speeds of up to 140mph while testing high performance cars for foreign magazines – and thereby making my personal contribution to the export drive. Now I crawl along between 70 and 80mph, often with no other traffic in sight except parked police cars, and then turn off to attempt maximum speed runs on narrow, ill-surfaced but unpoliced country lanes. Doesn't make sense, now does it?

I have spoken to several people who don't take any notice of the 70 signs, and they've had no trouble from the police. I even know someone who got away with passing a police car at over 120mph. (Okay – they couldn't have caught him, and they wouldn't attempt to chase him anyway, but they could have taken his number.) Nevertheless I don't propose to emulate either him or CAR's bold editor, not even with a dirty rear number plate, because I value my driving licence more than Britain's export drive. But if the 70 limit doesn't come off I think I shall go and live on the Continent and make a living out of extolling the virtues of Continental cars.

The car which really brings home the fatuity of the 70 limit is the new 2 + 2 version of the Jaguar E. At 70mph this is doing less than 3000rpm, and feels almost as if it is straining at the leash. Its natural cruising speed is in the region of 3500 or 4000rpm (85 to 100mph) and it will maintain this rate indefinitely – at the same time returning over 20mpg.

However annoying it is to have to stay below 70 on motorways, it's even more difficult to do so on normal roads. The slightest burst of acceleration makes you a lawbreaker, even though it may enable you to complete overtaking manoeuvres *far* more safely than in almost any other car, and if you are really conscientious you will spend more time looking at the speedometer than the road.

If the speed limit becomes permanent, and is rigorously enforced, sales of high performance cars must suffer. Jaguar say this hasn't happened yet, and point out that many people buy E-types for their appearance, comfort and handling rather than their performance. But I certainly wouldn't buy a car like the E-type if I couldn't legally exceed 70mph. *David PHIPPS*

Twice a day, 365 days a year, year after year, the **Post Office advertises the Reliant Motor Company.** Just dial TIM, and if you wait long enough you'll hear the magic words 'Three twenty-five precisely.' It's the word 'precisely' that we like. The Reliant Regal 3/25 is a **precisely built** job. This three-wheel family car has a 600 c.c. engine to give **up to 65 m.p.g.** and achieves 100,000 mile reliability. But we **can't persuade the Post Office** to add the word 'Super' *(or to tell callers they can drive the car on a motor cycle licence)*. So we have to advertise in print the **new looks, inside and out,** of the Regal 3/25 Super—the new version that costs **only the same** as the standard 3/25 used to. (We've **reduced the price** of the standard model at the same time.) THE TIME IS NOW to *write for the new brochure* to:

The Reliant Motor Company Limited (S.) Tamworth, Staffs.

Reliant 3/25 Super

(shown here)
New styling and comfort
65 miles to the gallon

Tear around the dotted line!

Independent suspension on all four wheels gives Imp its safety, its firm grip, its controlled stability round the tightest corner. Wide, low-profile tyres and a low centre of gravity make even more certain that Imp holds the road surely and safely. Imp has its sting in the tail with an 875 c.c. aluminium engine. The 4-speed all-synchromesh gearbox gives a change for the better each time, urges Imp along till the needle nudges the 80 m.p.h. mark. Generous on space (room for 4 adults all with freedom of movement).

Imp is a miser with your petrol money. 40/45 m.p.g. Routine servicing only once every 5000 miles. Testing is believing. Arrange this with your Rootes dealer today. **SALOON £420** plus p.t. **DE LUXE £440** plus p.t.

Recommended ex-works prices.

HILLMAN IMP

MADE IN SCOTLAND BY ROOTES MOTORS LIMITED

HILLMAN MOTOR CAR CO. LTD · LONDON SHOWROOMS AND EXPORT DIVISION: ROOTES LTD · DEVONSHIRE HOUSE · PICCADILLY · LONDON · W1

MOKE A LA MODE

it mayn't be much in the mud – but in Chelsea it's fab, gear, rave

We sent Jan Condel, CAR's kinkiest staffer, to try the Mini-jeep that flopped in the country but drew every eye in Town

THIS IS YOUR CHANCE TO jump right in with the jet set – so the ads ought to say, but don't. This is the top gear car for people on the move. It's also the coldest, the wettest, the most useless cross-country vehicle since 1898 . . . but to hell with the wide open spaces. We fell in love with it strictly as a fun about-town car. We begged Henry Manney to prolong a stay in London to photograph it. We conned the prettiest birds we know (ex-art associate Hawkins's wife Jackie, and her sister Jennifer) to come and smile. We borrowed that pvc trouser suit from a Hampstead boutique, fixed a Chelsea rendezvous for a mammoth photo session, sat back – and watched the rain pour down.

This, then, is the tale of moking the mast of a Mini Moke.

Yes, it was raining. We had a week to find out why this tent-on-wheels had become the darling of the Chelsea set. The week stretched damply away into a cumulus nimbus future. Then we noticed a smile, the first for days. Our chin went up and we gave the engine a few more revs in third before doubling down showily for the next hold-up. We collected a feeble wolf-whistle, carved up a staring taxi driver and decided we'd found most of the answer already.

In fact, completely unintentionally, the Moke has most of the properties inseparable from our much-vaunted ideal town car – far more for this special use than the Mini itself. The fact that it's not exactly a success outside the Royal Borough of Kensington and Chelsea must have come as something of a shock – a shock that apparently BMC's ad-men still haven't got over, judging from the agricultural nature of their literature.

Even in traffic, though, complete contact with the outside is by far the Moke's biggest advantage. It's a quality that would be lost with even the side-screens available from Barton Motor Company. True, you get traffic fumes blowing through your hair – but you can join in kerbside conversations. You can nip in and out (or is it on and off ?) at will. Parcels can be dumped unceremoniously, friends quickly piled aboard. There's more space than in a sports car, no doors to be locked, no windows to be wound, no claustrophobic iron sheet an inch or two above your head. The scanty hood is instant up, instant down – just like an English sun.

Perhaps surprisingly, this is enough to overcome the myriad disadvantages. You can get far colder and wetter in a Moke than in any sports car. We quickly learned that we pickled if we pulled up near belching diesels, that buses made welcome shelters from searing cross-winds, that if we parked left side to kerb the camber threw water from the roof over our passengers and not ourselves . . . For £406 (£4 cheaper than a Fiat 500, £34 dearer than the barest Minivan or pick-up) the Moke is delivered in the crudest possible form. All three passenger seats are extras at £25 the set, and so are the grab handles. Girt tubular bumper bars front and rear are standard, though: they have a psychological effect all round in a butchery session – which can, in any case, be carried out with surgical precision in a vehicle where all four corners are not only visible but almost within reach. Occupants sit rather precariously on a level with the wide pontoon sides. If the seats are removed, the well forms a flat baggage area. Two moulded rubber catches hold the lift-off bonnet firmly in place and seem far more practical than the Mini set-up. On the test Moke's engine, plugs and so on were waterproofed – probably with the money saved in fitting a single windscreen wiper which is little use anyway, as the inside of the screen gets just as wet.

The only chrome is around lights and speedo. There are, if possible, even fewer knobs than on the basic Mini. The only luxury is the turn-key starter à la Cooper, which long ago dispensed with the old fingernail-saving trick of using a well-placed stiletto heel on the Mini's rubber whatsit. Lucky: stilettos are out, too. The seats are all adjustable – with a spanner. Driving comfort is a dirty word. Nonetheless, just buzzing about town can be fun for its own sake, though the usual raucous first gear graunch brings more than its fair share of kerbside ribaldry. A passenger's life is even more hair-raising, especially in the front where shortage of room →

Tom Northey

makes a poor wight feel unbalanced. In anything but high summer *all* occupants need protective clothing – gloves, wind- and rainproof moking jacket, rugs and foot-warmers, as all north winds make straight for the foot well.

All hell breaks loose on the open road at anything over 58mph. The pvc hood flaps dementedly and the whole outfit shivers and shakes like an ancient biplane lumbering up for takeoff. Passing gusts of wind will lend an extra burst of speed, but passing under a bridge will as quickly rob you of five hard-earned mph. The cause is all aerodynamic as the Moke, hood and windscreen in position, is three inches higher than the Mini. In fact, although none of the ratios are altered, the little car wouldn't keep up a steady 60mph over the test track's measured quarter-mile.

We drove it round our sodden skidpan and only succeeded in filling the foot well with water while proving that its roadholding is no different from a standard Mini's, despite the optional cleat-tread tyres. Suspension, incidentally, is the old rubber cone and shock absorber setup. In the quest for action, we headed for our favourite stretch of broken *pave*. Like learning to rise to the trot, the Moke and its rider were never airborne together. But we failed to bottom the heavily guarded sump, and nothing fell off except the wiper switch.

Finally someone suggested a short session in the mud. The idea! We'd heard about the vehicle's cross-country background, but really. Beaming gaily at the camera, we plopped off the tarmac and into the mire – and stopped dead, six feet from the edge. Mud flew, wheels spun and we stayed right there. None of the schoolbook theories worked, but after a time we found we could go anywhere the Moke wanted to, crabwise in reverse if we used lots of revs.

Not for farmers, this one. But we'll remember how the Moke turned city sceptics into fans. We'll remember, too, the earthy Morgan feelings. Best of all we'll remember the effect on thrusting London drivers. A touch of the horn and rush-hour traffic would halt with polite hand signals to let us cross their bows. Why, one soaking night a car drew up as we parked and a deep base voice boomed 'Madam, we admire your courage'. Seconds later four large hands had grabbed suitcases, parcels and gub and two large umbrellas escorted us to our door. In a week we found that chivalry's not really dead.

Windblown? So would you be (top left). Mini-Moke is more exposed than the starkest sports car, for better or worse

Styling at its simplest. BMC's newest Mini-variant has the same air of uncompromising fitness as a London bus

Room for many more. Moke's capacity for people and luggage (left) is limited only by what discomfort you can stand

Hairy performer (right). Actually, low weight gives Moke lots of acceleration although shape sadly limits its top speed

Top gear car. Reason for Moke's success with the Chelsea set (below) is its relaxed air. Hollow sides serve as boot

photographed by Henry Manney III in and around Chelsea, London

Bill Hartley talks about Antifreeze

Can anyone afford to drive in a British winter without antifreeze?
"No, the risk is too great" says Bill Hartley.

"People are always asking me that question and I always say the same thing. No matter what Insurance policy they have or what other precautions they take — and that covers rugs, blankets, heaters, draining out, the lot — the only sure way to prevent winter damage in the cooling system is with a good antifreeze."

Is it true that freeze-ups can actually occur while driving?

"**If you don't use antifreeze, certainly they can.** There are people lucky enough to have heated garages who may think they don't need to take precautions against frost because the car will either be in the nice warm garage or in use, with the engine running. This is a dangerous assumption. Many a car's radiator has frozen up while on the move.
Running into a biting cold east-wind, for instance, is liable to limit the circulation and cause serious overheating of the engine or even freezing and boiling at the same time. This can lead to serious engine damage such as a cracked head or block – and nobody in their right mind wants that, do they?"

This business of flushing out before putting in antifreeze, is it really necessary?

"**Well, it's not essential, of course, but not to do it is simply spoiling the job.** Present day pressurised systems which are not often topped up are particularly liable to rust and corrosion. This means obstruction of the water passages and the ideal way to remove it is to add a tin of Holts Speedflush and run the car for a few days – not less than 50 miles. When the car is drained out you can actually see the muck you've shifted and now all is ready for the antifreeze treatment. YES – I believe in chemically cleaned cooling systems anyway, but specially before using antifreeze."

Which type of antifreeze do you think is best?

"**Simply one that has the right balance of Ethylene Glycol and Methanol.** You see Ethylene Glycol – acknowledged as the finest antifreeze – is very expensive and Methanol much less so. So the right balance of the two gives you an antifreeze that's just as effective but far cheaper. It's fine for protecting your car from frost for the longest of British winters. This is what Holts Glycolmaster is and does. It's a scientific blend specially for the job."

Does Glycolmaster Inhibit Corrosion?

"**Yes, but I don't like the word 'inhibit'. I prefer 'prevent',**" **says Bill Hartley.** "It seems to be a sort of blinding with science the way the word 'inhibit' is used these days. I think 'prevent' is simpler and much more to the point. Certainly it expresses exactly what Glycolmaster does. And that is to protect the engine metal, whether it's aluminium or anything else. By the way, the only other trouble that might occur – and it's never the fault of the antifreeze itself – is the possibility of excess acidity. But, of course, that's no problem because you have the visual colour guard."

What is this visual colour guard exactly?

"**Well, it's a sort of early warning system.** It tells you when there's an excess of acid in the cooling system. You know, there might be a slightly leaking gasket or something to set up dangerous acid conditions. I reckon any antifreeze worth its name should give you this added protection. What happens – it's rather ingenious really – when you put the Glycolmaster in, the water goes red. If too much acid builds up it turns yellow, and this is your cue for action. Top up with a little more Glycolmaster and bring up the red again – couldn't be simpler, could it!"

Do many people use Glycolmaster?

"**Good gracious, yes. It's so terribly economical,**" **says Bill Hartley.** "I know that many of the country's top motor engineers, the men responsible for operating big fleets of vehicles of all kinds for Government Departments, Municipal Authorities, and Bus fleets, all use Glycolmaster. Economy is a commercial necessity to them, provided the results are always safe and reliable. That's why so many of them have chosen Glycolmaster year after year."

Glycolmaster Antifreeze

1 pint 3/9 **2 pints 6/9** **3 pints 9/6** **1 gallon 25/0**

from garages Halfords and autoshops everywhere

'I LOVE STATION WAGONS. They're for people who spend a lot of time in their cars. Comfort in a car is very important. You can't drive fast today anyway, but I like to go on holiday and not count the suitcases. I like to take anything that's fun – my sled, a boat on top . . .'

That's fine, of course, for a watchful, carefully-spoken, successful young car stylist (who also designed the glassfibre sled as a matter of fact). With a name like Ferry Porsche III you are one of the few 30year-old Germans who can afford to run a Pontiac station wagon, even if only a compact. But not to drive the sacred Porsche? 'The only car I do a clean-sheet sports car with a middle engine. With extra seats it's a compromise and a touring car would be wrong; the engine would have to be in front because of the luggage'.

A very brief chat – the only kind he grudgingly grants – with this bearded, dedicated backroom boy soon convinced us that the eldest son of Dr Porsche is an idealist with the firm, almost dogmatic convictions of a young man who started at the top and then proved his right to stay – the hardest of all commercial tasks. He believes in current design, not the history of form. 'Styling is too young for postwar Germans. But I don't the family studio without the corruption of higher formal education because 'I think a car is enough for the designer, it has so many parts. If a man only does tape recorders, say, he would do well to try a car'.

After half a dozen years in Porsche's embryonic styling branch (three of them as its head) he remains impatient of team efforts or even comments from other bureaux. The small, tradition-conscious Porsche laboratory has always mirrored just one family. Prof (honorary) Ferdinand Porsche founded it, his son Dr Ferry Porsche runs it today and *his* eldest son is Ferry III, the stylist. As Butzi remarks: very well together to style a car, and many things will still be falsified. I could work as part of a team but it wouldn't be my own work and therefore it wouldn't be as good.' You sense a conflict here with the old guard – in a firm where some department heads settled into the red brickwork the day they followed his grandfather, Porsche's original pragmatist, from Austria.

'After all' Butzi points out, 'we have to build a car we can count on for at least 10 years. The 911 shape goes back to 1959/60, but there were many similar ideas before that'. He feels most definitely that 'our cars must be Porsches first, not just German.

THE 3RD MR PORSCHE

The elusive Butzi tells our man Sloniger about the cars in his life

ever owned from our range was a Speedster. Why should I buy a Porsche when they're everywhere around me?'

If the Porsche heir drives big wagons, what can his select circle of customers expect from the intense young head of their beloved marque's seldom-discussed styling studio? A Porsche station wagon some day? 'I *have* tried one on a Porsche basis, but it would be difficult with our customers. We wouldn't build a real four-seater. There are so many things we couldn't do with it. We would need a larger engine, the car would be heavier and the boot insufficient for four people. We're a sports car firm'. He sounded almost regretful.

But in reality 'Butzi', as he's known privately within the close-knit Porsche ranks, is wholeheartedly dedicated to doing things quite the opposite way – at least during designing hours. 'I'd do away with the occasional seats entirely if I had my way. If you ask a man to sit on a box he knows it's a box, hard and temporary. But if you put in a chair he expects comfort. The occasional rear seat is like that. 'In fact, given the chance, I'd feel I have to bring more style to Germany, just better – so we can learn what is basically good'. As an afterthought: 'Of course, our generation recognises styling.

'Perhaps it wasn't needed before in Germany. America has to have it to sell cars – their kind of life demands it. But styling doesn't exist to provide new faces. It must strive for what's truly good'. His work is entirely company-oriented because there was no alternative. 'I didn't really have any personal gods as a boy.'

Dependence on private wellsprings still marks Ferry Porsche. In a firm where the chiefs are seldom on display he sets some sort of record for shunning public exposure. Tucked into his studio, protected by two guarded gates and hidden behind the already inaccessible racing department, Ferry III seldom poses with one of his own designs – although both the current 911/912 road car and the highly successful but now obsolete 904 GTS track bolide were his. Motor shows? 'I don't go often, except for Turin of course. That's a must.'

Ferry is the complete pragmatist – the boy who doodled cars in the schoolroom and went into 'I would insist that my grandfather had a great deal to do with car styling. In his day a designer did everything. But the current road Porsches were more the cars of my father. Particularly the recently-retired 356. The 911 is his car, too, technically, but not so much as the 356. The 911 is a more modern car – a team effort, descended from the 356'.

But it was styled originally by Ferry III, part of that team. Rather ruefully he concedes 'styling is the new baby in our firm, so you hear a lot about it right now. Everybody knew about the technical side already. I don't know if there would have been a styling studio if I hadn't been inclined that way, but it would certainly have been necessary. Any firm building cars today needs one – and not necessarily just for its own cars. We work for outside people, too'. In fact Porsche devotes roughly half its overall staff time to consultation contracts, though the company is even cagier about naming clients than admitting the bhp of next year's racer.

This is only one reason he insists it is better for one man to do one car. 'A committee must work

'It could be interesting for us to build a high-quality car not in competition with any other' he muses carefully. Both form and technology might come together then, but it would cost £5000 or even £6000.

'All right, any firm should take an interest in being a leader but there are so many new things which would come better from a large company. They are too risky from a small one. If VW brought sliding doors to the market it would make them more popular than, say, Farina could.

Getting down to specifics, how did he go about maintaining the family image when the original purely aerodynamic 356 design was turned into his 'styled' 911? 'For the 911 we wanted a falling tail line like the 356 first of all. And to keep the rear engine of course. That dictated our form.

Ferry admits 'sales people have a say, too, sadly enough. They control a lot – like those instrument surrounds in the 911'. (These were styled in matt black but changed to chrome for production.) 'Sales say they look richer now. I think they should say "we do it this way →

→ because it is better". If it *is* better everyone will agree in the end . . .' To be fair he added firmly 'but nobody has complained about either the chrome or the reflections'.

The new Targa convertible with fixed, flat roll-over bar behind the seats was another car young Porsche couldn't really do entirely his own way. 'The whole Targa was more of a compromise than it needed to be, because of tooling costs. To me it should have been a pure cabriolet alongside the coupe'.

To a man who only yearns for open transport when it is limited to two seats – first a scooter, then a motorcycle and eventually a Speedster, the most minimal Porsche of all – the immutable Porsche insistence on rear engines can be a frustration. 'There has never been a successfull rear-engined cabriolet. This is a major factor here and the failing in my Targa. Still, I think it looks better than one first thinks – and could be better still'.

As with the original 911, 'there was plenty of time for that job and we got a lot of opinions from people outside the studio. Father had a word, but he left it largely to me. He has taste but is not a stylist'. Allowing his favourite almost-smile to expand into a rare puckish grin, bearded Butzi added: 'I don't think you'll find many men who say they have no taste'.

The 904 sports/racing car was another matter. It remains a memory that lights his eye. 'It was my favourite because I did it and there wasn't this fight to change it or make it newer. It was designed and finished. Time was very short. I didn't have a *free* hand but it had to appear so soon after the scale model was built that there was really no time for interference'.

The corollary is clear without words: it ruffles him that the 904 was discarded, still a winner, for the newer Carrera-6 coupe (CAR August). 'I think there was still room for development there, in the 904' he says. 'Admittedly, it was heavier than it might have been. Glassfibre was too new to us. We were the first in Germany to make a famous series that way, remember. Now we work a lot with the stuff – on models. It all goes back to the Formula One car. I think you could say we have included glassfibre in our system. Perhaps there will even be a road Porsche in glassfibre one day, but I think it will be a long time. The quality is not good enough here. In America they have gone further and quality demands are not as high from their customers'. And in England, too?

New materials can mean new shapes – such as his 904, which was a winning racer yet not a copy of any other track machine. We asked if Ferry III would design a clean-sheet road Porsche in glassfibre to look like the 904 two-seater, partly since it is his obvious favourite from the studio and partly since he favours two seats for all Porsches anyway. 'No' flatly. 'I believe that as soon as an architect or stylist does something new he must try and do it better. Any designer knows, once a project is finished, how it could have been made better'.

While his legendary grandfather (whom Ferry III knew, but never as an employee) was an instinctive engineer, stylist and even winning Alpine Trial driver, the third generation says 'Oh, I like to drive fast but only comfortably fast. Why should I race or test cars? I try a car for space and comfort, not speed. Of course I notice if it leaks water or the engine doesn't go, but my problem is form'.

But for a born and bred Porsche, dedicated to rear engines in the £3000 kind of car, mechanical abstracts such as the worldwide swing to front-wheel drive do have some significance. He says flatly 'I'd have to see if the Toronado works before talking about front-wheel drive. I do think a heavier car will be better with front drive than a light one. But rear engines remain better on hills (there speaks the born Austrian ski enthusiast). 'You can't drive a light car up or down a hill as well with extreme understeer. If your Porsche gets stuck in the snow, don't bother with any other car. It won't get through'.

Reminded of the argument that average drivers find front drive safer in side winds and self-slowing in corners, Ferry III says 'All right, safer until they begin to skid. But once they go you can never catch them again'. With his characteristic musing leap, young Porsche adds: 'A car is usually tailored to the people and landscape where it must be sold'.

Considering that Porsche only sells half its cars at home, how does he evaluate their features? 'I don't think top speed is the answer today, while acceleration and manoeuvrability rule in modern traffic. But a large engine is difficult with Germany's tax structure. A Porsche must be the fastest car, the one out in front. That's why I want only two seats – with our engine limitations'.

Would that rule out automatics at Porsche? 'We are trying automatic gearboxes, but they won't come until we are entirely happy. I have one in my wagon because I like to look out the windows and not think about changing gear. And when my wife drives a Porsche she uses the four-speed kind. I find them more comfortable in town'. (The vast majority of current Porsche buyers opt for the five-speed.)

Deprecating his own taste for simplicity refined, Ferry III insists 'Porsche is not a standard for styling in the first place, but for the technical side. We really aren't moving towards a 'styled' car here. On the other hand, people who say German form is heavy see only Mercedes. Ours is heavier than Italian, true, but styling is becoming less nationalistic. It is hard for me to tell an American Ford from a GM product – harder than it used to be. Even Italy will be influenced by the Americans soon'.

Reiterating a pet theme, he went on: 'Many stylists today come from architecture, but they must still learn to work with automobile materials. An entirely square glassfibre car is wrong, for instance'. Asked how this might bear on his quoted comment that the 904 is 'sexy', since it obviously isn't square in either the outmoded jazz sense or the architectural, Ferry returned to a suspended dialogue on masculine and feminine in cars. 'I think the 904 was typically masculine – and the 911 is more masculine than the 356 was. I don't know precisely how. It lies in the personality of the designer'.

First deferring the problem of whether a car could be altered consciously towards either the male or the female persuasion, Ferry said on another occasion: 'The feminine car would be soft overall . . . I don't believe you can change a line or a grille and alter the car's character. A soft car might be more masculine as a convertible, of course, but while *I* find the Mercedes 230 SL a hard car I could imagine that it would be soft to some buyers. Performance is a part of this concept'.

He added: 'The Targa is masculine and certainly more sporting or roadster-like because of its roll bar. Whether a manly man would buy it depends on his age. A man of 50 or 60 wants a car that gives him a young, sporting image. A very young man wants that image too'. (Ferry Porsche III is an ageless, married 30.)

Sex changes apart, how would he make a car more German? 'I would make it look more expensive for our market, but I don't think you can fool Americans so easily – at least not in Porsche's kind of buyer circle. I think Porsches are bought more often in American families where the man picks the car.' Even its colour? Ferry notes wryly 'We invent new colours but there are always too many requests for special ones. Orange is my favourite. I'd always have an orange Porsche. First for safety. And then, why not? A sports car can have a perky colour. Why should it be German racing silver? Besides' he added almost parenthetically, 'there's a quality problem with metallic colours like silver'.

When your name is Ferry Porsche, aesthetics may rule your whims but quality control, house image and production parameters still dictate sales. The future owner and autocrat of perhaps the second smallest motor firm of true world-wide renown actually melts into his chosen background of clay models and drawing boards in a two-storey, glass-walled room called the Studio. Eschewing colour-keyed doors, glamorous receptionists and (best of all) intruders, this son of the boss, grandson of one of the true and few dogmatic geniuses in automotive history, rules his own way there. ❋

Henry Manney III

LAMBORGHINI REVISITED PART 2

Disaster in the Sicilian mountains! George Bishop continues CAR's Lambo saga

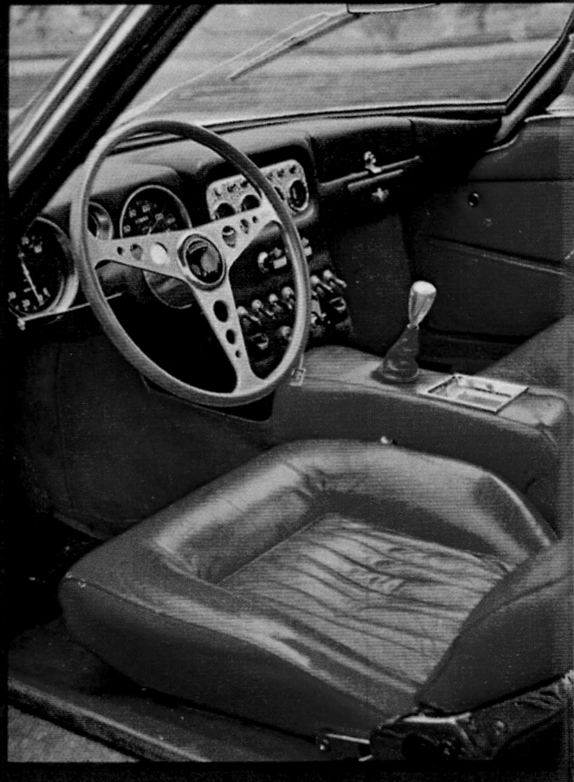

At rest, the Lambo may be ugly but on the move (top) it comes alive. Squat profile gives it a road-hugging look that is borne out in excellent aerodynamics right up to 160-plus

Wottle she do, signor? In Modena they're used to rapid machinery but the Lambo still rates a second glance. Ours was painted silver-grey with subtle hints of royal purple

A frequent scene, this (left), during our five days and 1500 miles at the wheel. Average consumption worked out at about 15mph – which isn't bad for six carbs and 250hp

Lambo interior puts all the essentials neatly to hand (above) and throws in real reclining seats complete with headrests so that a passenger can relax even at high speed

Driving through Italy, you'll find plenty of roadside hoardings proclaiming the merits of Lamborghini. But they don't mean motor cars – at least not yet. So far the Cavalliere is best known for his tractors (opposite page), which range from small general-purpose farm workhorses to middleweight crawler types such as the 5C at top left. It's a two-litre, three-cylinder diesel with no less than eight forward gears and two reverse! Other Lambo products include hot-air burners for household heating (top right) and complete home air conditioning systems. You, too, can own a Lamborghini . . .

IF YOU DON'T KNOW THE story already, it seems Lamborghini cut up army surplus trucks after the war and made them into tractors, thus founding his fortune. Then he bought three Ferraris at different times, and being displeased with the service he received decided to make a better car himself. He went two better with four cams instead of two, and three better with six carbs instead of three, then added an independent rear end instead of a live axle, and a great deal of silence by cutting out wind noise and engine racket.

Having collected our 350GT from the good Cavaliere himself, we started to find out for ourselves how it works. There are about 250 genuine horses to propel this light two plus two wind-cheating carriage, a five-speed box, a redline at 7000, and it's very *wide*. To the driver it feels like Todd AO, because unless he's kangaroo tall he can't see the far wing without sitting up. There's plenty of prod, and if I never drive a nicer car I shan't complain.

I don't want to go into too much detail about the car as that's the subject of another treatise in this very journal (to come! – *Ed*) except to note that the seats with built-in headrest are just what the doctor ordered, and that all the clutch travel is needed to sort the cogs neatly. Handling is just about neutral and steering hands-off at any speed you care to name. And so to the Autostrade del sole for hour upon hour of cruising at a rate you don't get too many chances to enjoy. Wallace Bob said fuel consumption would stay better than 20mpg (what, with *six* double-choke Webers?) if we kept down to 160/180km/h, but over that it would use a bit.

I was allowed a burst at max speed for the let's-see-what-she'll-do bit, and it turned out to be an indicated 280km/h, later found to be a 20km exaggeration due to a change of gearing. 'You have just driven' said Blyne, twiddling the km/miles converter 'at about 173 miles an hour.' On the way up I changed from fourth to fifth at 200km/h just for the hell of it. With this out of our system we settled to using only about 5000 of the available 7000rpm, and when we compared notes decided neither of us had extracted more than about 60percent of the car's potential. For those who can do sums maybe I should explain I'm talking now about percentage in terms of handling.

After very few hours of this kind of juvenile activity we ran out of motorway around Naboli, or rather eschewed it in favour of the left-lock, right-lock stretch through Calabria, motoring through the scent of honeysuckle in the hedgerows and savouring the absence of any kind of noise unless driver-provoked by stirring levers and pedals or torturing the tyres. We flipped out to Paestum to see the Greek temples on the coast, but, deciding we didn't like the look of the German-owned hotel vaunted by M Michelin (who didn't mention the salacious beach) we pushed on again to a seafront place at Sapri, where the Lambo looked a little lost amid the rusty dustbins and Dauphines in the backyard.

The last stretch to the night-stop from south of Salerno will not be soon forgotten. It was the old right-lock, left-lock story all right, but in the dark with a beeg drop on one or both sides, and the Lambo did not climb higher than third gear for more than two hours. I sat behind a relaxed indigenous gentleman who held his Fiat's roof on with one hand and twirled with the other with the dexterity of a croupier. He knew the tortuous route so well that every time we rounded a corner with a straight ahead of it – there he was, gone. I learned then the lightness of the Lambo's steering, and marvelled at its suppleness and agility.

And so to Reggio, where we told the Auto Club we needed more petrol coupons, having used 18 days' supply in about the same number of hours. They laughed and said have a good time, or something like that, and come back in 17 days. There's not much point in going into miles and speeds and such in detail, since the Lambo will cruise at what you will up to about 170mph. So far we had returned better than 15mpg.

We'd done about 800 miles London-Modena in the Tiger, then about 750 Modena-Reggio in the Lambo, all between Tuesday afternoon and Friday afternoon. We stopped to switch cars, eat, fill with fuel, pay tolls, talk to people, sleep, and kept down to what is for the Lambo a slow cruising speed of 180km/h on the autostrade – much slower on the locky bits. This was genteel cruising, not do-or-die stuff, but it shows what Italy's sun route has done to distance.

In Reggio there was high comedy with the ferry, which it turned out went better from Villa san Giovanni a few miles back. The Italians kept shunting trains across the road, through which your scribe had to climb in order to buy tickets for the brief 10-minute crossing to Messina. Meanwhile Blyne had scrounged the car on without tickets, but they found out and held the ferry while the train-climbing proceeded. All done with a light operatic laugh. Ah, the sun! In truth we had much rain on the sun road.

So from Messina in the evening we purred on towards distant Palermo, as they probably say in the brochures. But by God the Sicilians didn't purr. They're all mad, the whole bloody nation, when they get behind a wheel, and are not likely to live the week out. Blind bends, bridges, mountains – nothing stops them trying to overtake a Lambo in a Fiat 500 with six aboard. But why don't they hit each other more often? It must be the Mafia keeping evil at bay.

Roadside flower-beds sprouting geraniums and other such growths are a feature of the Sicilian scene, and there's plenty of time to contemplate the beauties of nature while sitting in the giant economy-size traffic jams engendered by the Targa. The locals don't help matters by dashing up the offside until the road is blocked solid in both directions. I'd like to send a posse from one of Britain's most anti-motorist counties over there for a week: they'd lose their reason, if nothing more.

This account is going to have to be shorthanded if it's to fit even into the white acres allocated, so let's get over the crisis. We made our night stop at a vast caravanserai dominating a hillside, wreathed in flowering shrubs and faded glory. This was the Grand Hotel Terme at Castroreale Terme, a great white elephant glaring over the village. We appeared to be the only occupants, yet somebody's belongings had to be moved out of our room before we could go in. There was a private spa or pump-room or health bath or →

A MOST ATTRACTIVE PROPOSITION!

POUR IN POWER POUR IN LUBYSIL

world's most advanced oil treatment

LUBYSIL SC100

The revolutionary silicone-oil treatment, gives power plus to your engine. Just add Lubysil to your engine oil and you get:

★ MORE MILES PER GALLON
★ GREATER ACCELERATION
★ SMOOTHER RUNNING
★ LESS OIL CONSUMPTION
★ EASIER STARTING
★ LESS WEAR AND MAINTENANCE

TEST-PROVED AGAIN AND AGAIN!

★ Anti-seize properties shown on test before B.B.C. — Sunbeam Alpine ran 34 miles without oil.
★ The Technical Editor of *Popular Motoring* found LUBYSIL SC100 to give a 14% increase in miles per gallon PLUS a 12% increase in acceleration.
★ Tests on Crypton Heenan Rolling Road, Acton, showed 12½% more miles per gallon.
★ Lubysil car came 4th in class, 19th overall in the 1965 RAC Rally.
★ Lubysil car came 3rd overall in the Welsh Rally.

Lubysil SC100 costs **12/6** and gives engine protection for up to 10,000 miles!

Available from **HALFORDS**, all good garages and accessory shops. If you prefer to get Lubysil direct from Silicone Lubrications Limited, post coupon below.

SILICONE LUBRICATIONS LIMITED (Dept. CR46) Abbey Barn Road, HIGH WYCOMBE, Bucks. Telephone: High Wycombe 21922/3/4
Please send me..........bottles of Lubysil SC100 at 12/6 each.
Please send me..........aerosols of Lubysil 717 at 8/8 each.
I enclose PO/Cheque/Money Order value..........
(delete as necessary)
NAME ....
ADDRESS ....

LUBYSIL 717 AEROSIL

RUST-PROOFING LUBRICANT

for lasting protection against rust and corrosion, apply behind body panels, door trims, wheel arches, bumpers etc. · unique penetrating action will prevent rust forming in hidden joints and cavities · stops squeaks · insulates · waterproofs · resists salt water spray · reduces battery corrosion · for CARS, machinery and boats **8/8** per 10 oz. can

→ summat in the lower rock-garden, and the major-domo who doubled as porter-receptionist-waiter in a home-made Esperanto of four tongues was a most sinister figure. Your guess is as good as Alfred Hitchcock's.

Next morning, Saturday and race-eve, we headed light-hearted for Palermo to collect tickets and such and were smote by a sudden rain-shower. A local Fiat 500 was going slowly, but the penny did not drop as to why he was betraying the habits of a nation and a lifetime; Sicilians *never* go slowly. So Bishop bangs it into second and overtakes, at a moderate 50mph or so, and away goes the Lambo's tail to the left. Driver and passenger exchange surprised glances, the tail is put back where it belongs, and promptly takes off in the other direction. Once more it is collected, but now the Lambo waltzes round through a complete 180degrees with driver winding furiously and watching stone walls whistling perilous close. This is the moment of truth: the point of no return is past. Suddenly, we are going to hit something with some part of that glossy carrosserie. Very soon now. But Allah is with us, and the smooth-shanked tail clobbers the wall only a glancing blow as we are motoring backwards in the direction of Palermo.

Bishop sits stunned clutching the splintered remnants of the woodrim wheel, not even feeling the splinters in his numbed thumb. White-faced Blyne climbs out to inspect the damage. Sixty-nine Fiat drivers materialise and offer advice, condolence, threats. The big truck looming the other way has stopped in time. We drive off slowly to find a quiet road and lick our wounds before complications set in. The leftside rear wing is clobbered, the rear-lamp cluster shattered, the flap over one filler-cap stares skywards, the boot is locked upon our luggage. It might be worse, but *why* did it happen? Blyne offers no word of recrimination and says: 'I thought you held it very well.'

He binds the limp steering-wheel rim with handkerchiefs, and chastened we limp, too – on towards Palermo. I ask him to drive. There is more thought than talk going on. Why, why? I ask myself.

Down the road Henry Manney's maroon Ferrari flashes by. We both brake, turn round, shoot past each other again, scream to a halt. Henry, polite as ever, asks 'Who shunted you?' We are not strong on the chit-chat, make plans, both press on. Later we soul-search, ask questions, analyse. Italian asphalt, and even more so Sicilian asphalt, is not so hot in the wet we learn. The Pirelli HS tyres have a hard mix to stand 150-plus cruising, are also not so hot in the wet. I ask any odd racing drivers around what they do when the spin begins. Most say they slap the brakes on and hope. Slotemaker, I recall, says declutch. All this is opposed to my upbringing, which says lift off the throttle, don't touch clutch or brakes, steer out of trouble if you can . . .

While we cruise at slackened speed a Ford Corsair roars by. Later we find the driver was Paul Hawkins, who cannot be quoted verbatim even here, but the gist of his terse talk was that he passed a couple of rich idiots with too much money who couldn't drive and had shunted their Lamborghini even before they'd had time to get it registered; it was still on Prova plates. Sorry, cobber, didn't know it was yew . . .

Black Saturday pursued its dreary rain-soaked course. We couldn't extricate our luggage at the hotel, trekked around to a Lancia agent who found an emergency catch underneath, put new bulbs in the shattered lamp cluster, bound up the steering wheel, could do no more.

Henry had found a new ferry sailing out of Palermo at eleven pip emma on race-night, which involved cancelling the Monday sailing, booking the new one, trying unsuccessfully to get money back. Wet and miserable we shunted around from one dock office to another, the Lambo so misted-up inside that we were driving blind. By evening we had race-tickets, ferry reservations, the boot open, a bed for the night, but realised we had quite forgotten to eat.

Sunday morning brought a five-thirty call for a six o'clock breakfast and the battle to the circuit. The race story, you know. Evening brought the 40mile battle in the reverse direction to catch the Blue Kangaroo. I didn't make it up; that ferry just happens to be called the *Canguro Azuro*. It's an 11hour sailing over about 150 miles costing 10 quid for a very big car, which makes the cross-channel boys look greedy. People cost a little over four quid each in cabins, and it's all new and shiny. Two snags: breakfast is a stand-up cup of coffee and roll, and it took an hour to get off although the boat's a drive-off.

Once Naboli's grime and traffic were shaken off we hit the Del Sole again and Henry offered me a go in his 330 GT. We swopped around, stopped to take dirt-track pictures of the two cars in a parking place, did the stopwatch session on speedo checks, standing starts, and the rest, and were still back at the Palace in Modena for a timely dinner. The Del Sole is a great engineering feat, sweeping across a whole country, but is a bit like airline travel and doesn't bring you to grips with the country. Fine with a very fast car if you are going places, but it must seem interminable else.

John Surtees was at the pub that night, Wallace Bob came in, and a good time was had by all talking about – guess what? Surtees really came to life when we switched to motor-bikes. He told me his first-ever ride was on a monster Vincent, of all things. When he had gone off to early bed we confessed our sins to Bob, who made light of the whole thing and relieved our nervous tension more than somewhat. Morning turned Henry's bedroom into an ersatz magazine office, with copy being phoned to London, his wife ringing from Paris to fix Monaco plans, typewriters thumping, and Henry writing a damn good race story against the clock, which he says he can't do. Judge for yourself from June's page four.

Meanwhile Blyne was dropping the Lambo at the works, making our peace, learning how they're made, and collecting the Tiger. After a snatched lunch we hit the Aosta trail in what felt like a kiddycar after the 12cylinder fare of the past days. This time we took the St Bernard tunnel, but nobody told us why all the trucks were missing. Reason? An hour-and-a-half's detour over the loose dirt surface of the Col des Blanches, which involved going up an alp and down again.

I suppose in bread-and-butter life we all think of a Tiger as a rorty beast, and you must shift scale a bit to find it tame, but you don't need words of one syllable to work it all out. It didn't put a foot wrong or use any oil even, so we plodded on by way of Lausanne this time to a night stop at Besancon where two hotels were full.

Next day a gendarme pulled us up for over-speeding a 40km bend, but let us go with a caution. Merci. Dammit, I've left so much out. Blyne never did find his zampone, and clashed with the Autostrada police when he wanted to cross on foot for a pig's foot. I've ignored the algemarin bath thoughtfully provided by the Cloche management at Dijon, which promised to be a fountain of youth to give us new elasticity. Hardly a word's been said about food and wine . . .

A few facts. To do the trip our way (ignoring the cost of acquiring V12s of assorted kinds) would cost two people about £200, nearly half of it in petrol, road and tunnel tolls, ferry fares. It could be done more cheaply. But would *you* have the face to go camping in a Ferrari or Lamborghini? ❊

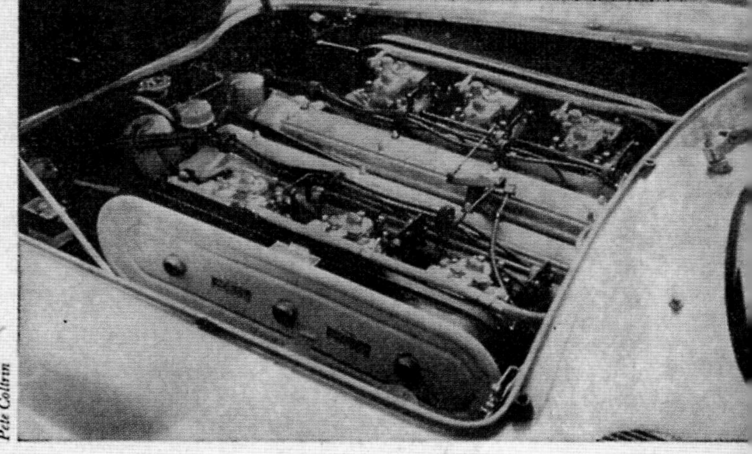

Pete Coltrin

Clearway '67

AC 121

Most car-makers shuffle their feet and er-um a bit when we ask them in high summer what they'll be putting on the show stand. Not so these old Surrey hands who have moved with the times from almost the fringe-on-top to rubber-burning Cobras, those forerunners of today's Le Mans winners. There will be three cars, they said, of which two will be open Cobra 289s with the 4227cc Ford V8 power units. Perhaps there will be a chassis too. There will also be the Frua Convertible or drophead coupe as you like, which has a Cobra chassis extended by six inches and power from the Ford V8 428, successor to the 427, with 7026cc. AC told us they showed this one last year when it was not quite ready, but it has now been improved. Other manufacturers, they said, have been known to make the same mistake.

ALFA ROMEO 107

Five cars from the Milano maestros will include two not yet seen in Britain, both tried out by CAR in sunny Italy and faithfully reported upon in our June issue. One is the new-style GT Veloce, which really does live up to that now debased name of grand tourer, and the other the open car similar mechanically but shorter and possessed of marginally more power. This one was the subject of the find-a-name contest which brought a free Duetto (the one he chose) to some lucky Italian. Other exhibits will be those well-tried and

Flying greenhouse for two – Duetto hardtop

successful examples of the twin-cam art, the Giulia in both Super and TI forms and the roomier though not all-that-much faster 2600 Sprint in two-door coupe form. Alfas confirm existence of the V8 about which CAR told all, but say it is not yet ready and would you please make-do meanwhile with those little ole twin-cam five-speed devices? Willingly.

ALVIS 148

Last year we reported speculation about a sporting Rover to be called an Alvis as a possible fruit of the merger of two of the industry's oldest remaining names. In the event the sporting Rover did emerge, but under the banner of the TC for twin-carb. It seems logical that something should be done about the ancient Alvis name – either decent burial, a splendid new image, or relegation to the field of multi-wheel soldiers' toys where they do so well. Meanwhile they soldier on on the civvie side with the very-very-small-production prestige three-litre with six cylinders and five ZF speeds, slightly tarted-up since Geneva. Now, if Rover really come up with that all-alloy General Motors V8 – not this year – could this be the salvation of Alvis? Predictably, they're not telling.

Old-style wheel is linked to ZF servo

AMERICAN MOTORS 127

They make Ramblers, and are having a thin time in the States, but are bravely bringing a bigger model over here. This is the Ambassador V8, with either 200 or 275bhp, and will be one of four exhibits – the others being hardtop, station wagon and convertible in the smaller size. The old Classic 770 is dropped in favour of the Rebel 770, which you may have with either a 155bhp cooking in-line six or either of the two V8s. They are the typical modern US product, very quiet but not what we are used to in the brakes and handling department.

ASTON MARTIN 114

The DB5 has faded away, but they are making (or were, before our Current Troubles) 14 DB6s a week down at Newport Pagnell, and a profit to boot at just over £5000 a throw. Maybe to give credit where it's due they'll put a bust of Ian Fleming in the hall. There will be four cars on the stand, mostly DBs with either the 280bhp cooking engine with three SUs or the Vantage giving a claimed 325 from twin double-choke Webers, all with twin ohc and five-speed ZF box. There used to be a convertible DB5; so far we haven't been passed by a chop-tail version, though Astons hint darkly that there might be something new. One could also expect H Radford to update the station wagon, but no one will say until show eve so you'll have to wait.

Another now with ZF power steering

AUTO UNION 108

This slightly eccentric outfit (who used to be the biggest two-stroke merchants in the business) say that the British are no longer falling over themselves to buy phut-phuts, so the three-cylinder front-drive F102 is now made in LHD only and stays over the water. Sales here are confined to the interesting but somewhat costly Audi, which they see slotting into

Audi super-compression is for economy

the market as the poor man's Mercedes. This year's stand will feature both two- and four-door versions of this 1.7 four-stroke fwd, and also the Variant or wagon model which is so far unsighted in the UK. Now's your chance to see one.

BENTLEY/RR 153/152

Bentley alias Rolls-Royce have no doubt shot their bolt for some time to come with the Silver Shadow alias T series, for not lightly do they make changes, and what was billed as the first really new model for 49 years really was some change. Bodybuilders (and £8000 cheques) being somewhat thin on the ground nowadays we shall probably see only the two-door versions made by James Young and Mulliner by way of special bodywork. They appeared at Geneva this year in addition to the standard hacks, but coachbuilders are a secretive lot and someone may spring a special surprise.

BMC 125/139/115/130/119

Mr Edwards's Midlands giant is known to be playing with several basic new designs and variants on old ones which will appear in Austin, Morris, Riley, MG and Wolseley versions, but just which ones will be at the show depends upon how his marketing people see the situation. The *Daily Mirror* said back in August that the Morris Oxford and Austin Cambridge were to be replaced by a new Issigonis-style fwd 1300cc model, then in a later story that the Oxford and Cambridge would stay. Our information is that the 1300 is not due yet, and neither the Wolseley version of the 1800 nor yet the automatic ditto. In fact the only changes seem to be minor ones (wind-up windows) to the little Elf and Hornet plus a couple of revamped sports cars about which we'll speak later.

BMW 96

This German firm who staged such a come-back with the 1800 (now joined by the 1600 and 2000 variants) can hardly ring any more changes on that theme, but you probably haven't seen the luxury version of the 2000 TI, the latest one to emerge. There's already a bewildering variety of models in standard, TI (sporting) and coupe form with two alternative engine sizes, an automatic and the newly scaled-down two-door 1600 saloon on the same chassis as the shortened 1800/2000 coupe. All use variations of the same light-alloy ohc engine plus running gear which leads many people to number them among the best-handling carriages on the market. The ultimate is probably the funny-frontal two-door 2000 Coupe Sport with automatic transmission, if you rank rakish lines as well as rock-like handling high on the list.

1600 body is reduced for performance

BOND 111

These split-personality people divide their talents between a bizarre device for marginal motorists (aren't we all?) with a glassfibre body on three wheels powered by a Hillman Imp engine and something for a different slice of the market in the well known if not to all tastes Equipe GT. This is a Herald with a Spitfire engine covered in a fastback glassfibre envelope, one-time advertised: 'Is this the best-looking, etc . . .?' The answer is that it seems to sell, and the original two-seat version was followed by a two-plus-two-halves. There are rumours of further ameliorations before too long along lines that should raise the Equipe's status among the cognoscenti, but for '67 the only novelty is an optional sunshine roof.

Cosmetic with non-fattening base

EARLS COURT STAND BY STAND

ROOMY DAF. 44 Daf, perfect transmission and 40 gross Dutch cheese horses for sparkle, wider track for stability

BRISTOL 116

The Businessman's Express has lived up to its name since in the long-ago the old two-litre gave way to a V8, although those early models were certainly the prettiest. At more than £5000 the 409(A) has a small slice of the market, but is nicely made in aircraft style for those who want something different. There is talk of smaller wheels but otherwise changes are likely to be minor.

Relent! This is the ugliest angle

CHRYSLER 147

Our American spies say the Barracuda is all-new for '67 but they don't mention the mechanicals, which is normal practice in a country where shape is all. Will Chrysler push their big models in Europe now that they have Rootes and Simca to carry the flag? Probably not. The man who styles for them, Elwood P Engle (yes, really), was with Ford one-time and produced the Continental – and Engle goes for angles. In addition to the Barracuda, which is the two-door one with a Le Mans-looking fastback, the other model listed over this side is the Valiant. Like all US makers Chrysler offer a soup-up kit known as the S-Pack, and if you said there are 439 variations we wouldn't argue.

Hottest V8s get 5-year warranty

CITROEN 129

The traction avant people down at Sluff have given up making cars here as you know and now import rhd conversions from France. The single-rotor Wankel (to be built with NSU help) is nowhere near sale-ready yet and will not be here. Meanwhile they will be showing five of the 10 alternatives on the still-advanced ID/DS/Pallas range: two Pallas 21s – one leather, one Jersey nylon seat-coverings; one Safari; one ID Confort; one Decapotable or *(very expensive)* drophead coupe. The ID now has the newer five-bearing engine in its smaller 1985cc form, and all Citroens have gone over from vegetable oil to mineral in their hydraulics after solving the seal problem. This means longer oil life and ease of supply; you try getting vegetable oil in Nether Wallop.

Pallas for five, boot to match

DAF 99

Have new car said to be livelier, more attractive (thanks to Michelotti) and powered by an 850cc edition of their twin-cylinder four-stroke which previously came in 750 form. Three or four will be at the show. We know the Dutch truck firm have future plans for something more sophisticated than the original elastic car driven by rubber bands, but that's way ahead. Meanwhile the cheerful but rather rowdy two-belt saloons are catching on as second cars, and if you still have reservations about the drive system – well, it works in a racer.

DAIMLER/JAGUAR 120/138

BMC have not yet had time to put the E-type engine sideways, nor Jag to commercialise that long-rumoured V12, but there were to be two new models from Coventry under the Lyons banner. One has been put off until Geneva '67, leaving only an S-type with 4.2-litre engine. There are changes to the Mark IIs as well. All are permutations on existing body-shells and machinery rather than brand-new cars, but when you're selling all you can make, why monkey with the product? The V12 with single overhead cam per bank is still for the future and will be raced before production, as will future Aston Martin novelties.

FERRARI 160

That Le Mans business will not take the gloss off the gingerbread in the road-car market because a Ferrari is always unique, after all. Proof of this is that in '64 and '65 the English concessionaires had the gall to show the same five cars, and who else can get away with that? This year the 330GTC seen at Geneva with all-independent suspension will come over by way of augmentation, and the Fiat/Ferrari Dino front-engined six should be nearing production – but nobody is sure who will sell it here.

Long-legged car for short-legged men

FIAT 140

Six cars, two not so far seen in Britain, will grace the Italian stand, but there is no truth in the rumour that the salesmen will be bearded Russians. The new ones are the 1100R, which is a modified version of our old friend the 1100D, and the 124, introduced in Italy not so long ago. Both will be in rhd form, with UK price tags. Old friends include the 500 and 600, this latter modified with a grille like that on the 850, rubber overriders and bigger headlamps. The 1500, still going strong in spite of gossip, makes up the quorum, together with several pretty 850 coupes and other assorted confectionary (no, no Dino). The 1800 and 2300 will be absent temporarily although they continue in production. Fiat are sore about the publicity other people are getting on safety measures, and say they were first with the most – eg, burstproof locks ('63) and a progressively deformable front and rear. They crash cars on the road by remote control from a helicopter, which they say is more realistic than what some others do. We promised to tell you, and have.

Dino by Fiat out of Ferrari

FORD USA 97

As successor to the Mustang they've cobbled up something called a Cougar, as predicted here earlier in the year. It shares pressings, but this does not mean that the Mustang disappears. The Americans say the Cougar is pretty, but the drawings we've seen don't bear this out so you must judge if it makes the trip. Otherwise the smallish Fairlane has a new grille, and the all-conquering Galaxie is revamped with plastic bits around the headlamps instead of plated metal. The Maquis and the Panther join the completely rerigged Thunderbird, but we don't know which ones will come to play at the Court – or between ourselves if we could tell the difference. It's all mostly a styling exercise covering lusty V8s in varying degrees of tune, with the odd in-line six thrown in for the peasants in the cheaper compact and super-compact ranges.

FORD GERMANY 95

No new powerplant this year, and Taunus don't sell over here very much in spite of the enormous range of models they have back in the beer-cellar. The previously-banished (to Holland) 12M has squared up its body boxer-style and returned to production in Cologne. It still has the fwd powerpack which Saab now shares. Also promised soon: a revamped V6 range.

Ford smooth the edges in Germany

FORD 143

You got the big news when the entire British press suddenly had dates in Tunisia and the Mark IV appeared looking like a cross between a coke-bottle and a Cresta. By now it has settled down and will possibly even be joined by an augmented version to match Vauxhall's Viscount. We don't think the Anglia replacement (long tipped for a rear engine) will come yet, but think of the other British Ford which has remained unchanged the longest and you may be on to something. Meanwhile the V4 Corsair station wagon will be there to add interest even if nothing else transpires. We're testing one at this moment and will report before long.

Zodiac/Zephyr: i.r.s. at last

GENERAL MOTORS 134/5/6/7

Chevrolet is the one which the world's biggest car-firm markets most over here, apart of course from the products of their British branch at Luton. The top model is the Canadian-built rhd Impala, a two-door on what we used to call sports coupe lines but about twice as big. This one too is all-new according to spies over the Atlantic, but again it takes an expert to see the difference. It has the dipping waistline and steeply-slanting back a la Buick Riviera, plus kicked-out front corners and horizontal rear-lamp clusters instead of the round ones formerly favoured by Chev. More dramatic GM exhibits will include the front-drive Toronado and Cadillac Eldorado and the glamorous but more conventional Camaro coupe (below).

Camaro: enough power for an aeroplane

GILBERN 110

Makers of a serious kit-car which is quite handsome and has used various power units including MG. It offered substantial performance and occasional room for four at modest cost. Now there's talk of a V6, which should lift it up a class; a V4 is optional already.

GLAS 124

Welcome newcomer from Germany, with a concessionaire appointed at last in (of all places) Kings Lynn. Current range includes a BMW-like 1700 saloon and a great number of sporting coupes both beautiful and otherwise, all with the remarkable belt-driven ohc engine that has caused much thought among British designers. Latest novelties are the V8 coupe (two of the same engine, siamesed) and an R16-like semi-estate version of the boxy 1301 saloon – still with live axle.

Yet another fastback

ISO RIVOLTA 123A

Peter Agg's Lambretta-Trojan group is handling distribution for this Chevrolet-powered Italian model, which takes over as the Aston's major four-seat competitor now that Gordon Keeble has suffered its second (reported) demise. Companion model is the sensational-looking Grifo two-seat coupe, a sort of US-powered Lambo which good friends of ours say is a winner. They promised us one to play with but so far have failed to cough up.

Grifo: suave Chevrolet power

JENSEN 147

Forbidden, alas, to talk yet about the thrilling new developments promised from this go-ahead Midland crowd. But we can divulge that last year's mistaken Interceptor convertible is no more, and that the FF is destined for new and greater things.

LANCIA 156

Rumours keep coming to us of dramatic changes to this fine firm's staple range, but we suspect they're being kept for Turin next month. Meanwhile don't fail to ogle the pert new Fulvia Zagato coupe together with all the familiar variants on V4, flat-four, front-drive and rear-drive-rear-gearbox formulae.

LAMBORGHINI 162

Loud cheers for CAR's favourite purveyor of closed carriages to the nobility and gentry, who will be there to let you see and slaver over his entire range from the sensational transverse-V12 Miura (well over 200mph guaranteed) right down to the cooking model 350GT which we tested in Italy this year. Look out, too, for delectable Dottorina Baldessari – a living lesson to rival makers in what a press officer should look like. Mmm!

LOTUS 146

Another firm from which great things are expected – but later in the year, and not affecting the present range one wit (cries of 'Bring back the Elite!'). Sole novelty for here and now is a cheaper and starker version of the Elan, ostensibly for ricers but in fact a commendable effort at getting under the Chancellor's guard. Oh, and the Lotus Cortina is NOT to be dropped. So there.

MARCOS 159

We've lost count of the permutations on this fine-looking and well-conceived West Country coupe, and no doubt there'll be a few more come Showtime together with the ugly but purposeful (remember Le Mans?) BMC-based Mini-Marcos.

MASERATI 144

Selling luxury cars is not a get-rich-quick occupation in today's economic climate, but maybe the Cooper/Maser's racing successes may help the old firm. We hope to see the revised Quattroporte saloon with a rigid-axle rear instead of the De Dion, and four headlamps, powered by the 4.2-litre V8. They have a solid setup over here, with their own service workshops down in Chelsea.

Quattroporte: silence in the rear!

MERCEDES 109

These one-time giants of the race track are following a 'nothing under £3000' policy for this year's Earls Court. They will feature the peasants' edition of the 600, which is aimed at the Silver Shadow market but is over £2000 costlier at £9080. The big one with the card-playing saloon in the back costs even more. Then there will be the Belgian-made IMA estate car on the 230S (£3047), the 250SE (£3050), and the newest one, the 300SEL (£5767), all good solid value for that sort of money if your strike-happy tenantry will let you aim high.

Uppercrust cars with common body shells

MORGAN 132

Nothing new, we hope, from this most lovable of all surviving British builders. The National Trust should take over the Malvern factory and prevent them from making mistakes such as that last glassfibre effort, thus guaranteeing a steady flow of wood-framed square-rigged open *sports* cars for the legions who are daily growing more ready and able to appreciate them. And isn't it time Peter Morgan got rid of that Ferrari of his? It's a pernicious influence.

MOSKVITCH 122

Farmers are about the only types whom we can see showing interest in this tremendously rugged but mechanically crude Soviet family bolide, although new styling (first seen last year) and a four-headlamp de luxe version superficially increase its appeal. Lots of goodies for the money, though, including a free radio.

PANHARD 129

The one-time multiplicity of models with twin-cylinder engines driving the front wheels of enormous bolides has fined down to the good-looking 24CT and BT 2 plus 2, which are selling well in France as anyone can see. They are both up against it a bit pricewise over here at nearly £1500, but if you must be different they can offer looks and novelty and are something of a man's car to drive even if performance and finesse are conspicuously lacking.

PEUGEOT 151

One million Frenchmen can't be wrong, and that (believe it or not) is the number of 404s made at this

writing – although many, of course, have been sold Abroad. This solid, reliable and pleasant barouche gets a new instrument panel with proper round dials for '67, plus a much-needed anti-roll bar at the back. Little brother 204's rump is restyled (below). The latest coupe and convertible (introduced at Paris and very nice too) you will certainly not have seen. We will by the time this appears, and can comment before long.

Full-width bumper on newer 204

PORSCHE 117

The ultimate shopping car has settled down to one basic shell with three alternative engines – the old flat-four, the newer flat six, and the 911S which has 30 more bhp than the normal 1991cc six, giving 160 at 61000rpm. The new one will be around £3500 in Britain, which is not much car for the money, but what there is is good. Recognition point for car-spotters on the S is to look for the odd magnesium wheels. All models can also be had in semi-open sports car form known as Targas, but they are all lhd and not yet sold here.

911S has cast alloy wheels

RELIANT 157/158

The next-door stand belongs to Autocars of Haifa, the Israeli outfit which provides much gold by building Reliant designs in a Reliant-built factory for the untapped wastes out east. Much of the interest here will centre on the models which aren't for home consumption, but meanwhile there's talk of changes to the sexy Scimitar (including that V6 of Ford's, perhaps?).

RENAULT 155

Well, what else can they do? They've tried rear-engine driving rear wheels and front engine driving front wheels, and even a different wheelbase on each side of the car before the accident. Both the R16 and the R4 estate are having their insides (the people part) changed a bit, but that's about it. In the R4 the idea is to make it more like a motor-car and less like a 2CV, which may not be a bad idea.

R4L, arch bottom-nurturer

ROOTES 113/118/131

There's quite a bit buzzing in this corner of Chrysler's empire (page 28), mostly bodywork rather than mechanical, and some of it you will know already. The programme for the major changes went on under the code name Arrow, but the actual name of the new Hillman turned out to be the old Singer one of Hunter. It still has the 1725 engine and such under a Corsairish new shell, plus a Borg-Warner automatic option and some subtle changes to boost power and aid fuel consumption. Estate cars are unchanged, and the old big Humbers and 1600 Minx de luxe linger for the time being. Humber also soldier on with the likeable Sceptre, ditto Rapier, Alpine and Tiger. We mustn't talk about the Singers yet, but at least they keep the same name. In the Mini firing line there's a souped-up Imp known appropriately as the Sport, but without the Rally version's

Hillman Hunter: good and simple

bigger engine or disc brakes. Not much sign of anything radical like Simca power plants or Chrysler V8s, for reasons which will no doubt become apparent.

ROVER 149

News from Solihull is that the twin-carburetter 2000TC mit rev counter, so far reserved for Americans with

1 Every knob is different

sporting inclinations and a love of fine British cars, is now to be let loose for the natives here too. It gives the 2000 what it needs – more poke – but has few of the US version's external signs, like tach and mag wheels, so that the neighbours will have to look hard to tell you bought the dear one. The 2000 will also go automatic for the first time with a Borg-Warner Model 35 option. Rover men have been sneaking about with a light alloy V8 as once used in Buick (and now Repco-Brabham they say) stuffed into a 2000, but that's another one for the future.

2 TC motor – more intakes more output

SAAB 100

These Swedish three-cylinder two-stroke merchants are, like so many others, known to be working on something new and *very* different and have admitted as much, but it is still a long way off. The new car will have a four-cylinder single ohc Ricardo engine which will be made by Standard-Triumph. Meanwhile it looks as if the two-stroke is going for a minor burton as befits its falling home sales, with its thunder stolen by a stop-gap newcomer featuring the V4 engine and four-speed fwd transaxle from Ford of Cologne's 12m. It could just be more interesting than it looks, especially in the rapid little glassfibre Sonnett coupe.

4-pot 4-stroke, much more urge

SIMCA 112

Despite all rumours of front-wheel drive and such, the only changes likely are in the 1300 and 1500 range, which become the 1301 and 1501. They will have new styling front and

Longer warranty, Chrysler-style

Cadillac, long bonnet, lower roof, shorter tail, a new 'European look' that was really started by the Olds Toronado

rear, a strip facia instead of a binnacle, better seats and airflow ventilation a la Citroen/Renault/Ford, plus proper rear extractors like the ones in Rootes's Hunter. This is a good move as people complain about the noise in the current ones if you open the windows. The 1000 is unchanged since last autumn.

STEYR-PUCH 106

Another delightful newcomer – the Fiat 500-like 650TR from Austria, which qualifies as the greatest Q-car of all time on account of the horizontally-opposed hemi-head twin in the tail which propels it to an honest 90mph with more noise and drama than you would willingly credit. Stand back! Corner-gobbling power is likewise high, thanks to Alpine breeding.

Always faster than seems probable

SKODA 104

They went from front-engine to rear-engine with the 1000MB and are still selling that one, which is not known to be due for any changes. It doesn't seem to have caught on over here as well as the knock-kneed old banger that became Czechoslovakia's answer to Ford's Popular and the eternal Standard Ten.

TOYOTA 105

John Pride's company in Brixton who used to handle Skodas have taken over the Toyota concession and are pushing these slick Japanese family four-seaters in Britain. They have all the usual range: saloon, twin-carb saloon, coupe, and wagon, with much power from 1.5 litres and very fair results all round – although, as with most imported cars, prices are elevated. Minor changes are going on all the time to eliminate things like gear-lever rattle (for steel read nylon bush) but we expect no dramatic '67 mods.

TRIUMPH 128

The 2000 continues, with we suspect a more potent engine up their sleeves for issue in better times. We thought at first that this show might see a GT six-cyl 2000, but instead we're presented with the exciting GT-6 which is the 2000 engine imposed upon the suffering Spitfire frame. It should go like – er, scalded cakes. The Vitesse, too, joins the club and is stretched to two litres. Meanwhile the Herald and derivatives move on towards their target of being a 10-year model like Mr Stokes said.

2-litre Vitesse: hairy-legged Herald

VAUXHALL 141

The Luton firm have done a Mr Ten Per Cent on the Viva and given it that much more of everything – size, performance, engine capacity (up to 1200cc) and probably price, not announced as we write. There is also an SL version with different cylinder head. The whole range look like

New Viva (top) is taut and lively; 101 remains milder-mannered

scaled-down Victors to fit in with the family image and are intended to lift Vauxhall neatly out of the economy-car field at a time when sales are dropping. Hidden changes include coil springs at the back, and there are some new safety features. Otherwise the others, already modded within recent memory, continue much as before apart from detail prettifying of the brightwork.

VW 133

Beetles have grown bigger already, with 1500cc to wag the tail now, and the show will show no change. The quicker ones of course have a cross-wise compensator spring, otherwise this incredible 30-year-old (give or take a year) marches on taking a big slice out of export business and is still far and away the biggest foreign seller in the States, Nader or no. Maybe service and spares do count? VW are known to have their own design of automatic transmission, but this is not for release yet.

1500 – more Kraft, less Freude?

VOLVO 103

The Swedish firm have changed the bodyshell first, with engine to follow. Their new 144 has a modern safety shell (its ends collapse) with lower waistline and bigger glass area. It is longer, lower and wider. Power still comes from the old 1778cc four-cylinder in one- or two-carb forms giving 85 or 115bhp; a 2000 engine to go with the new shell will not come until 1968, since Volvo are old-fashioned people who like to prove everything first instead of leaving it to the customer.

WARTBURG 161

Pictures in the less highly principled foreign weeklies show an all-new model from this East German monopoly, crisply styled in the Volvo manner. But last we heard the British importers were denying all knowledge and urging us to queue up for their dated two-stroke offering – tremendous value for money to the mimser fraternity.

AFTER LAST YEAR, WHEN foreigners took most of the lemons at the Tokyo motor show, the nine Japanese firms had the stage to themselves for the 13th Nippon salon. That the wares on display added up to an important and exciting collection is a pretty fair indication of the liveliness of the Japanese market. Main emphasis this year on the new model side was on cars up to 1000cc, though most stands had a sleek GT or racer as an eyestopper. Synchromesh appeared on all cars, even the 360cc babies, as a matter of course. Disc brakes, Borg-Warner automatic transmission and air conditioning were offered as extras even on quite lowly vehicles.

Honda had a certain crowdgetter with its Formula One car and engine, but the profits were expected to come from its new baby the N360. Most manufacturers are producing these less-than-Mini-sized vehicles at prices between £300 and £400 in Japan, with dimensions and engine size strictly controlled through cunning taxation. The Honda is quite a breakaway from the firm's ideal-dominated attempts to build small engines for light sports cars and trucks. It looks surprisingly like a Mini, has front-wheel drive and a transversely-mounted engine. There the similarity ends. The 360cc twin-cylinder air-cooled unit develops 31bhp at 8500 rpm. It has a four-bearing crankshaft, four-speed gearbox and overhead cam. Claimed top speed: 72mph. Price around £320.

The other new baby, the Daihatsu Fellow, is more conventional, slower (four-up 60 mph maximum) and dearer (£400). A Vignale-styled glassfibre coupe prototype was the other attraction on the stand, hurriedly codded up with the chassis and engine from the same firm's Berlina 1000 GT saloon. A bigger engine and fuel injection are scheduled for production cars.

The definitely-for-export Toyota 2000 GT (potential E-type eater, some say) appeared again in even more luxurious and faster form with cast alloy wheels now standard. Unexpected eve-of-show news was that Toyota has taken Hino, the ex-Renault assembler, under its wing. Hino's only new offering was a mid-engined prototype racing coupe using an experimental twin-cam four-cylinder engine. Toyota, once again, expect the money to come from a small car, the new Corolla – young sister of the Corona – which enters the lists at the top end of the one-litre market where it directly challenges Nissan's Sunny 1000. Anyway, the new

1 DAIHATSU SPORT. *A Vignale-styled 2+2 prototype to be built in glassfibre* 2 GROUP SIX HINO *sports prototype has experimental four-cylinder dohc 1.3litre engine fitted amidships in the spaceframe chassis* 3 MAZDA COSMO SPORT *from Toyo Kogyo may be for sale this year. Wankel engine is said to give 106mph maximum* 4 *E-type rival, the* TOYOTA 2000GT, *will go on sale this spring. It has six-cylinder, seven-bearing dohc engine of 1488cc. Claimed top: 140mph* 5 *Japan's biggest. The* NISSAN PRINCE ROYAL *was built for HIM the Emperor. Its 6373cc V8 whisks the three-ton eight-seat monster to 100mph or ambles at 5mph for hours on end* 6 DAIHATSU FELLOW *has 360cc two stroke two-cylinder engine and costs around £400. These babies get special road fund tax concessions* 7 ISUZU 117 SPORT *first seen at Geneva is by Ghia – unlikely to go into production, unlike* 8 *the factory-adapted saloon version. Both are built round the existing all-independent Bellett chassis*

1

2

4

photography: Car Graphic, Tokyo

Corolla is a neat two-door five (occidental size) seater saloon selling in basic form for £430. The front suspension is by Macpherson struts and coil springs with an unusual two-leaf transverse leaf spring to do double duty as an anti-roll bar. It will definitely come to Britain, perhaps next year.

Toyo Kogyo is the giant firm behind Mazda cars. Once again, the exciting twin-Wankel-engined Mazda Cosmo Sport dominated the stand. And once again the firm promised it would soon be on general sale. If NSU withdraws its own Wankel spider, this could be the only rotary engine in production. Also on the Mazda stand were estate and twin-carb versions of the beautiful and successful Bertone-styled Luce 1500. We're amazed that no enterprising British firm has taken on distribution for this make.

While Mazda was giving the Luce a sporting image, Isuzu was trying to get rid of one on its Bellet – producing the Bellet B with oblong headlamps and a subtly redesigned rear suspension using a rigid rear axle with semi-elliptic springs in place of the other model's independent, semi-trailing arm system. So as not to lose its sporting following completely, though, it also had on show a very neatly done fastback version of the 1600GT tourer and two prototypes: a lovely Ghia-designed and built 117 coupe and a four-door 117 saloon based on the coupe – an approach completely opposite to the European.

Fuji have had great successes with their BMC 1100 rival, the Subaro, and so produced only an odd new slogan – 'high-class people's car'. Suzuki had nothing new either, but Mitsubishi's star attraction was a Colt one-litre engine fitted to a Brabham-influenced F3 monoposto for Formule Libre racing. A road version of this engine has been put into the fastback body that used to belong to the unsuccessful two-stroke Colt 800. The resultant hybrid also replaces the old Colt 1000, which was upgraded to 1500cc in 1965.

Besides the Toyota/Hino tie-up, the other important merger during the year was between Nissan and Prince last August. This meant that the monster Royal produced by Prince to supercede the Japanese Emperor's 30year-old grosser Mercedes actually appeared under the Nissan label and takes over from that firm's President as Japan's most prestigious car – which must prove something. As there are more presidents than emperors it's doubtful if the Royal will go into production . . .

10 Tokyo way out

5

6

7

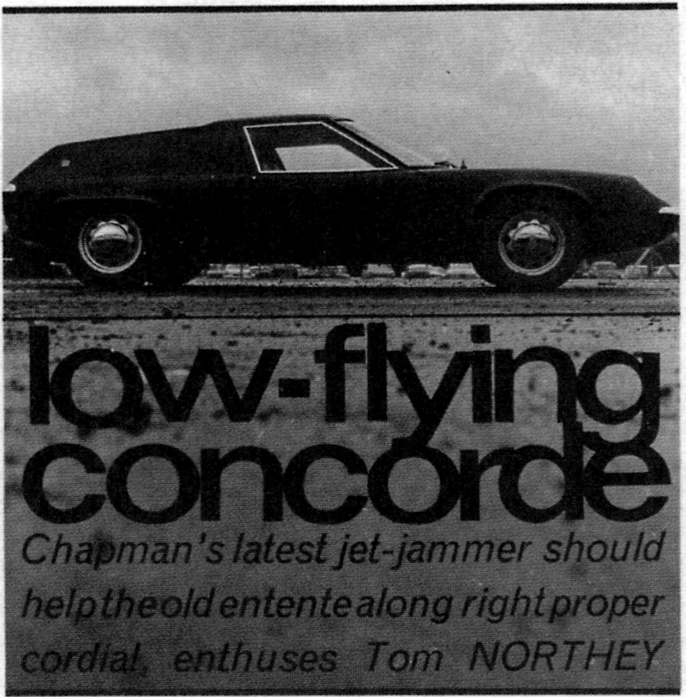

low-flying concorde
Chapman's latest jet-jammer should help the old entente along right proper cordial, enthuses Tom NORTHEY
Tom Northey

IS IT A PLANE? IS IT A CAR? Hardly – it's a Chapmobile. Which raises another question. Is Colin Chapman human? If he is, what is his game? Wot wif G Hill joining the Flying Scot to form what is *almost* the most talented racing team in history, building himself a brand new air-conditioned factory with its own landing strip and generally bringing gloom and despondency to other manufacturers of high-speed carriages for the sporting gentry, our hero has now beaten the Great Harold and the British Aircraft Corp by going European and getting his own Concorde awf de graand before too many others have even sharpened their pencils after the Elan.

However, as with all things Loti there seems to be a lot more going on in the background than appears on the plastic surface. So okay, maybe you have already seen the car at Brands (the P15 racing version that is), but that has very little to do with the one you may be allowed to buy. The entente, initially, seems to go all one way. Read on.

Let's start by examining the overall image of the Chapman outfit. Sure he can build racing cars and sure he can build splendidly sporty roadsters with sticky feet and fabulous suspensions – but from the angle of producing a viable, marketable product he has things going against him. The biggest of these is the by now unwarranted accusation of lack of after sales facilities, and in the hard faced markets of the world – to which Chapman must go to expand – that is a very big problem indeed. Memories last for a long time.

Therefore what he really needs is a ready-made, fully organised after sales organization into which he can infiltrate his motor cars. Current links with Ford go part of the way, but the primary purpose there has always been to guarantee a steady source of basic components at the right price. Next step is to combine supply with sales – in volume.

Basis of Concorde's wild-looking body is a one-piece glassfibre moulding which is produced by Lotus. On this are hung the doors and the front and back lids for luggage and engine compartments. The windows are fixed in and are not even removable. Strike one – no rust, easy to repair by anyone and reasonably cheap to produce. The chassis is a logical development of the one used on the Elan, with wider forks to take the engine and other bits. Strike two – well-proven principles incorporated in the design assure extremely good roadholding and simplified servicing procedures as the engine and gearbox can be lifted in and out at will. Another bonus of the central location is that routine maintenance is easily accomplished around the big engine bay. Thinks – a Porsche unit will fit in there a treat!

But Chappers has no intention of remaining in the proverbial dugout and has managed to pull off a big offensive by using a proprietary engine and a damned good one at that. Working on the principle of what looks right is right he has taken the Renault R16 engine and gearbox, turned it round the other way and produced a mid-engined poor man's Miura in which the only components that could go seriously wrong and require expensive medicine are already catered for by a worldwide sales, service and spare parts organization.

Modifications to the engine are minimal, the only outstanding feature being the use of a double-choke carb. But just look at what he has done. In one stroke of pure design and sales genius he has produced a most enviable car which anyone put off by twin-cams and twin-carbs can buy with complete confidence. You, too, can blast along the roads of Europe looking for all the world like Jack the Lad in a steamy refugee from the 'Ring or the Sarthe, a little bomb with superb roadholding that will have any bird doing her nut for a ride. And if the little beast gets a trifle off song or decides it wants a new set of bearings for the Easter Parade, just run it along to Jacques, park it alongside the R8s and 4Ls and bob's your uncle. Anyone trying to pull a stroker by charging Maranello prices for fiddling with a very standard motor can be told where to stuff his addition. And if things get really desperate just buy a recon engine and lower it in yourself, raising two fingers to the mercenary swine that get fat off the flesh which enthusiasts sell to keep their beloved toys in running order.

But there's a catch. We Brits are to play second fiddle in the world's market places. Now whisper slowly after me – Matra Jet. That is the enemy and that is where the initial battle is going to be fought. In France.

As with all good movies, you have to wait your turn. The question is whether you consider the wait really worthwhile. Meanwhile let's examine the Concorde in slightly greater detail. Up at the front Chapman has used wishbones with telescopic shock absorbers while at the rear stickability and transmitability are provided by the use of wishbones with trailing radius arms, again with telescopic shock absorbers. Wheels are the 4½J type (without which no go-faster type will consider taking the road) and these are fitted with 155 by 15 radial ply tyres – SP41 on the prototype. Pressures front and rear are 18lb and 28lb respecters which, so they say, gives neutral handling characteristics. Hum! Brakes are 8in by 1.5 drum at the rear and 9.75in disc at the front. Styling is by Chapman himself and John Frayling and the complete car should turn out at about 1350lb at the weigh-in. Claimed bhp for the R16 engine is 80 at 6000rpm, which should make it quite quick. Sorry to be so vague but even James Bond would have great trouble getting a drive in a Lotus prototype.

Overall, the Concorde measures just over 13ft; in production it should be 42in high and 64in wide. The fuel tank holds 7 gallons and an optional extra will be another 7-gallon tank which, at a claimed 35/40mpg, could give a really usable range of 500miles per fill-up. Whether you can stand being at the wheel for that distance is another matter. The seats in the prova car were not the ones to be fitted in the production versions. Even so, Concorde's seats will be fixed and adjustable pedals are there to accommodate any dwarfs that come along, dictionary definition of a dwarf being anyone who isn't the same size as C C. Ventilation is claimed to be accomplished by the dazzling, Ford Lotus Airflow ducted fresh cool breeze system. We have all heard that one before, and not having been allowed to take a run in it we ain't saying. A heater/demister is fitted as standard, by Harry, and adequate luggage accommodation is said to be provided in the nose of the car and in a tray behind the engine. It all depends on your definition of adequate. But let's face it, the car is not being produced for mum and dad – at an approximate figure of £1100, Lotus sales people will have enough trouble on their hands trying to keep ahead of youngsters' orders.

On looks alone the car is a winner. If you have ever drooled over one of Carlo Abarth's creations or lusted after a Le Mans type body with no concessions to standard ideas then this Concorde is for you. When deliveries start in England the Kings Road on a Saturday afternoon will never be the same. On comfort we cannot comment for reasons we've already mentioned. Visibility forward is extremely good, although London's traffic may be a little frightening from such a low position. Visibility rearwards is surprising, too, through the pillbox-type slit behind the driver's bonce, so avoiding the peasants who will litter the path of this bolide will not be much of a problem. But C C does not really make cars for commuting in. Lotus owners always dream of beautiful quiet, sunny dawns with the open road stretching before them, memories of the Targa and the Mille Miglia chasing the adrenelin through the system.

So rush along to the Racing Car Show and crawl all over it. Take along a bag of gold and join the queue – the one forming behind us. ✻

SAR 857D
SAR 857

Question: where does the industry's top talent go in spring? Answer: Geneva. Geneva is also where catch it can be fierce. Behind this annual ritual lurk weeks of frenzy, months of application—and visit the star performers on home ground. We drove secret prototypes, talked to key engineers, pene curtain-raiser racing show. In the next 17 pages we present a sort of potted anatomy, kicking-off with

ALTHOUGH I MAKE A POINT OF NEVER reading Dickens, I am given to understand that he wrote of a Mrs Boffin that she was a 'high flier at Fashion'. If so, she was surely the only member of the tribe of whom this could be said. One's mental picture of the typical boffin is seldom of a man to whom the niceties of attire and customs appeal: our figurative boffin, polishing his seat on a chair and his elbows on a desk, his hands full of pencils and his head full of the calculus, surely has a rumpled collar, a clumsy necktie and ill-cut clothes?

There is another type of boffin, even more spartan in his apparel because more active in his work—the chief tester-cum-development engineer, of whom Lamborghini's Bob Wallace is at present perhaps the most fascinating example. Such a man in a suit is more anomalous than a wet Quaker; but this is not to say that he has no pride. One of the most impressive pieces of repartee I have ever heard came from the lips of Mr Wallace when we were chatting in Modena one night: a drunken American volunteered the estimate that when Wallace first came to Italy he did not have so much as a pair of shorts. Without hesitation, without apparent rancour, but with the right kind of pride, BW quietly responded: *No, but I had a tool kit and a pair of overalls.* This was magnificent, especially when you consider his order of priority.

The man is bung full of automotive engineering *savoir faire* and is by all accounts a terrific driver, so it is scarcely to be wondered at that each Lamborghini makes itself a reputation as a car without peer. Nevertheless even Wallace's most fervent friends would never credit him with an awareness of those arts that are in thrall to fashion, and I suppose it is the same with his opposite numbers in many other companies. This is why the special coachbuilders wax fat—and of course the ephemeral nature of fashion explains why few of them wax fat for very long. This is why the big Lago-Talbots never looked much good as standard, but were real stunners when clad by Figoni et Falaschi or Saoutchik; why a Delage always looked better after it had been through the workshops of Henri Chapron, or a Bentley after attention from Gurney Nutting. It is also the reason for the Lamborghini Miura owing as much to the imagination of Carrozzeria Bertone as to the inspiration of Ford or Eric Broadley. So, when the time came for Lamborghini to essay a four-seater two-litre variant on the rear-engine Miura theme, using what was virtually half of the V12 Miura engine, it was only natural that they should go again to Bertone for a nice dramatic body.

They certainly got one. Mr Editor Blain and I were invited to the Bertone factory to see the new demi-Lambo in its final stages of preparation a few days before the opening of the Geneva show. This, we told ourselves, ought to be good. It must surely be fascinating to see the craftsmen of a great carrossier adding the last lingering touches that make ideal something that is already nigh perfect, or alternatively working flat out in the effort to compress into perhaps a week or two all the work that should normally occupy a couple of months.

When, under close escort, we penetrated into the inner sanctum of the Bertone factory a little outside Turin, there was certainly a mild sort of pandemonium going on. There was the new car, all closed up with five men crouched or supine inside it, banging it in 10 places at once, others rushing to and fro, or hovering with spraygun and pieces of ticky-tacky at the ready. It would have been exciting enough to be present during the final stages of labour if even a fairly ordinary vehicle were being born; but to be accoucheurs during the parturition of a car so extraordinary as the demi-Lambo was almost too much. It is impossible to concentrate on the activities of the men swarming in and around it, so intriguing, so exciting, so utterly absorbing is the car itself.

The *spinto* or competition version of the four-litre Miura engine is good for 430bhp net at 8500rpm, with the torque curve peaking at 6750 and drooping very little thereafter. It is all done by revs and camshaft, the normal Miura having a cam profile identical with that of the earlier 350 Lambo and giving its maximum power output (350bhp) at 7000rpm. This is equivalent to a bmep at that speed of 166lb/sq in, a figure that may be compared instructively with the 151 of the current E-type Jaguar. A more useful comparison might be with the corresponding figure for the four-litre Lamborghini engine in its softer tune, as installed in the front-engined 2+2, for in this case the bmep at maximum power is 163lb/sq in, and this commendable figure is only 7.5

the money goes, and competition to this year CAR took time beforehand to trated styling sancta, *looked-in on Turin's an at-home analysis by LJK Setright of the*

Lamborghini 2000

percent lower than the pressure at 4500rpm when maximum torque is being engendered.

From all this it may be deduced that the engine of the Marzal, derived as it is from the touring Miura, will render its 89bhp per litre in a manner calculated to satisfy any likely purchaser. It will be crisp, but not brittle. However, if 89bhp per litre seems a high figure for what is ostensibly a four-seater tourer it must be realised that the engine's performance has been achieved without recourse to any extremes in design. Good breathing accounts for much of it, Ing Dallara justifying once again in a road car the reversed-port cylinder head design that is now common in racing cars but has vanished from roadsters since the demise of the old Bristol and even older BMW. In other respects the Lambo engine marks no departure from common practice, its stroke and bore being in the ratio of 0.755 to one, so that in the Marzal there are 49sq in of piston area, each square inch being responsible for 3.57bhp.

Such a quota is high but not extravagant. The average of all 1966 Formula One racers was 4.55bhpg/sq in, and indeed this has been a typical level ever since 1958 when GP cars became petrol-burners. Three years before that, the cars that finished in the first three places in the two-litre class at Le Mans, as they had also done a year earlier, had engines rated at 4.75bhp/sq in. No need to worry about the Marzal straining itself. Even the mean piston speed is only 2850ft/min at maximum-power rpm, and nothing detrimental has happened to piston accelerations as a result of the designer's attempts to minimise the engine's height, for the connecting rods measure between big- and little-end centres a full 2.05 times the piston stroke.

Since it shares the same proportions and camshafts as certain of the V12s, the Marzal engine will have a torque curve of similar shape and will thus be able to get along nicely with the same gearbox ratios. These involve engine-speed increments of 18, 22, 41 and 47percent as you change methodically down from fifth to first. If you are not methodical, Porsche-type synchromesh is there to help you. Believe it or not, there is even synchromesh on reverse gear! You see, for most men who can afford one of Lamborghini's creations, time is worth money—indeed, that is one of the best reasons for buying one. So the driver may not only lack the inclination to wait but even resent the cost of waiting two or three seconds after declutching before he can slip the gearlever into reverse, and he would be ashamed to produce graunching noises in his haste. Therefore, reasoned BW after an enforced delay of a second or two when he was out in the car one day, reverse gear *must* be synchronised.

It would be easy to dismiss the Marzal as little more than a lengthened Miura with a cropped engine. It would also be ludicrous meiosis, as though one were to say that Beethoven's Ninth Symphony was like his C minor Fantasia but bigger. In fact the demi-Lambo of Bertone, largely the work of the young Italian Gandini, is perhaps the most extravagant piece of virtuoso styling to have come out of Europe since the war, surpassing even the Saoutchik Berlin on Pegaso's immortal V8 chassis 13 years ago.

In many of its details the car betrays that temperamental artistry so typical of the Italians who (perhaps rightly) will sacrifice convenience to beauty where the two are mutually inconsistent. Thus there is precious ▶

The lines are fallen unto me in pleasant places; yea, I have a goodly heritage (Psalms 16:6)

photography: Humphrey Sutton

Lift up your heads, O ye gates; and be ye lift up, ye everlasting doors (Psalms 24:7)

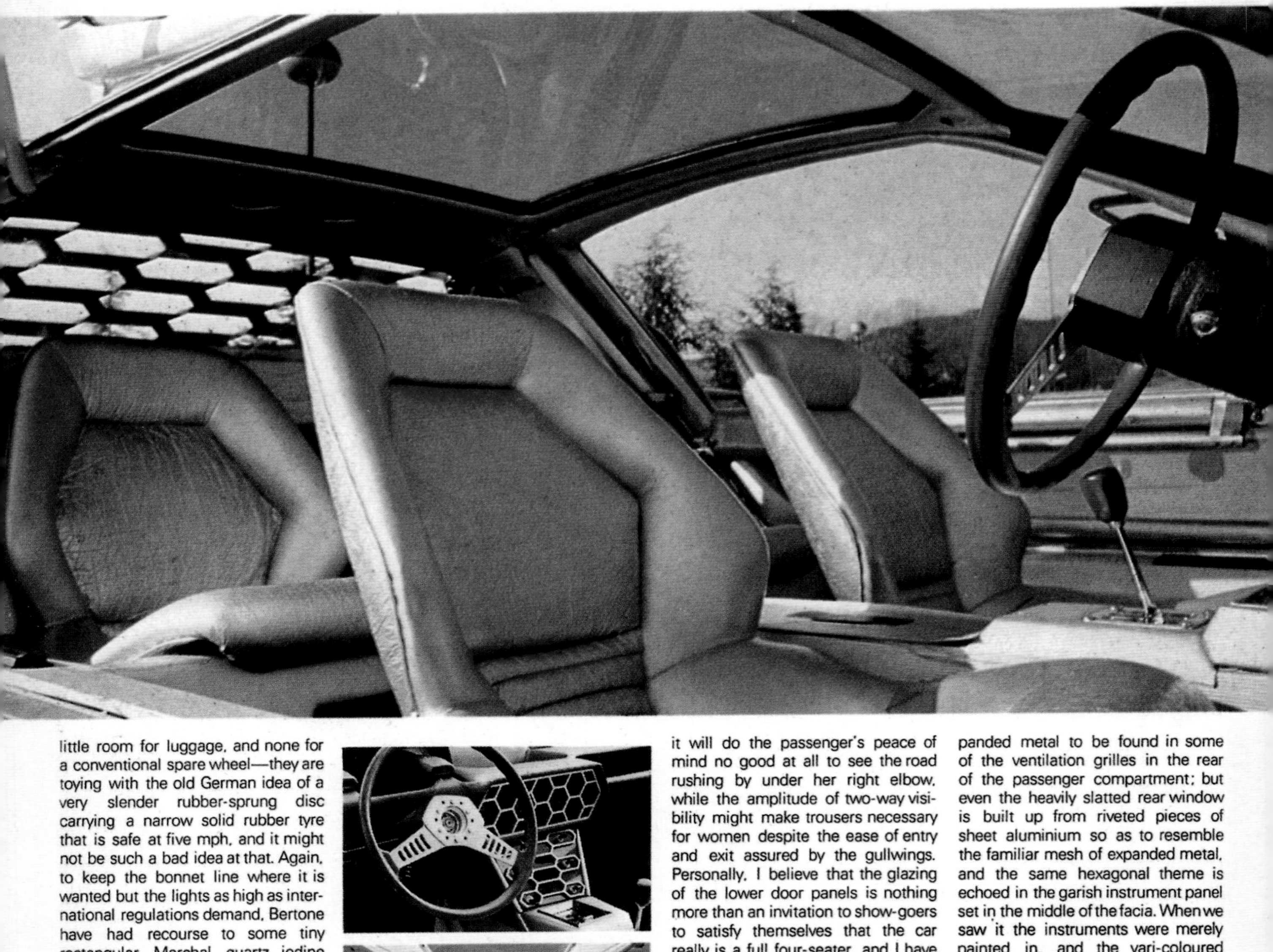

little room for luggage, and none for a conventional spare wheel—they are toying with the old German idea of a very slender rubber-sprung disc carrying a narrow solid rubber tyre that is safe at five mph, and it might not be such a bad idea at that. Again, to keep the bonnet line where it is wanted but the lights as high as international regulations demand, Bertone have had recourse to some tiny rectangular Marchal quartz iodine auxiliaries, half a dozen of which are hung under the upper edge of the snout. Quartz iodine lamps are bright, we know, but the adequacy of these little things for this slowest of all Lamborghinis (140 perhaps) must be questionable.

By contrast, many of the features of the car are extremely practical. The widest point of the body is protected by a slender black rubber strake that extends from nose to tail, and is only interrupted by the front wheel arch. The gullwing doors are built that way because the four-seater interior demands great door width, which would make disembarkation impossible unless you first removed your second car from the garage. Almost the entire door area is glazed, and this is certainly impractical, for

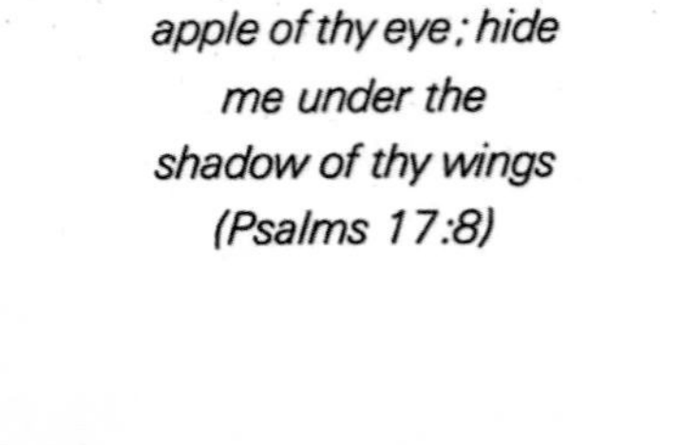

Keep me as the apple of thy eye; hide me under the shadow of thy wings (Psalms 17:8)

it will do the passenger's peace of mind no good at all to see the road rushing by under her right elbow, while the amplitude of two-way visibility might make trousers necessary for women despite the ease of entry and exit assured by the gullwings. Personally, I believe that the glazing of the lower door panels is nothing more than an invitation to show-goers to satisfy themselves that the car really is a full four-seater, and I have no doubt that any but the most exhibitionist of purchasers would demand that these panels be obscured to provide some fundamental privacy.

Be that as it may, the glazing certainly does emphasise that the new car really is a genuine four-seater—though my comfort at the wheel when I tried the thing for size might have been diminished had the pedals been fitted. There is not really much legroom to spare, but the seats are at least deeply bucketed to hold each occupant firmly against the tremendous cornering forces that the car could assuredly generate. Each of the seat squabs echoes the hexagon theme that permeates the entire car, as though the designer had a congenital passion for honeycomb or expanded metal. There is in fact expanded metal to be found in some of the ventilation grilles in the rear of the passenger compartment; but even the heavily slatted rear window is built up from riveted pieces of sheet aluminium so as to resemble the familiar mesh of expanded metal, and the same hexagonal theme is echoed in the garish instrument panel set in the middle of the facia. When we saw it the instruments were merely painted in, and the vari-coloured translucent plastics elements in the hexagonal panels of the auxiliary switchgear binnacle went further to create the impression of sitting in a mobile Espresso machine. Even the hub of the two-spoked steering wheel was assymetrically six-sided, and it was with some anxiety that I looked at the wheel rim itself every now and then to take some assurance from the fact that it, at least, was circular. Do MG men have this worry?

Being one who is inclined to think that the only hexagons proper in a motor car are nuts and bolt heads, I found the engine compartment in the tail of the demi-Lambo rather less disturbing. The power unit is basically the crankcase and transmission of the V12 four-litre Miura surmounted by the forward cylinder

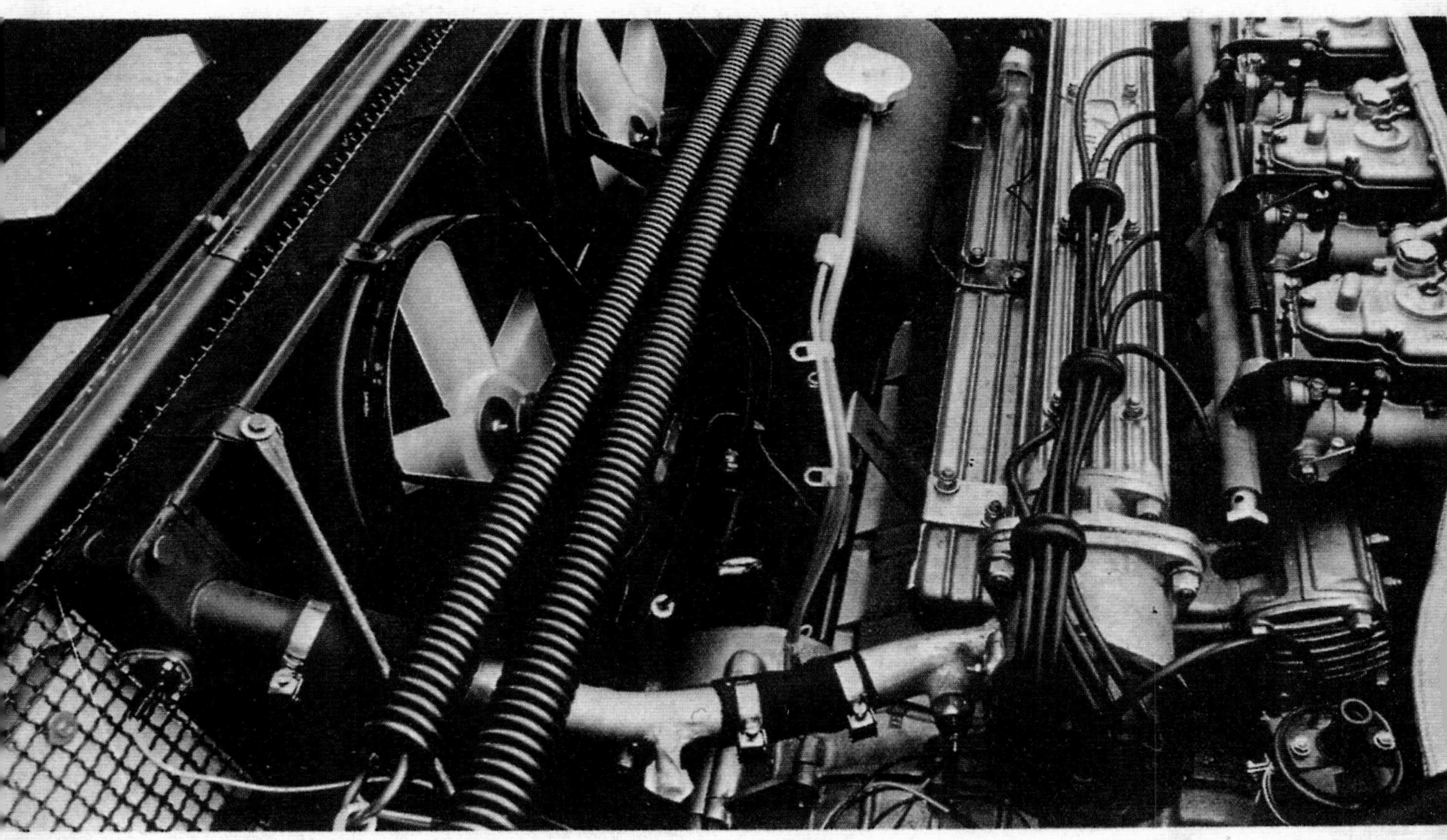

bank of that engine, thus constituting a transverse six-cylinder twin-overhead-camshaft apparatus claimed to produce precisely half of the 350bhp that the four-litre Lamborghini engine develops with such legendary absence of fuss. The reason for the good manners is that this is a detuned racing engine, the much more powerful original having been designed for competition by Bizzarini. This new two-litre version is a sort of castrated mutant of the original, but it fits the car well enough, and according to Bob Wallace the abrupt corner in the inlet tracts (allowing the use of horizontal Weber carburettors instead of the downdraught variety and thus improving the rearward vision) actually improves combustion in the middle and lower speed ranges by creating a measure of turbulence that a racing engine usually lacks in this régime.

Glamour on wheels has never been pursued more successfully: the thing is all highlights of glass and silver, relieved by touches of dull black. As a result, this long and low and wide car looks almost paper-thin and weightless. It is called Marzal, which like Miura is a strain of fighting bull, echoing Lamborghini's charging-bull trade mark; but as any convalescent matador will hasten to assure you, no fighting bull may weigh less than 542kg (1192lb) and this Marzal probably turns the scales nearly twice as far—for the Miura weighs nearly a ton.

It is not only to the engine qua power unit that one's interest is confined. Some of the auxiliary detail is equally noteworthy, such as the installation of a hefty refrigerant pump (driven by a cogged belt from the nose of the inlet camshaft) for the air conditioning unit that is to be standard. Apparatus of this sort is second nature to Lamborghini, and the installation in this car is claimed to be lighter than the usual run of air conditioning equipment. The heat exchanger is intended to sit in the nose of the car and, while being charitably inclined to believe the claim for lightness, it was nevertheless with no little amusement that I watched the empty space being packed with five large blocks of metal and a moderately small anvil before the bonnet was fastened. Of course it could be that somebody had miscalculated the front spring rates, and it would not be the first time that a car was exhibited with plenty of hidden ballast to make it look low and more or less horizontal.

A slightly more disturbing sight under the nose was a fairly substantial steering damper coupled to the rack and pinion mechanism, for I am always inclined to view a steering damper as an admission of failure. These devices are often owned by cars that do not steer well, though one is forced to recognise that there are examples also among those that steer very well indeed—such as Mercedes Benz, the Anglo-American Eagle, and the 2.5litre Vanwall.

There isn't much more in the nose of the car but there is plenty more in the tail. The water radiator is there, for instance, with a brace of thermostatically controlled electric fans ahead of it. Over all there are stretched a pair of long helical springs which do duty in lieu of counter-balance weights to hold the doors open when they are pushed up. The connection between door and spring is a length of wire, a grooved pulley and a shaft with two universal joints which communicate with the door hinges. This is typical of the Italian love for unnecessary engineering, for the same job could have been done equally effectively and with less cost in weight, space and money by the use of pneumatics, of flexible wire drive shafts and coil springs, or of any of several other alternatives. Perhaps it was time that forced this particular mechanism on Bertone, the suggestion being endorsed by Mr Wallace's observation that the universally jointed shafts were bits of old steering-column assemblies that they had found lying around.

The compulsively honest Wallace was not over-enthusiastic about the car when we saw him, but that might easily be explained by the disillusion he suffered while thrashing his Mark 10 Jaguar up to Turin from Modena that morning, during the course of which trip he succeeded in de-treading two Dunlops. Did he think the car was a sound practical buyable proposition? He didn't know: it had been built to find out. *Built* was really the word, rather than *designed*, as far as the mechanical elements were concerned, for it was little more than the front end of one Miura chassis mated to the rear end of another. When it was driven it might go very well; when it was exhibited it might prove to have considerable appeal. On the other hand, it might not, and there was only one way to find out. Whatever you think about boffins, they are often practical.

222 seconds per Miles

How to win at Le Mans: just repeat this (saving a second somewhere) 392 times

A FORD GT2 DRIVEN BY McLAREN AND AMON WON LE Mans '66 at an average of over 125mph. A mixture of technicalities and bungling put the sister car of Miles and Hulme in second place after it dropped back from its lead to try for a dead heat. Miles had been trying for a record lap in the opening hours, and succeeded four times over; but Gurney took it from him by 0.9sec with another Ford in 3min 30.6sec. As a consolation, Miles had the distinction of being the first ever to be officially clocked at over 200mph during a race.

Maybe Ken Miles was the moral victor at Le Mans last year. Alas, he isn't around any more to have another try—but over a year ago, he was at Le Mans more or less winning the race in advance. It was at the practice weekend, when Ford turned up in strength to get their cars *au point* good and early. The very new and experimental J-type stole most of the publicity thunder, despite Ford's assurance that it was not for the 1966 race; but while it was being belted around by Amon and McLaren, serious work was going on with the GT mark 2, the 7-litre derivative of Ford's original Lola-inspired coupé. Fastest driver of this was Miles, and electronic recorders monitored his every move.

Ford later published one of the lap charts transcribed from Miles's tapes. It logged engine speed all around the circuit during a lap that took 3min 42sec. That is just one second longer than the winning race average per lap; Miles could hardly have been more representative. But really to see what the chart-recorder had to tell, another piece of transcription is necessary to relate the fleeting seconds to the car's road speed. The operation is not altogether straightforward: I had for instance to allow for the tyres' centrifugal growth of 3percent per 100mph, to recognise and allow for the wild-looking acceleration out of Mulsanne corner where in fact the car broke traction, and again to smooth some crazy kinks where the back wheels must have become airborne over bumps, 10 seconds before White House corner.

There remains plenty at which to marvel. Along the Mulsanne straight, where the engine was making its full 485bhp at 6200rev/min, the car was holding 205mph for six seconds, over more than a third of a mile. Then look at the braking for the Mulsanne corner; unremitting 0.7*g* deceleration for nine long, long seconds, punctuated by three downward gearchanges spaced two seconds apart, double-declutching and all, and the dear Lord help you if you make a mistake. Then hard acceleration for 25 seconds, much of it at about 0.4*g*, before the still-hot discs are clamped yet again at 180mph for the 60mph Indianapolis corner. This time the deceleration is only 0.39*g*: have the brakes weakened, or has the driver? Eight seconds later we have the answer: 100mph to 40 in four seconds, 0.68*g* while picking up bottom gear for Arnage.

Watch Miles accelerate out of Arnage: as usual, he hits his gearchange smack on the nose at 6200 rev/min. In bottom that is 89mph, in second 140, in third 170. No time for top before White House, though the peak is reached in third. The engine is in fact safe to 7400 rev/min, but Miles is too good an engineer to be led astray: the world may be careering headlong by, but he will have his 6200, neither less nor more. ❋

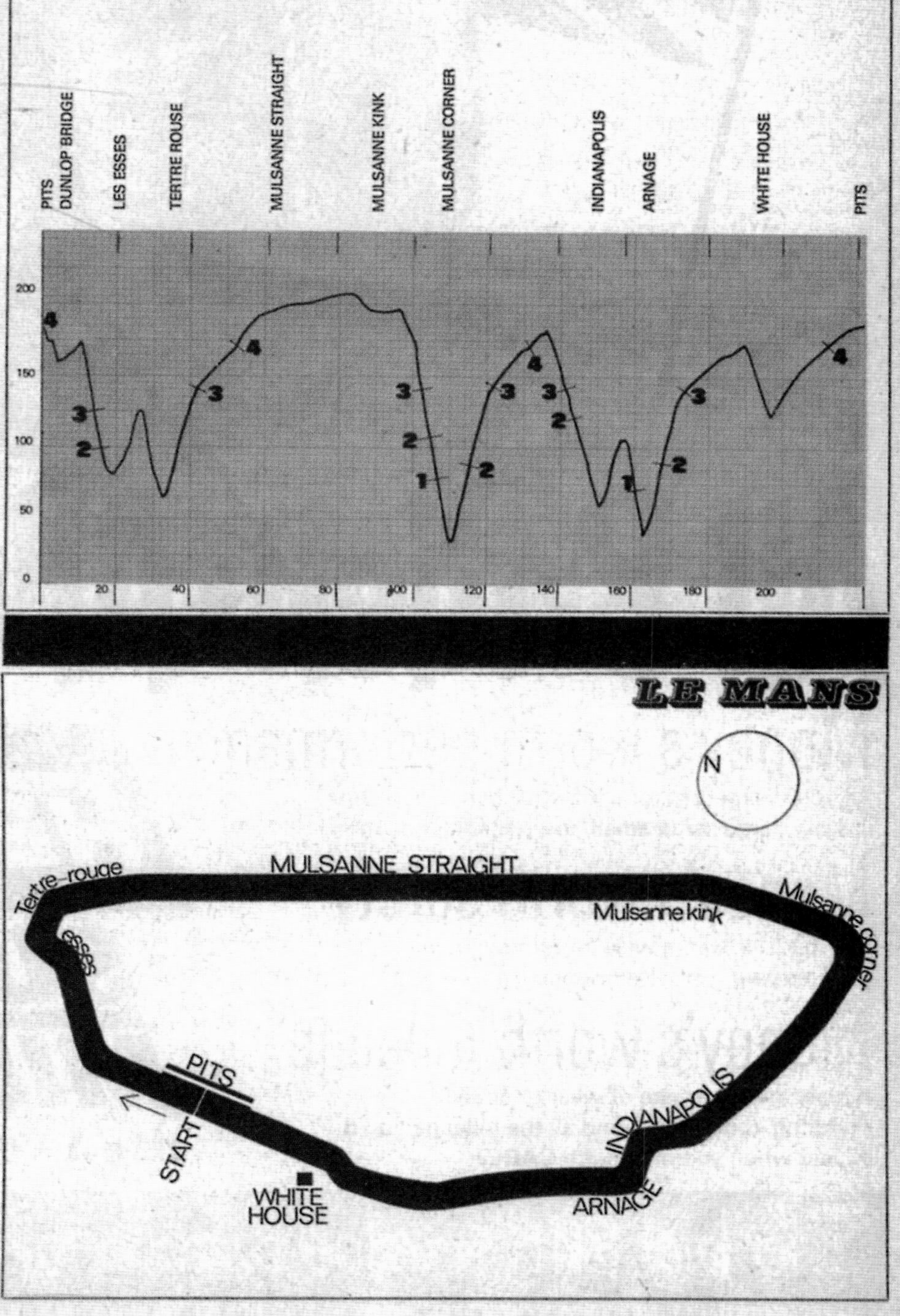

Psychedelic is the in-word these days for anything from a bad poem to a loud tie. It takes in the growing sub-cult you see illustrated here, though we're told on good authority that you don't need to be psyched-up to do a decent job (non-ravers can buy stick-on patterns as at top right for 27s 6d per repeat). One-off efforts currently touring the capital range from the frankly amateur (bottom right) to the coolly professional (sunburst Mini, right, by Binder, Edwards and Vaughan). We like the schizo E-type (bottom left)—done, the owner says, 'to confuse the fuzz—and the witnesses'.

FILL
ME UP WITH
LSD

Championship Partnership

For fifteen years, Esso and Lotus have made a champion team. Together they've won the World Championship twice, and Lotus has been the only British car to win at Indianapolis. Lotus relies on the Esso Tiger for fuel and lubrication. Get the Champion Tiger in your tank. For race-proved power and performance.

PUT A TIGER IN YOUR TANK Esso

Do you have trouble getting her going first thing in the morning?

You do? Well, Holts have something for you.
It's called Cold Start; and it starts cold engines with amazing speed.

All you do is spray Cold Start into the air intake, and it goes to work. In seconds. Even on the frostiest morning.

Get a can before the next cold snap. 14/6 will get her going all winter long.

Holts **The best friends a car ever had.**

Obtainable from Garages and Accessory Stores.

IF YOU'RE AN EXTROVERT YOU'LL LOVE IT, for it gets more attention than Batmobile and the James Bond Aston rolled into one. If you're an introvert like one or two members of CAR's staff you'll cringe down as low as possible in the seat and pretend you're not with it. If you're out on the open road trying to cram more than 60 on the speedo without going off the road you'll begin to wonder why you bothered, but when you get to the beach and nearly make yourself sick with laughing at its antics, suddenly you'll find you're glad you did.

What is IT? It's a Beach Buggy, the latest of the thousands of American crazes that have hit these shores—and what's more it's better than bubble gum or the hula-hoop although a lot more expensive. Now that the Buggies are here you can hop down to your local Buggy store and get yourself mobile for around £350 —less if you're ingenious, or lucky, or both.

Those of you who study the American magazines will have seen how the Buggy craze has grown from a one-off special into a whole industry (complete with legal battles over who designed the thing) in the space of a few years. Now, as Henry Manney III tells us over the page, they run full-blown cross-country races in California and Mexico, and although they cannot perhaps compete with four-wheel drive vehicles in really sticky going they cost a quarter the price and are twice as much fun.

People have been building special off-the-road cars on the west coast of America for many years, largely using big V8s and various other large capacity engines, the idea being to explore the deserts of California and Mexico. The coming of four-wheel drive vehicles, during and after the war, tended to kill interest in the specials somewhat, but in 1964 a gent by the name of Bruce Meyers built the first car recognisable as a Beach or Dune Buggy, and from then on his one-off special mushroomed into the huge industry which is now calculated to sell over 5000 kits a year in the States. Many other firms copied Meyers's design for the Meyers Manx, but as he had taken the trouble to patent the shape he is furiously sueing everyone in sight. In spite of this the Beach Buggy is here to stay and examples are reaching our rainswept shores in increasing numbers.

So far we know of two firms dealing in Buggies, Volksrod of Doncaster, who import the American Buggy of that name and GP Beach Buggies of The Ham, Brentford, who build their own car. Since we know little of the Volksrod and since we didn't fancy hieing ourselves to Doncaster to drive one back to London we popped down to Brentford to find out all about these plastic VWs. The proprietor of the GP Speed Shop is Paul du Plessis, a fair-haired young man whose accent immediately betrays him as a South African. He was (and still is for that matter when time permits) a racing mechanic who has ministered to many a famous machine, specialising in big hairy sports cars like Lolas, Ferraris and the like. He has helped out David Piper on occasion and it was whilst mechanicing for Piper during the Kyalami Nine Hour race in Johannesburg a couple of years ago that he spotted his first Beach Buggy. He passed this machine parked outside a garage for day after day without taking much notice,

BEACH BUGGY

but one day he stopped to have a look and straightaway decided that he could do a better job. So he sank all his meagre savings into the project, designed and built the mould for the glassfibre body, and came to England with all the bits and pieces to see if the streets of London really are paved with gold.

Like so many predecessors he found that they are not, and the project has nearly foundered on one or two occasions due to lack of cash. Fortunately a sale has come along just when it looked as if the shutters would have to go up, or he has gone off to do a bit of lucrative mechanicing to make a bit more money. He even had to sell the Porsche engine out of his most rapid Autocross device on one occasion as he had a good offer for it, but like most pioneers he keeps grinding on. Having no money he cannot advertise the machine and no advertising means no customers—just about the worst sort of vicious circle you can have. However, he managed to build up a car and enter it in the Player's Autocross Championship. With a VW engine it had little success but when he forked out for the Porsche unit he soon began to blow off some experienced Autocross men. No one likes to be beaten and one or two of them have placed orders for replica racers, while a few orders from people who want to use them on the road makes Paul feel he may have turned the corner.

What is a Beach Buggy? You may well ask. Basically it's a VW platform chassis to which has been bolted a glassfibre open body, looking more like a bathtub than anything else. That's just about it really—nothing to get excited about you might say but once you start driving one it's like a good book: difficult to put down.

There are several ways of building a Buggy to the GP formula. ▶

▶ Firstly, you can go to Paul du Plessis with a bundle of pound notes and tell him to get on with it, but this will probably cost you a lot more than you want to pay and in any case he is not too keen on building complete cars as he has to spend lots of time finding a suitable crashed VW and even more time prising the reluctant body from its rustbound chassis—if it's an old one of course. So what he would prefer you to do is to buy all the necessary bits from him and you undertake the task of finding the shunted Beetle. When you have found the VW you must remove the body and throw it away, unless by some miracle you know someone who wants a chassis-less VW with a smashed body. When you have the chassis laid bare it is necessary to do a cut and shut job at the rear, taking a 15¾in chunk out of the chassis. This has to be done pretty accurately or it won't steer straight so Paul will do this for you for £30 and for another fiver he will sell you the necessary shortened cables, pipes and things which you have just chopped in half with the blowtorch.

You now hand £140 to Paul, who will rush down to the bank with it to keep the accounts out of the red, and when he comes back he will hand over one glassfibre body in assorted colours, complete with windscreen, dashboard and a few other odds and ends. Believe it or not, this bolts straight on to the VW frame and there is your motor car. The front bonnet is added afterwards when you have got the petrol tank installed (this must be from a 1961 or later VW or it won't fit) and you are ready for the road. There are lots of other things you need but you can either bodge them up from the VW parts or buy special bits from Paul. A pair of bucket seats could cost you £25, a leather rimmed wheel £10 10s, Marchal head/side lights £8 the pair, wiring harness £12, roll over bar £10 5s, while if you hand him your old skinny wheels they can be given 7in rims for £4 18s each or 8in for £5 8s. You need huge racing tyres to fit these, which will cost you £14 each new but there are plenty of part worn racing tyres to be found.

So if you go the whole hog you could end up spending £500 without any trouble, but sensible use of existing components could get the price down to the £350 limit without skimping too much. Certainly £400 should buy a pretty good car. Paul supplies detailed instructions on how to fillet a VW and tells you what bits to keep, so the assembly job is merely bolting on the body, connecting up cables, wires and pipes and off you go.

To see what Buggy driving was all about we borrowed one of the two Buggies that Paul had in the workshop and set off for a few days' driving, including a session on the beach near Dungeness. This in itself was an epic drive, for the VW engine of our car had covered 90,000 ordinary road miles and was exhibiting every sign of senile decay. The 80-odd mile journey from London to the south coast was a four-hour marathon, interrupted by frequent stops to fill up with oil (about 20 miles per pint by our reckoning!) and to coax it back on to four cylinders. Unfortunately there was practically no power left due to burnt valves, worn bores and various other maladies so it was quite an achievement to get it to go over 50mph downhill. Obviously *you* wouldn't buy an engine like that and Paul says that a VW engine in reasonable tune will propel it at 80mph comfortably. On the road it rides remarkably well, despite stock suspension components with standard spring rates, etc. Paul did try to soften the suspension but directional stability was worsened and with huge Firestone racing tyres pumped up to a mere 9psi at the front and 18 at the back who needs suspension? They cushion all but the most vicious bumps yet are not deflected from their chosen path at all easily. Handling at low and medium speeds is quite fantastic, for the enormous tyres just will not lose their grip at all; the writer was blown off in no uncertain fashion following the Buggy through a roundabout in a fairly exotic GT coupé.

We could not find a decent stretch of sand so resorted to the stones of Dungeness where the Buggy would rush about in great understeering slides, flinging stones everywhere, even down its own carburettor, until it gradually lost way, whereupon the spinning wheels would quickly dig their own grave, leaving the engine resting on the stony beach. The lack of power of our car told in this respect for it was not keen to keep up any speed at all, especially with the four bodies on board demanded by the photographer. The GP Buggy can be counted as a four-seater although you might not want to occupy the glassfibre bench at the rear for very long periods. Paul reckons that the Buggy is at its best on fine sand, which it covers very quickly; he has even taken it into shallow water without disaster . . . ❋

BARMY BUGGY RACING

A postscript by Henry Manney III

ONCRE PUNNER TIME ALL the yokels used to jounce along over the cow paths in their rude carts, cursing the bumps and the springing (still used by sundry automobiles) as they went. Comes the Romans already who had the idea of cutting a straight road through the cow pasture, paving it with stale macaroni, so that Mrs Roman could have a smoother ride. One thing led to another and soon people are happy to ride around in Citroëns thanks to which they don't feel even the slightest cobble. So just the other day we travel out to Las Vegas of slot machine fame to see over a hundred vehicles do two laps of 320 miles each across the naked desert. None of your jewel carriageways or even as good as Forestry Commission roads but two bare ruts in the tulies, when it isn't tracks up a dry wash that is. June in the Nevada desert hard by Death Valley? Had they lost their cotton pickin' brains? What did the Romans build roads for?

Well actually it was one of those special events dreamed up for dune buggies and four-wheel-drive enthusiasts with a few motorcycles thrown in for seasoning. Quite frankly we didn't expect it to be such a Thing as 150 entries is pretty big for an event nearly as esoteric as an egg candling contest. Factory support, if not actual factory teams, was available in bikes from Triumph, Husqvarna and Honda; the buggies had factory entries from practically all organised makes and/or speed shops including Volvo of all people; and the 4wd chaps were really loaded with a really strong Jeep under Brian Chuchua and no less than Ford Motor Company (in the guise of Holman and Moody) entering several jeep-like Broncos with full helicopter escort and the lot. Technical descriptions are really out of the question as there must be 10 different makes of buggies alone, the chief being the Meyers Manx and the Burro; most powered by bored-out VWs (up to 1800 cc), Porsches, and Corvairs although one Burro did have a Volvo Stage 2 1800 installed therein. Besides these there was lots of absolute junk (including a T-bodied V8 roadster with Franklin rad shell), various ramifications on the 4wd theme including several with big V8s installed, and even a passenger car class which had a Mexican Studebaker, two Chevrolets, and what looked like an absolutely stock Toronado.

The rigours of practice whittled the field down to 135 starters in eight classes, the under-and-over 250cc bikes occupying the last two. It is also useless to describe the route as few of you have a map of Southern Nevada but suffice it to say that it went down a 'pole line road' (a two-ply track following telegraph poles) to Stateline and then cut over the low Kearon Pass down a dry wash (a desert creek bed that enjoys intermittent water) to Mesquite Dry Lake and Pahrump, the last named town being called after the noise a wagon made going across a cattle grid. From there it was around Black Butte across another dry lake and then across desert on virgin territory to Ash Meadows Rancho, a community that enjoys (because of local option and the peculiarity of Las Vegas laws) the distinction of being the only whorehouse in the US with its own lighted landing strip. And from there it was across the boonies again (boonie and clod?) [Ouch! Ed] *to the aptly named Big Dune and Beatty before returning down to the raceway via Latrop Wells, Johnnie, Green Dragon Mine Wash, Goodsprings, and Blue Diamond Wash.*

The competitors didn't have time to enjoy the desert scenery much as the first runners set up vast clouds of dust which made passing difficult to say the least, things fell off unprepared vehicles, others ran out of gas or oil, throttles stuck, sumps (and sump guards) succumbed from craftily placed rocks, and others simply lost their way, as odd as that seems. Most of the bikes were having a great time as your California hare-and-hound specialist does this sort of thing every weekend, skittering down the washes dodging the most important boulders and flitting across the desert standing on the pegs. The four-wheeled stuff was having a rougher ride as your buggy man usually picks his way at a modest speed, relying on the soft suspension and even softer earth-mover tyres to save him from harm. The 4wd rely on brute force and could be heard coming miles off. Other surprises were in store though on the dry lakes . . . these are usually a thin crust of salt or other hard stuff over talcum-like salt and the first heavy chap to break through made colossal ruts. Next along fell into them and it is Boggsville in that floury stuff without a tow as there is literally no bottom; the car is just resting on the transmission.

Thus by dark a goodly number of the entry had already turned up missing or retired at Ash Meadows, not only because of the company (the madam looked like Baroness Steel) but because Ash Meadows is one of the few places you can get a decent meal within a hundred miles. The others kept on, though, with Oetggvist's Honda and Dean's TR6 Triumph stretching out an ever-increasing lead over the remaining Bronco and the buggy which had started third on the road. The large part of the competitors still going were considerably behind schedule . . . a modest 30mph . . . as nobody had avoided spending half an hour at the side of the road carrying out more or less major repairs. The leading Honda in fact led the Bronco into the Raceway to complete the first lap at about 10pm (about 10½ hours of running) with 2½ hours in hand. The Swedish rider was eased off so that his mate could take his place and quoth 'Yeesus what a country to run a race! Now ve go to town'.

The two bikes sped around to consolidate their lead, stretching the gap over FoMoCo's Bronco to 4½ hours, and finished easily the next morning. This is really remarkable when you consider how inefficient the usual cycle headlight is on a fairly smooth road, let alone a lunar landscape like the black and bumpy desert. The buggies and cars found the second lap even more difficult, not only because of the extreme heat and dryness (you can easily drink a dozen beers and never go looking for a tree) but also because the track was so chewed up that 50mph stretches on the first lap became 20mph stretches on the second. At 9 ayem approximately some 45 vehicles of all sorts had arrived at the Raceway to start the second lap and 10 of those retired on the spot! In fact, two classes had no finishers. Meanwhile the Honda was whizzing along and actually took the flag, around 10.30 ayem on its second lap. Behind them all sorts of derring do was taking place; the Volvo buggy broke its rad, blew a generator (and used up several batteries), fiended its shifting linkage, and driver Thompson had a heart attack but carried on. A Manx-Porsche with whom it was scrapping had to clean dust out of the distributor several times (endemic with the buggies) and wound up changing the engine to a VW.

They sure make them tough out there, even if a small percentage finished. It was a keen event, worth being on the International Calendar, and I couldn't help thinking what Makinen, Aaltonen, Trana, Hopkirk, Roger Clark et al would do. Now that would really make it interesting . . . the next Baja California run is in November! ❋

Housewives: This is your world...

the world of Good Housekeeping

More and more housewives are turning to GOOD HOUSEKEEPING because it's the best magazine for expert, up-to-date advice on all aspects of a busy wife's world. How to run your home successfully. Cook with confidence. Furnish with flair. Shop wisely. Keep husband and children happy—and healthy. Save money.

Take next month's issue on sale mid-February. For only 2/6, you get two big magazines for the price of one. 'BRIDES HOME-MAKER' is a full-sized colour magazine for young home-makers furnishing on a budget. The main issue is packed with lots of other exciting features. How to give a superb dinner-party. Furnish a country-style kitchen. Shop *and* save via the fabulous bargain offers in GOOD HOUSEKEEPING'S exclusive Shopping Club.

The hidden ingredient that makes the undecided housewife turn to GOOD HOUSEKEEPING? The fully-equipped test kitchens, the clever cooks, the domestic scientists and all the facilities of the famous GOOD HOUSEKEEPING Institute (at your personal service any time).

Make sure you get your copy of the double-value March issue. Still only 2/6

GOOD HOUSEKEEPING

The new Escort might appear to be a small car.
It has a price like a small car price. It parks in a small car space. It will cost you as much to run as a small car does.
But otherwise, a small car the Escort isn't.
There's room to stretch and yawn without getting the small car neck cramp.
There's enough room for the kids to wriggle and romp without getting a clout.
Our 15 cu. ft. boot is something of an oddity in the smaller car market: it holds luggage.
The engine has a five bearing crankshaft. So it runs smoothly. Lasts longer.
And doesn't burst your eardrums at 50 mph.
The gearshift is short and racy. The gears are all synchromesh. So when it comes to the crunch, there isn't one.
We offer our new Escort in 4 models.
De Luxe, Super, Super 1300 cc and GT.
Our GT does a roaring 92 mph and takes you from 0 to 60 mph in 13.7 seconds.
The De Luxe and Supers aren't far behind.
All four have a very modest price, speed, extra room, and all.
So you won't feel the pinch either way.

The new Ford Escort.

The small car that isn't.

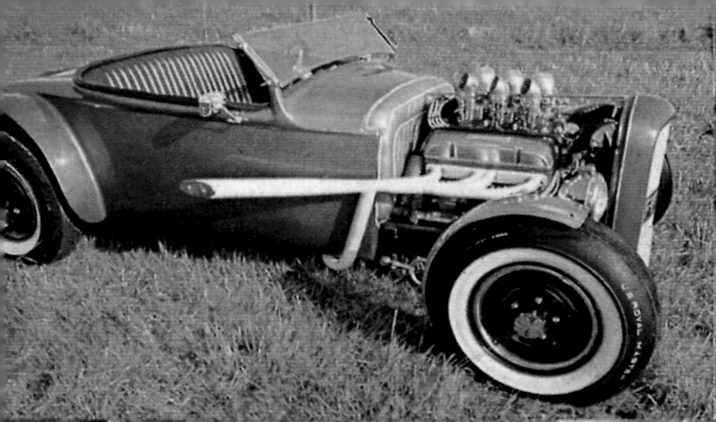

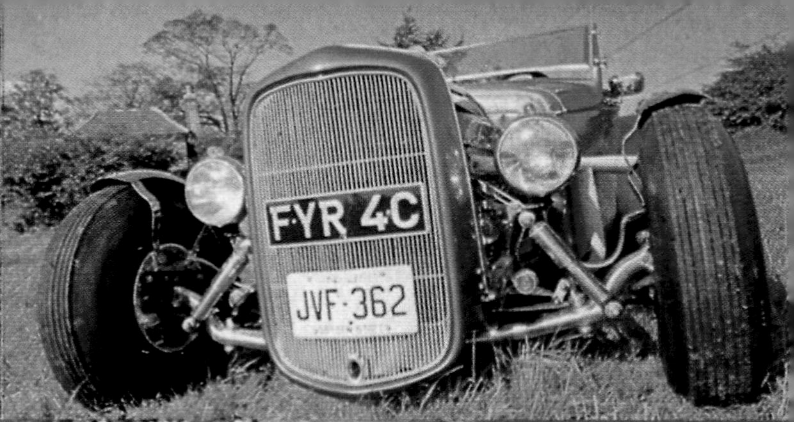
FYR 4C
JVF 362

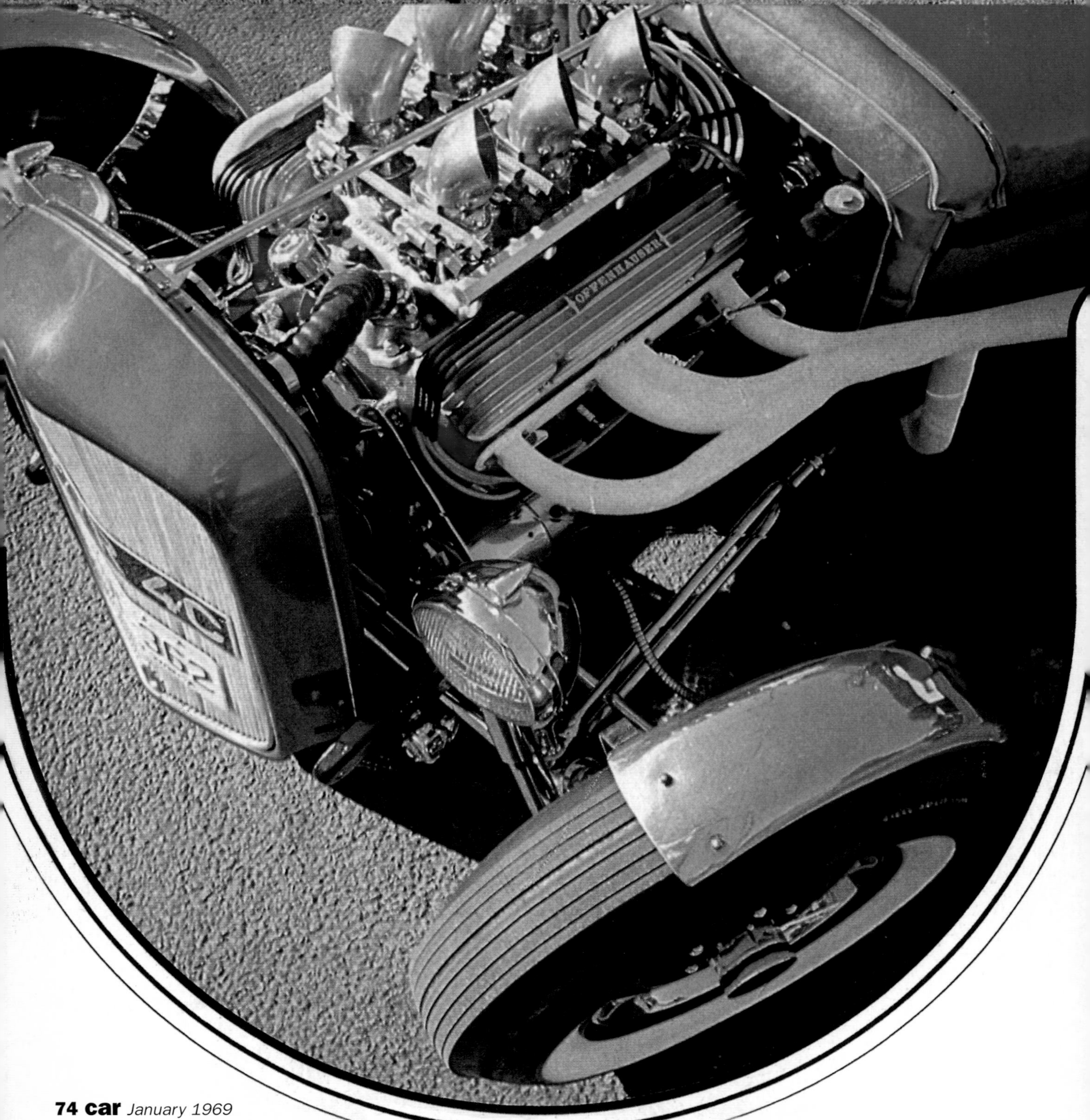
OFFENHAUSER

photographs: Charles Pocklington

THE COFFEE GRINDER IS ALIVE AND WELL

THOSE OF US WHO SAW THE ORIGINAL stupendous display of Drag Racing several years ago at Blackbushe fondly imagined that the flood gates would be opened to a whole new facet of the sport, but although everyone went away promising to build themselves a dragster and belt through the quarter mile at 200mph the sheer expense, lack of a good big V8 and suitable facilities saw to it that hardly a dragster was built for two or three years.

So we were somewhat surprised to receive a call from a young man who announced himself as Godfrey Langrish-Smith, then offered us his 1930 Ford Model A roadster fitted with a 283 Chevrolet Corvette engine for road test. We rather fancied that this branch of the dragging crowd was virtually non-existent in Britain, as the stolid British temperament seems far removed from all this frivolity. So soon afterwards we were standing outside a quiet suburban house eyeballing the polychromatic blue creation of Mr Langrish-Smith. In fact it was not his creation at all because it had been built as long ago as 1959 in Pennsylvania by one Adam Coffee, who named it the Coffee Grinder. This car apparently became quite famous and won many awards throughout the States, but in 1962 an English artist bought the car and imported it into England where he used it for a while before letting it fall into disuse.

Mr Langrish-Smith bought it in a rather dilapidated state in 1965 and has spent some time in renovating the car.

Basically a show car, Coffee Grinder is a 1930 Model A Ford roadster on which the chassis has been 'chopped 'n channelled' which means that the chassis has been shortened and strengthened, in this case by inserting a Z-shape section in the rear of the chassis. The rear section of the original body is retained, but lowered by nine inches while the old rear wings were replaced by glassfibre mouldings.

For some unaccountable reason the running gear is taken from a 1939 V12 Lincoln with transverse leaf front spring, a solid dropped H-beam axle modified by Linwood Welding, radius arms of the type used on midget racers, Monroe shock absorbers and huge 12in Lincoln drum brakes. The wheels are from a 1950 Mercedes of uncertain model with $5\frac{1}{2}J$ rims at the front and $6\frac{1}{2}J$ at the rear, shod with US Royal Master tyres of rather ancient aspect. A Lincoln Zephyr rear axle on a transverse leaf spring is fitted, together with Monroe shockers.

Motive power is provided by a highly bulled up 1955 4.75litre Chevrolet Corvette engine with hydraulic tappets, modified heads with Duntov cams and a 10 to 1 compression ratio and an Offenhauser manifold on which are mounted no less than 6 twin choke 8BA Holley carburettors. A Corvette distributor and Mallory coil look after the electrical side and a lightened flywheel transmits power through a Borg and Beck clutch to a 1939 Lincoln Zephyr three speed crash gearbox. Cooling is looked after by a Chevrolet radiator block housed in a modified Ford V8 cowling. At the moment, in the interests of fuel economy, only the two centre carburettors are connected to the throttle linkage which reduces the available horsepower from 280 to about 240. With all the carbs connected up it has been timed over a standing start $\frac{1}{4}$ mile in 14.83sec at a terminal velocity of 97.68mph and its lowish gearing gives a top speed of about 105mph.

Seating is catered for with one wide bench seat while the whole of the interior is trimmed

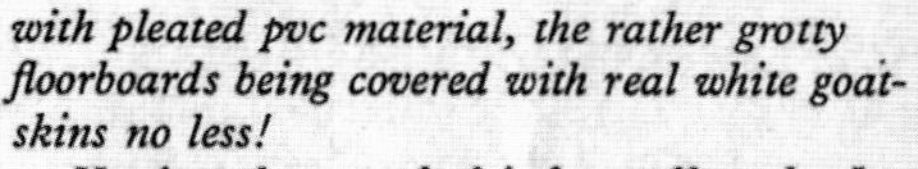

with pleated pvc material, the rather grotty floorboards being covered with real white goat-skins no less!

Having photographed it from all angles I climbed aboard for a drive, after being warned by the owner that it wasn't much fun on bumpy roads, the reason being that the shockers had no innards inside their nice chrome cases!

The driving position is quite horrible, being far too cramped and offset to the left (it's a left hand drive car), while the crash gearbox needs to be treated extremely carefully to avoid the most ginormous graunching noises. The leather rimmed steering wheel has some vague connection with the front wheels but it steers itself quite nicely from bump to bump, each bump being announced by enormous crashes from the front end. Being attached to the suspension mostly by the bolts in the centre of the front and rear transverse leaves body roll is something of a problem but as cornering at any speed is not recommended you have only yourself to blame if it falls over.

So what good is it? Well, owner Langrish-Smith finds it's irresistible to young maidens on a fine summer evening's cruise in the West End while film companies have forked out to use it in feature and advertising films.

As transport the Coffee Grinder is quite useless, as a unique (in Britain) example of the latest American art form as glorified by Tom Woolf it's—well, unique.

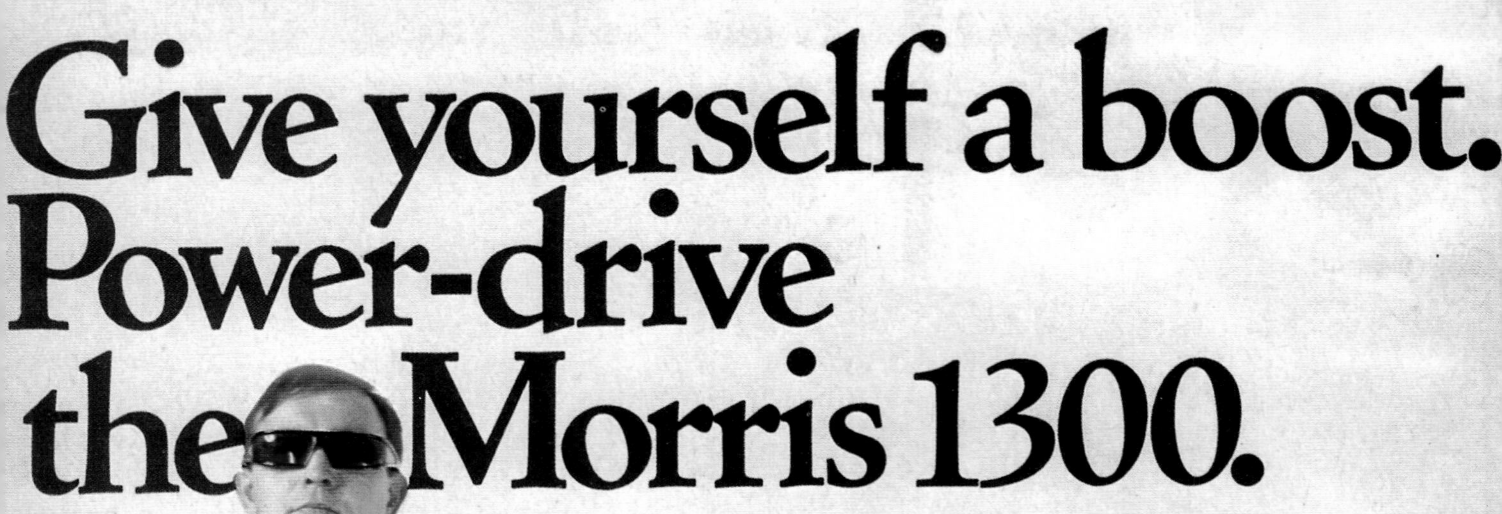

Give yourself a boost.
Power-drive
the Morris 1300.

Great cars don't happen overnight. They come from a line of great cars.

So if you see the famous Morris 1100 unmistakably in the 1300, you're unmistakably right. The 1300 gives you all the 1100 gives you – and more.

Mainly, more power. Power where you need it today. Power to get you out of the line, past, and back in line – quickly, safely. Power to conquer hills, power to whip you off the mark faster when fast-off-the mark can make all the difference. This is the meaning of the extra power in the 1300.

But there's a lot more than a bigger engine. Super comfort seats. Revised fascia – with safety padding No-nonsense controls. Extra safe braking system.

(You'd like all these with the regular 1100 engine? We can even arrange that.)

See your Morris dealer soon. can give you just the boost you need.

BRITISH LEYLAND **MORRIS**

Is CanAm racing the beginning of the end for Formula 1? As Bruce McLaren says: "For every pound we spend on Formula 1 racing we make three pounds out of the CanAm series." *story: Mike Twite, photography: Charles Pocklington*

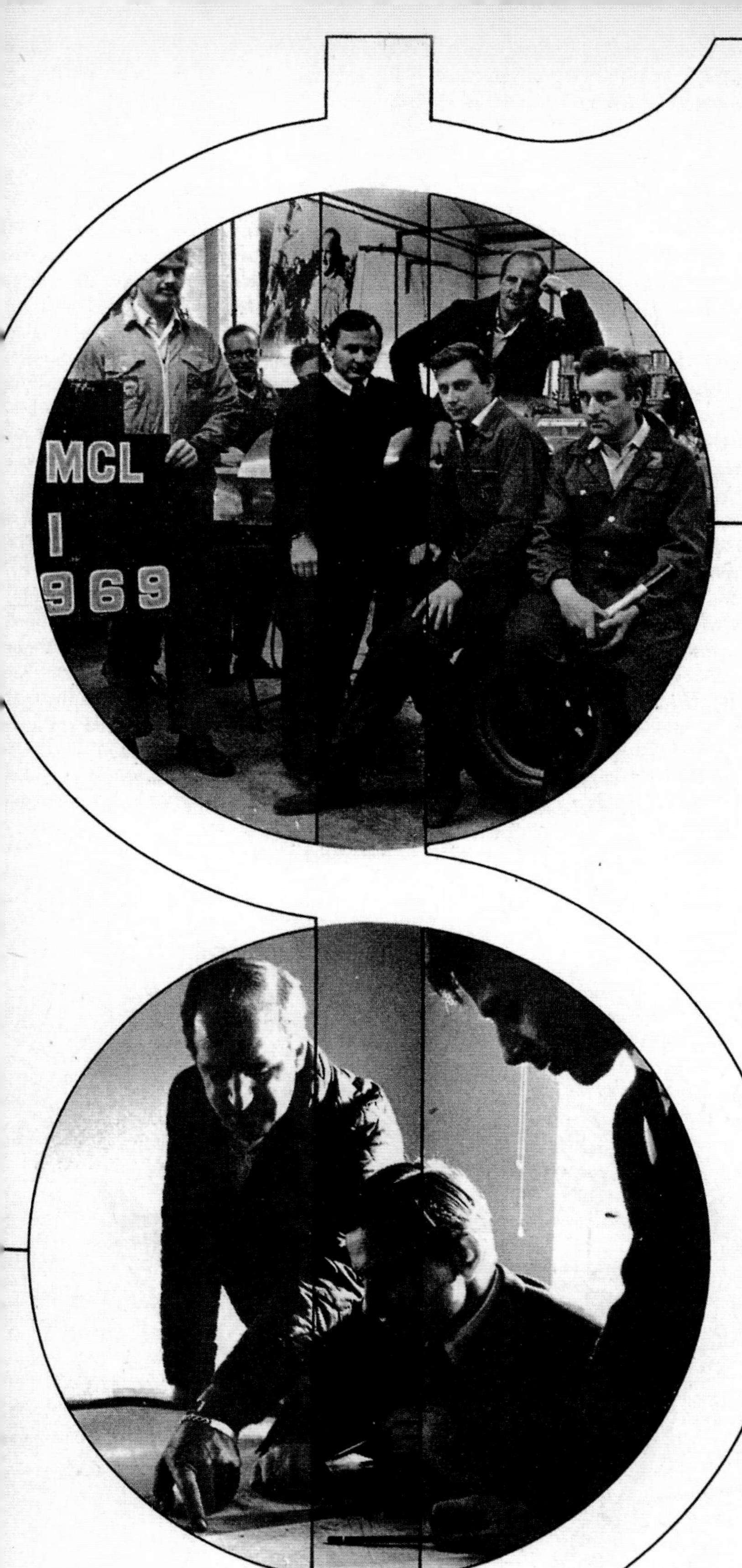

The clever young men of McLAREN

THE CHAIRMAN OF McLAREN MOTOR Racing was sitting relaxed in his office at the McLaren factory on a trading estate near London Airport; opposite him with feet irreverently placed on the boss's desk sat Denny Hulme, taking it easy after the strenuous CanAm series, while joint Managing Director Phil Kerr and design man Gordon Coppuck popped in and out as Bruce and Denny talked to us about the CanAm series which had just finished and the season which lies ahead.

Conversation soon turned to the $95,560 that Denny won and the $69,370 that Bruce brought home, together with various other prizes which put their combined earnings at around $170,000 (about £71,000); they are both a little embarrassed about talking about such a large sum because everyone tends to think of it as all profit, whereas in actual fact they spent more than *£71,000 in preparing the cars! Bruce pushed a photostat of an article from* Time *magazine across the table which insinuated that he was worth over $1,000,000.* 'If we realised all our assets and sold all the cars for what they cost us we might just be worth a million but unfortunately we have to absorb development costs—you can't sell cars at £30,000 apiece. For a start we spent $75,000 on our CanAm engine programme, then the two new cars cost us $70,000 each, taking development costs and overheads into account, so you can see that we had spent more than our $170,000 prize money before we even got to the States! Far from being wealthy young men we only made a profit on the trip because of our sponsors out there, Goodyear and Gulf—without them we would be in trouble. We could have done it more cheaply, of course, but we couldn't have guaranteed to win.'

It's obvious that Bruce sees the future of his team more and more closely allied with the American racing scene, so much so that if there was a clash between an F1 and a CanAm race the American race would win hands down—fortunately, by adroit planning it looks as if there won't be any clashes despite the fact that the 10 race 1969 CanAm series starts as early as June. As Bruce says 'Finding support for Formula 1 has become very, very difficult ▶

and unless you have good sponsorship you cannot make money. In fact for every pound we spend in Formula 1 we make three pounds out of CanAm racing. You just don't make money out of Formula 1.

'While we're not beating sponsors away in America there are plenty of people prepared to listen to you and if you've got a good case you have a chance of getting a sponsor, but in Europe very few people are interested. The general news media is more interested in racing in the States too, and although we're very appreciative of the detailed job the motoring press does, it's articles like this one in *Time* which catch the eye of potential sponsors who haven't previously been interested in racing.'

At this point Bruce and Denny became absorbed in a cutting from the Auckland Star which lauded their exploits in America. 'We made the editorial column,' *said Denny in wonderment,* 'and they're praising us.' *Both of them obviously regard themselves as prophets without honour in their own country.*

Talking of their success in the recent series in which Denny won three of the races, finished second in one, fifth in another and retired in the remaining one and Bruce won one, finished second in two, fifth in one, sixth in another and retired in the sixth, Bruce made the point that they were really the only professionally organised team to take part in the series. 'We have some basic rules which may sound childishly simple but I'm going to hang them up on the drawing office wall because they are essential. The first is that you've got to get to the race and be on the starting line. This is obvious but so many of the teams in the CanAm series were just not ready in time because they were busy playing with new cars, engines, transmissions and a hundred and one other new ideas with the result that they started the races with untried machinery which was destined to fail. The other problem is transporting all the men and machinery over the vast distances involved in getting from Northern Canada to Southern United States—we have complicated movement schedules for everyone, with the result that we were generally in the right place at the right time.

> **"A turbine engine would be great for a production car. Kinda tempting for the future"**

'The second point is that if you want to win a race you have to finish—again almost stupidly simple but many people lose sight of this fact by having way-out designs and experimenting right up to the last moment. We are often ribbed about the simplicity of our design but you cannot afford to play about with radical designs with the very short development period available.'

'Our simple monocoque chassis, which weighs a bare 70lb, proved to be very strong indeed and by bolting the engine to the back of the chassis as on the Formula 1 cars we saved some weight and had no trouble at all. We used the aluminium block 7litre Chevrolet engine which was produced by General Motors and which weighs 100lb less than the cast-iron version. Chevrolet sold complete engines with aluminium blocks at a sort of give away price of $3000 (about £1255) to any of the competitors who wanted them and I think they got rid of about 30. Our engine man Garry Knutson modified our five engines pretty thoroughly, converting them to Lucas fuel injection and so on, so that these 450lb engines were giving a comfortable 620bhp at 7000rpm'. *The engines had their problems as the team couldn't find the right combination of piston rings for a long while and the engines burned a great deal of oil which filled the combustion chambers with deposits, which in turn led to detonation and piston burning, followed rapidly by the bearings getting hammered out and the oil pressure disappearing. It wasn't until the penultimate race of the series that the team finally got the right combination and could rely 100percent on the engines. They had even got to the stage of fitting an auxiliary oil tank from which oil could be passed to the main tank when the engine had used up the initial supply—and it saved them from retirement at least once. So the team didn't have it all their own way. Fortunately other likely winners had even more problems—like John Surtees who fitted virtually untested Weslake heads to his ali block and had insurmountable problems.*

We asked Bruce if he liked the CanAm formula and whether he preferred designing to a virtually free formula as compared with the stricter limitations of Formula 1. He quickly came back: 'The success of any formula almost invariably depends on the availability of engines and if you have what amounts to Formule Libre rules you have a complete and open choice c engines. And this is good. Being able to buy big engines from Detroit and trying to persuade the big manufacturers to help out a b in supplying engines—not that it's ever worked in the past although we've always kidded ourselves it will—is a very cheap wa of getting a helluva lot of power. If there ha been a 4 or 5litre limit for CanAm racing w would all have been building four overhead cam engines and the expenses would have ru away with themselves.'

The next obvious question was whether Ferrari's intervention with a proper racing four cam 6litre engine which is giving over 600bhp with hardly any development could upset the CanAm apple cart. Bruce thought not. 'We ca go up to 8litres on the current pushrod V8 and end up with an engine that's as light if not lighter than the Ferrari's which will have a better torque curve. The criterion is more a matter of power for weight of engin than power for displacement. From that view point the pushrod is as good as the overheac cam engine. We're not too worried about it. There was a move some time ago—and we were partly behind it although I'm not sure we are now—to restrict overhead cam engin to say 5litres or even restrict the formula to stock blocks only, but

TECHNICAL DETAILS

CHASSIS:	Monocoque construction bonded and riveted aluminium skin with the engine attached to and forming part of chassis at rear
BODY:	Glassfibre with quickly detachable body sections
ENGINE:	7litre aluminium Chevrolet modified by McLaren fitted with Lucas fuel injection and developing 620bhp at 7000rpm
TRANSMISSION:	Hewland LG 500, four-speed gearbox/final drive unit
BRAKES:	Lockheed ventilated discs, 12in diam with twin piston callipers
SUSPENSION:	Front by wishbones and outboard coil springs damper units Rear by wishbone and top link with radius arms and outboard spring units, with transverse links attached to gearbox

Weight:	*1450lb.*
Track:	*F 4ft 9.6in* *R 4ft 6.7in*
Wheelbase:	*7ft 10in*
Steering:	*McLaren rack and pinion*
Wheels:	*McLaren*
Tyres:	*Goodyear*
Fuel:	*Gulf*

t is the Sports Car Club of America's wish that the CanAm series should become the biggest, best, fastest, greatest form of racing we've ever seen—even allowing Formula 1—and for this reason everyone agreed not to ask for any restrictions—just let it go!'

There was a strong rumour that McLaren would be running a turbine engined CanAm car but he scotched the story. 'No, we did look at a couple of turbines but by the time we started seriously looking and checked on their capacity equivalents under FIA rules—the engines were about 5litre equivalent and we were intending to use two of them—equal to 10litres—the SCCA had brought in their 3litre turbine limit which would have brought us more than three times over the capacity limit! Nobody could cheat that much!'

"The worst of the McLaren production cars was Dan Gurney's but that was because he *improved* it so much"

Bruce wasn't sure whether they would have used a turbine at each end of the car as they hadn't got that far but he opined that '... there really are some lovely engines around, real beauties, but we decided not to use them for racing—they'd be great for a production car I must admit. Kinda tempting for the future but expensive of course ...' *Since McLaren issued a brochure in early 1968 which made the enigmatic comment that: 'Later the McLaren design team may turn its attention to a high quality low volume road car', you may like us wish to draw your own conclusions and start saving your pennies for the McLaren M99A turbine road car!*

Another question which always crops up when the American racing scene is discussed is the amount of assistance given by the outspokenly anti-racing General Motors colossus to the racing fraternity. As far as Bruce McLaren is concerned the answer was short and sharp, 'None at all', *but he knew that Jim Hall's Chaparral team had received assistance in the past but he had no idea how far this went.* 'But Chevrolet did make that aluminium engine this year largely for CanAm, which had a fully nitrided crank, forged pistons, a damned good camshaft and a very good alloy in the block. They definitely went to some effort to make sure they kept the lead.'

Would Ford do anything to bolster their sagging reputation in the CanAm field? 'Very definitely. In the aluminium 7litre they've got what can be a good engine but time is so short now.

'We were toying with the idea of using Ford engines but there just isn't the development time, so we're sticking with the Chevy which was very reliable over the last two races this year.'

Rumours had percolated back to England that some of the owners of the twenty or so production versions of the M6A1967 car, which the Lambretta-Trojan group builds under licence for McLaren, were not too happy with the handling of their cars, caused by the front suspension geometry. This brought an explosive 'Bloody hell!' *from Bruce, and a quick rebuttal, as his experience was that everyone was delighted with the car as delivered by Trojan.* 'Bonnier had problems with his steering box but you give Bonnier anything and he has tremendous problems that no one else has. The cars that people left alone such as Jerry Titus's which was bog standard went beautifully and was the fastest of the M6Bs apart from Donohue who had the 7litre engine, and Titus was going round corners quicker even than Donohue. The worst of the production cars was Gurney's but that was because he had improved it so much!

'Most of the customers who left the cars alone were delighted with the way they were built. The only problems were with those people who wouldn't believe we run our cars the way we say in the sales brochure which gives information on setting up the suspension, tyre pressures, etc. There's always an American mechanic coming up to tell us that our recommendations are all wrong. We were terrified of selling cars to people like Gurney because if he had put in ▶

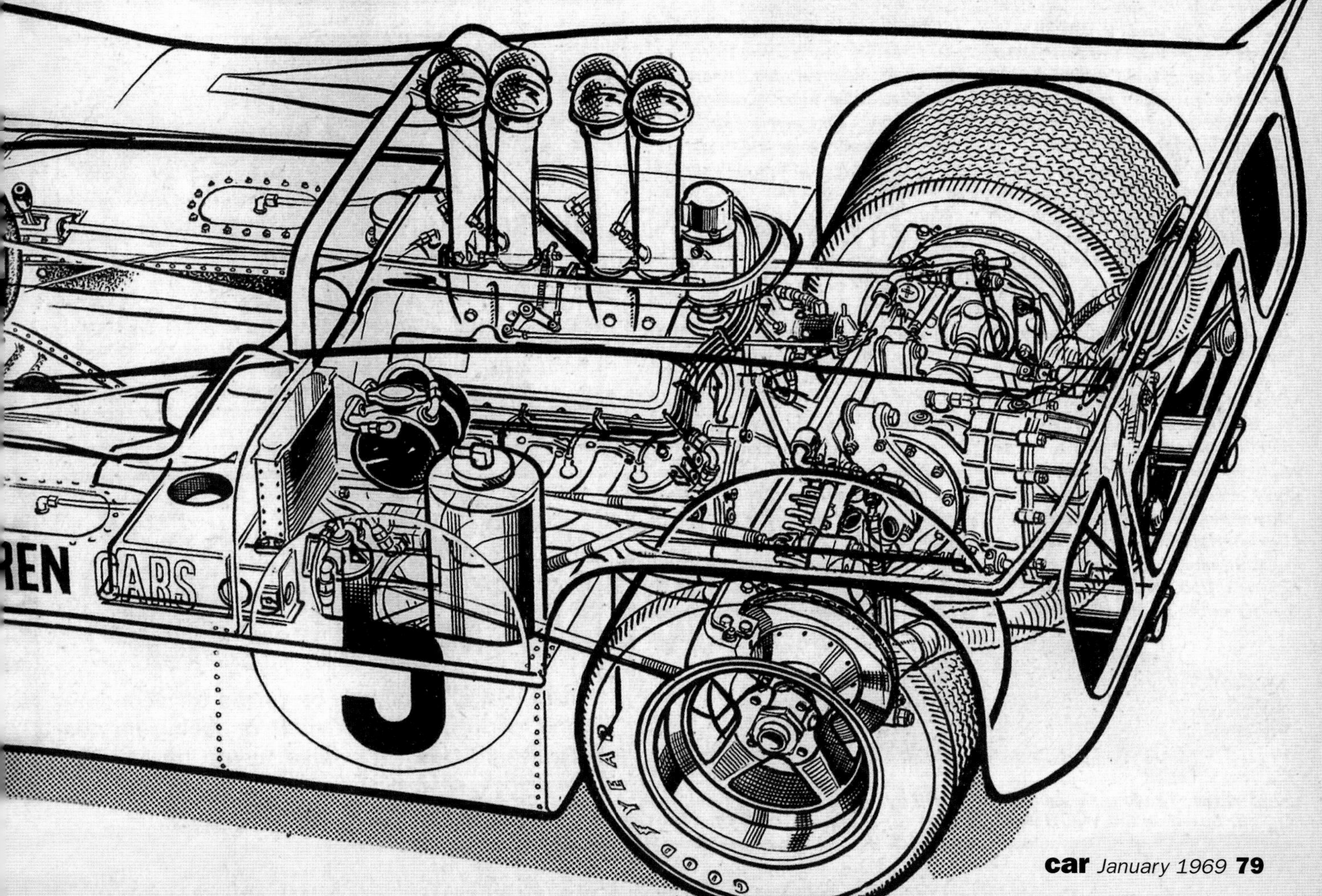

▶ his Weslake Ford with say 570bhp and left the car standard he could well have blown us off.

> **"The main difference between our team and the people racing our production cars was that they went to the cocktail parties and we worked all night"**

'We'll always get accusations of this sort while we're selling cars and in fact we were accused of selling different F2 cars to customers by one journalist but we were able to prove him wrong by showing him an old car of ours side by side with a production car. Trojan's build the cars to the same drawings we used for the works cars—we just haven't got time to make new drawings.'

Conversation turned to the 1969 season. As before, the current M8A will become the production car of 1969, to be known as the M12 which will sell for $15,000 less engine and gearbox. A number of improvements will be made mainly in the rear framework, for Bruce feels that hanging the engine on the back of the chassis is not ideal for selling to private owners—firstly because on the Chevrolet engine a great deal of machining has to be done on the bell housing to fit the suspension pick-ups and secondly it would be difficult to switch from a Chevy to a Ford engine as the bell housing would be different, so the monocoque chassis will be extended back below the engine as on the M6 and the rear suspension will be chassis mounted, but all the good bits of the M8A will be incorporated on the M12, and they should be every bit as quick as the 8As. A number of orders have already been received and Trojan will once again be building them. Bruce and Denny will start 1969 with the existing M8As highly modified but a radical new car may be ready by mid-season.

As well as the M12 there will be a Group 4 car based on the M6 chassis but fitted with a coupé body and 5litre engine to comply with the regulations. At least 25 of these have to be built for homologation but enquiries were already coming in during early December before the car had been officially announced. Another project is a Formula A/5000 car which Bruce reckons will be the big thing of 1969.

The first chassis was well on the way to completion at the time of our talk, the design being rather different from that of the Formula 1 car as the monocoque section extends below the engine and is also swept up as high as the driver's head, incorporating the roll over bar, while the cockpit area is much more enclosed than on the M7A F1 car. This car will sell for $10,750 less engine and gearbox.

In Formula 1 Bruce and Denny will start the season with the same 1968 M7As, one probably remaining very much the same, the other having a number of modifications which will be in the nature of a test bed for the all-new car which should be ready by mid season if all goes well. Naturally Bruce was reticent on the subject of the design but a sketch of a proposed car which we were able to look at showed a very wedge-shaped car, much more so than the Lotus 49, with fuel contained in large pontoon tanks very similar to the Lancia D50. The car will definitely have four wheel drive to a Hewland design and some new thoughts on suspension design, assuming they pass their trials.

We asked if four wheel drive wouldn't lead to even less spectacle in Formula 1 racing than there is now, where the vast tyres allow the cars to corner on rails most of the time. Both Denny and Bruce thought that this was a danger but as neither of them had raced a 4wd car they don't know anything about it as yet. However, there is a possibility, given sufficient power, that spectators would see all four wheels spinning coming out of a bend. They were unanimous that single seater racing could well become boring for watchers if the cars did not look more spectacular. 'In CanAm racing' said Denny, 'there are about six or eight people who can use the full 600 or 650bhp coming out of a bend, and it's pretty exciting sitting behind watching one of them going round a right-hander on full left lock with the rear wheels pouring out clouds of smoke. In fact even if a car is out of sight you can tell he has just gone round a bend by the long black lines on the track with clouds of smoke still rising.'

Lunch time intervened at this stage and while Bruce indulged in a real tycoon's lunch of a sandwich at his desk Denny chauffeured us expertly to the local pub in his Zodiac where the conversation became non-attributable! ❋

First coupé. The first closed car to be built by McLaren is this Group 4 GT car based on the Mk6B which should stir things up at Le Mans in '69 for the Fords and Lolas. It is NOT the whispered road car!

WEAR A MENDAC

JUST LOOK AT THIS PICTURE HERE . . . AND CHECK OFF ALL THOSE FEATURES.

for only 95/6

WIN A MINI for only 4d

THE NEW CAR COAT WITH THE STAR FEATURES READ THEM VERY CAREFULLY, THEY COULD WIN YOU A BRAND NEW MINI:

- *Warmth with Elegance – for only 95/6
- *Unique 'Phobotex'® processed poplin – to repel the rain
- *Zip pockets outside, breast pockets inside – a space for everything
- *Quilted duo-tone lining – for lightweight cosiness
- *Choice of three smooth colours – Midnight Blue, Mid Fawn, Steel Blue
- *Heavy duty fly front

We could go on about all the other features—button-up cuff flaps, side vents, angled pockets—but we want to make it easy for you to win that brand new Mini for only 4d.

ONLY 4d? Yes, when you buy a Mendac Car Coat from this advert and complete the entry form below, you can enter this competition.
So for 95/6 you get a six star Car Coat, and for the 4d. postage for your entry you could be lucky enough to win a Mini car.

TO ENTER THE COMPETITION
Simply list the six starred features mentioned above in the order you consider most important.
Write your answer on the coupon provided, e.g. if you think 'Phobotex'® processed poplin' is the number 1 feature, then mark '1' against it in the space on the entry form.
Complete – in not more than 8 words – the slogan. Send the full coupon, together with your remittance for 95/6. We will then send you by return your Mendac Car Coat and acknowledge that your entry has been accepted for the competition.

RULES

1. The above instructions form part of the official rules.
2. The winning entry will be the one which, in the opinion of the Judges, provides the best listing of the star features and the most appropriate slogan.
3. The competition is open to all customers purchasing a Mendac Car Coat from this advertisement **except** employees of Mendac, their agents and their respective families.
4. The competition closes on 14th March '69 The winner will be notified by post within 3 weeks of the closing date. The result will be published in the press.
5. The decision of the Competition judges is final and legally binding. No correspondence will be entered into. All entries become the sole property of Mendac and cannot be returned.
6. It is a condition of entry to this competition that all players agree to abide by the rules.

Snip

ENTRY for WIN-A-MINI Competition

List the following star features in order of importance:

*Warmth with elegance		*Quilted duo-tone lining	
*Phobotex processed poplin		*Choice of three colours	
*Pockets outside & inside		*Heavy duty fly front	

Complete in your own words (not more than eight) the slogan:

"Mendac Car Coats suit me best because ....

....

In entering this competition I agree to abide by the stipulated rules.

Signed ....

7 DAY MONEY BACK GUARANTEE

Try one for yourself. Use this coupon and send it to us with your remittance for 95/6. We will send your car coat by return. If you are not completely satisfied, return the coat within SEVEN DAYS, unused, in good condition and we will refund your money in full.

NAME ....

ADDRESS ....

TOWN ....

COUNTY ....

MID FAWN .... STEEL BLUE .... MIDNIGHT BLUE

Tick size: 36" . . . 38" . . . 40" . . . 42" . . . 44" . . . 46" . . .

MENDAC · HIPLEY STREET · OLD WOKING · SURREY · Tel: WOKING 64161/7

promise fulfilled?

It's the latest, the greatest, and just what you've always wanted—as long as you're Mr Average to the Ford market researchers.

SINCE WALTER HAYES CAME ON the scene Ford's stock has risen sky-high in the estimation of press men who get the kind of service they used to dream about. No longer do we receive an outline specification and a blurred photo two days after the announcement to inform us of an important new model (don't laugh—BMC did it to us once); now we get all the information we need, can drive the cars long before the announcement date and even talk to the men who designed them and make verbal and written criticism without fear of reprisals like cancelled advertising and the withholding of information. And *that's* happened to us before, as well.

But things didn't go too well for Ford this time. Normally when a new car is announced they like to have at least 20,000 cars in the showrooms so that you can go and look at one almost as soon as you've read about it in your morning paper. Unfortunately Britain's troubled components industry rose to this occasion beautifully and several firms were suffering from 'industrial action' (*ie* inaction) when the Capri was nearing its unveiling. The yards at Dagenham and Halewood were littered with brakeless cars because of the Girling strike and production of the Capri, which should have risen to over 200 a day at Halewood in December was trickling along at a heartbreaking four an hour, with the production line staff scratching brake parts from wherever they could find them.

Ford were committed to a launch date of January 24, which meant that both dealers and Press needed to know something about the car by late November, especially monthly journals like us who have long lead times. But with no cars to show us the Press Office was in a panic, while at the same time the sales people were screaming for enough cars to satisfy a dealer junket in Malta. The sales people got their cars and the dealers were whipped off on their spree—a fact which did not go unnoticed amongst our Maltese readers!

Then eventually in early December the Press Office managed to get hold of a few cars and invited the monthlies out to look at them and bash them round the Ford test track at Boreham. So rushed were they that one example on show had been completed at Halewood the previous night, driven straight to Warley, given a wash and shoved on stage. Evidence of the rush could be seen in the paintwork and detail finish which, we are sure, would not normally pass the Ford inspectors.

Usually we manage to get in a good long drive on the road before the release date of a new Ford but they had promised their dealers that no cars would be driven on the road in Britain before February 4, so we had to be content with many furious laps of Boreham. In any case virtually every car was being shipped off to Cyprus where the press were going to be lavishly entertained during January, with a spot of Capri driving thrown in during rare sober moments. Mr Editor Blain bravely volunteered to submit to this torture, instructing the rest of us to prepare the first road test report in his absence.

Of the seven-model Capri range only the 1600 and 1600GT were available for us to drive at Boreham. It seems that work has not even started on the Zodiac-engined device, while the first Cosworth-engined machine was being completed behind screens in the Competition Department on the day of our visit. The V4 car hasn't yet reached the production stage and we got the distinct impression that the Escort 1300-engined car is regarded very much as a loss leader, the £890 price tag tempting you into the showroom where the salesman will try to make sure you drive out with a £1041 1600 or a £1087 V4 two-litre.

The first car we laid our hands on at Boreham was the 1600; the immediate impression what that the car was exactly the same as a 1600 Cortina—it sounded the same, it rode the same, the gearbox felt the same—in fact to sum it up we felt it was just a Cortina with a different body. A quick check on performance, two up, showed that at 18sec for the 60mph dash it was unlikely to go into orbit on full throttle. A subsequent check on the GT (15sec to 60 indicated) confirmed our suspicions that any Capri version is a slower car than the equivalent Cortina.

Further acquaintance, however, showed that there are in reality a number of improvements over the Cortina. Most noticeable is the lower noise level: at 90mph the Cortina is reverberating madly while wind noise drowns both radio and conversation, but the Capri slices through the air very ▶

Capri specification—1600GT
ENGINE Inline four, 1599cc, pushrod ohv, all-iron; 93bhp at 5400rpm, 102ftlb at 3600rpm; Weber compound downdraught carburettor
TRANSMISSION Four-speed, all-synchromesh; ratios 2.97, 2.01, 1.40, 1.0; final drive ratio 3.77; tyres 165/13 radial
SUSPENSION Front Macpherson struts, lower links, anti-roll bar; rear live axle, semi-elliptic springs, telescopic dampers
STEERING Rack and pinion
BRAKES Disc front, drum rear, 9.6/9.0in

Part of the 'X' pack—twin rear seats Padded wheel boss is standard, reclining seats are not

cleanly and quietly with far fewer groans and buzzes from the chassis/body unit. We worked the GT Capri up to 95mph on Boreham's short straight, a speed at which it felt much more comfortable and rather more stable than a Cortina would.

A second big improvement is the seating. Gone are those dreadful devices which tilt the tallest among us infuriatingly forward as we try to get more arm room; they are replaced by much more comfortable seats, with deeper cushions and a better-shaped backrest (reclining seats are an optional extra). A full arms-stretched driving position can now be adopted (at the expense of back seat legroom) and we have no doubt that a long-distance drive will prove quite comfortable.

The rack and pinion steering is as light as that in the Escort, but its real benefit will be found on those cars which are fitted with wide-rimmed wheels and radials—Lotus Cortina owners will know what we mean. Without these aids to ultimate adhesion the handling is best described as very safe, with gradually increasing understeer. Even at what feels like the limit the steering wheel can be wrenched back and forth without any sign of loss of control, and cornering power is undoubtedly pretty high in the dry. In the wet it would depend far more on the tyres, and it remains to be seen how the thing will behave with a heavier engine up front. *MLT*

Technically speaking

The trouble is that technically there is little new to talk about in the Capri. It has, of course, been engineered to take a wider range of engines than ever before in a British car, but even this has only partially dictated the size of the bonnet; equally important, we are sure, was a feeling that this had to be the British Mustang. Certainly it looks astonishingly like American Ford's all-time jackpot winner in profile, even though it is so much lighter and smaller a car (19in shorter, seven inches less wheelbase, six inches narrower, and five hundredweight less than the 'base' Mustang, to be precise). Apart from width, room inside is about on a par with the American car—which bodes ill for six-footers riding behind six-footers. Structurally, of course, the cars are very different, the British model's unitary structure effectively ruling out a productionised convertible such as the Americans insist on. Ford have taken their NVH approach one stage further in their endeavour to produce a truly civilised car, and are very proud of the structural mods they have embodied to rid it of low-frequency boom and the damping employed to cut out the higher-frequency stuff. But all this detail effort could be said to underline the fact that there is not one wholly new idea in the Capri, and that the entire concept is a triumph of marketing over engineering. This is an approach which has paid Ford great dividends in the past, but in the Escort and now the Capri one can discern signs that the point of diminishing returns must be close indeed. Some aspects of the Capri can certainly be quibbled with: the ultra-small headlights, for instance, and a fuel capacity which is reasonable for the 1600 but derisory for the 3000 when it eventually appears.

In fact the Capri's range of engine sizes is relatively even greater than the Mustang's, running from 1298 to 2994cc (a 2.32 to one ratio) as compared with 3272 to 7003cc (which is only 2.14 to one). At least the V6 Capri will have a power/weight ratio superior to either of the straight-six 'base' Mustangs, and even the V4 promises to be a respectable performer; which is more than can be said of the 1300cc with its 32lb for every bhp to haul around. Just as in America nobody ever actually buys the basic Mustang, so Ford must be hoping that few people will take a fancy to the smallest Capri. Most surprising of all is Ford's decision to go ahead with a real sporting-image version with a productionised Cosworth FVA engine. Not that you should let your mouth water too much, because the published power is 120bhp; so that even if you can get one (unlikely, if the Escort TC is anything to go by) it will prove little faster than the slightly heavier 3000 with its 140bhp. The real point, of course, is to have a homologated touring car for prestige racing.

Really, you must admire the thing as a marketing concept, and as an economic one. Ford were adamant that they would never have gone ahead with the car on a British-only basis, for it would never have achieved a high enough production volume to justify its existence. But with costs split between Britain and Germany, and an immediate assault on the whole of Europe in prospect, matters looked different. One could be cynical and say that the emergence of Europe as an American-size market was the thing that justified an American-style assault with an American-type car. And you wouldn't be far wrong at that. *JRD*

MINIS. You just can't feel that way about any other car –when everything else goes wrong your **Mini** will still love you. **Austin-Morris MINIS from £573 (inc.tax).**

BRITISH LEYLAND AUSTIN MORRIS

A LAMBO
TO LOSE
YOURSELF IN...
MPH
9.4
11.5
13.7
7.9
16.7
5.9
21.0
4.5
25.1
3.3
31.2
2.4
30
40
50
60
70
80
90
100
110
120
130
140
150
160

Le Pur Sang

DAVID BURGESS WISE

Bugattis at Prescott on the occasion of the International Rally. The hill-climb was sponsored by W D & H O Wills, the fag kings (rumours that they are about to bring out a Castrol R-flavoured cigarette can be discounted) and attracted Bugs of all ages, as well as more modern machines. Outright winner was Bernard Kain driving his Type 51 with which Achille Varzi won the 1933 Monaco Grand Prix, and which was later owned by Lindsay Eccles. It hadn't run since 1938, but even so made fastest time on its first outing since then. Kain is seen in the centre picture on the right, driving another of his Bugs, a Type 35B. Large photo shows Jardine's Type 22

ETTORE BUGATTI WAS AN artist and architect by training and an engineer by instinct. His cars were therefore beautiful pieces of sculpture bristling with mechanical impossibilities which worked in spite of themselves.

Among the idiosyncratic features of the various Bugatti models were banana-shaped sliding tappets, reversed quarter-elliptic coster-barrow back springs, fixed cylinder-heads with minimal water passages and valves that could only be ground-in by removing the crank-shaft (but the often quoted aphorism that you can only grind-in the valves on a Bugatti by removing the back axle is actually a misquotation from Ian Hay's Edwardian motoring classic *A Knight on Wheels*, and refers to pre-Kaiser American cars) and oddly spaced firing intervals that contributed to the distinctive Bugatti exhaust note. Other novelties of the 1920 cars were the tapered side elevation of the chassis, the cast aluminium wheels with integral brake drums (ideal for racing but prone to develop fatigue cracks in old age), the tubular front axle through which the springs passed and, in the early 1930s, a front axle made in two halves screwed together by a collar to give an imperceptible degree of suspension independence. Yet Bugattis ran, and ran well, with only a few failures. (One was the 1922 Type 30, the first small straight-eight to enter production, which had a rough, rattly engine with only three main bearings but which formed the basis of the potent Type 35 of 1924.)

Ettore himself was an Italian resident in France who had built his first car at the age of 17 while apprenticed to the Milanese firm of Prinetti and Stucchi. He built a two-engined tricar, then a four-engined four-wheeler, fell out with his employers, joined Count Gulinelli and his brother and produced a four-cylinder ohv three-litre car which was seen by the Baron De Dietrich, who promptly engaged the 19year old designer at his factory in Neiderbronn, Alsace. When De Dietrich closed down at Neiderbronn to concentrate production at Luneville, Bugatti joined Mathis at Strasbourg but soon quarrelled with Emil Mathis, resigned and went to work for the old-established Deutz company. While he was there, and probably inspired by the 1.4litre *Coupe des Voiturettes* Isotta-Fraschini (IF, incidentally, were the Italian subsidiary of the Société Lorraine des Anciens Etablissements De Dietrich) Bugatti built a tiny, 6cwt, 1208cc car in the cellar of the house in Cologne where he was living. It was, of course, too big to get out of the door when it was finished. Like his latest full-size design for Deutz the little car, which he christened Pur Sang (thoroughbred), was shaft-driven and had an ohc monobloc engine; it was capable of 50mph, which was remarkable for the date. Probably the first outsider to drive the new Bugatti was Louis Blériot, who had just gained world fame with his cross-Channel flight. He persuaded Bugatti to set up in business on his own, and by 1910 Bugatti cars were in production in a converted dyeworks in Molsheim, Alsace. Five cars were sold in the first year and the company started to enter for races, where the speed and reliability of the 'toy' attracted much favourable comment and a good many orders despite a high selling price. From the start the Bugatti had a glamorous image—aviators were much addicted to the marque—and its elegant horse-shoe-shaped radiator (Bugatti originally was inspired by a chair-back designed by his father) was retained until the marque's demise in the early 1950s. There was a period in the late 1920s when Bugattis were virtually invincible in motor racing, although admittedly the frequent formula changes at that time meant that his cars were often unopposed.

Having acquired this glamorous racing record, Bugatti then turned his attention to producing an out-and-out 120mph luxury car, *La Royale,* destined for 'monarchs and captains of the automobile industry', none of whom actually bought one. It was a 12.8litre white elephant, only six were sold, and the engines ended up in high speed rail-cars with cable brakes, no less. At the other end of the scale, in 1943 he designed a 12.7cc cycle motor. He also turned his attention to yachts, aero-engines, motorboats, machine tools, clothing reform, boots, dog breeding, estate management, electricity, fishing reels, surgical instruments, horses, religious philosophy, interior decoration, bicycles and electric cars. He was, in short, the modern equivalent of the complete Renaissance gentleman. It was as much to honour the man as his machine that the Bugatti Owners' Club was formed in 1929, and Bugatti took an active interest in the club before his death in 1947. This summer, in token of the club's 40th anniversary, Bugattis from all over the world attended a rally in the Cheltenham area—the last such gathering was in 1963—and 100 of them took part in a hillclimb at Prescott, the BOC's own venue. Charles Pocklington's pictures of the event testify to the fact that the spirit of Pur Sang is still alive. ●

Photography: Charles Pocklington

british car american engine

story: L J K Setright
photography: John Perkins

There are certain definite advantages in building cars in small quantities slowly and one at a time. The mass producer, having cast his die and crossed the Rubicon, is wholly committed to a substantial ▸

▶ production run which must be indulged and encouraged to persist and continue for as long as possible before the introduction of any alterations involving extensive or expensive retooling. By contrast, the small producer can introduce improvements at almost any time by a simple process of infiltration. The economic horrors of retooling are absent because tooling itself is seldom substantially present. The only problem is that if, as is usually the case, certain components are bought from outside specialists (or at least contractors), no good will be done to the firm's reputation if the specifications of these be changed every couple of weeks. It is at least necessary for a reasonable quantity to be ordered, and for that batch to be consumed before the implementation of any alteration. So if you are building in really small quantities, by which I mean something like five cars a week, your difficulties may be almost as insuperable in their own scale as those of the big timer. Your little men with hammers and sewing machines may be able to wreak subtle modifications to the bodywork, but you may be stuck with (say) Salisbury axles or Mintex brake liners for the next 173 chassis before you can make any changes to those items. Once your factory has reached the dizzy heights of two cars a day, however, you have far more scope; and a continuous pattern of modifications and improvements can be indulged in without too much difficulty or expense provided only that your design and development men exercise reasonable forethought.

Such is the state of affairs in the Jensen establishment up at West Bromwich, where they currently churn out about 12 Interceptors and five FF cars a week. Superficially they are no different from what they were when they appeared back in 1966, and I suppose they would still be good cars even if they had not changed beneath the surface. But they have, and I think for the better, as recent experience in driving both versions has illustrated. It also shows that there is still some scope for improvement in several directions.

This suggestion may give offence to certain known parties of known pragmatism who are given to asserting (with excessive emotion) that Jensens are perfectly all right as they are, or (with insufficient logic) that anything costing that much money should be beyond criticism. Such protestations need not be taken seriously: you will not get perfection even in a £10,000 Lamborghini, and certainly not in an £11,000 Mercedes-Benz or a £13,000 Rolls-Royce, so the producers of the £7000 FF and £5000 Interceptor need not feel particularly slighted. More to their credit, they asked me what I thought might be wrong with it, and then presented me with the gratifying news that practically every object of my criticism was being worked upon by them and would be modified or amended before long. How nice, as the character in the Mikado found, to have one's views supported by an obvious authority!

Indignor quandoque bonus dormitat Homerus, as Horace once observed: there was one thing upon which Jensen and I did not quite agree. I felt that the rear axle of the Interceptor needed tying on to the car by some means geometrically more positive than the semi-elliptic springs upon which at present it relies for thrust, braking, suspension, steering, roll stiffness and sundry other functions. When you have as much torque available as is delivered by the big Chrysler engine, and then multiply it by the same firm's torque convertor and epicyclic transmission, you need something more than a mere limited-slip differential if you are to exploit that torque in any but the more favourable of circumstances. A stalled-convertor blast-off while trying for acceleration figures on a dry and only very slightly cambered road kept the Interceptor sideways for well over 20 yards—and as for opening the throttle early in emerging from a corner on wet roads, all I can say is that the consequences induced severe impairment of the zeal. Jensen's customers, it seems, do not find these faults, or do not consider them to be faults, for Chief Engineer Kevin Beattie assured me that he had had no complaints in this respect from any soul among them.

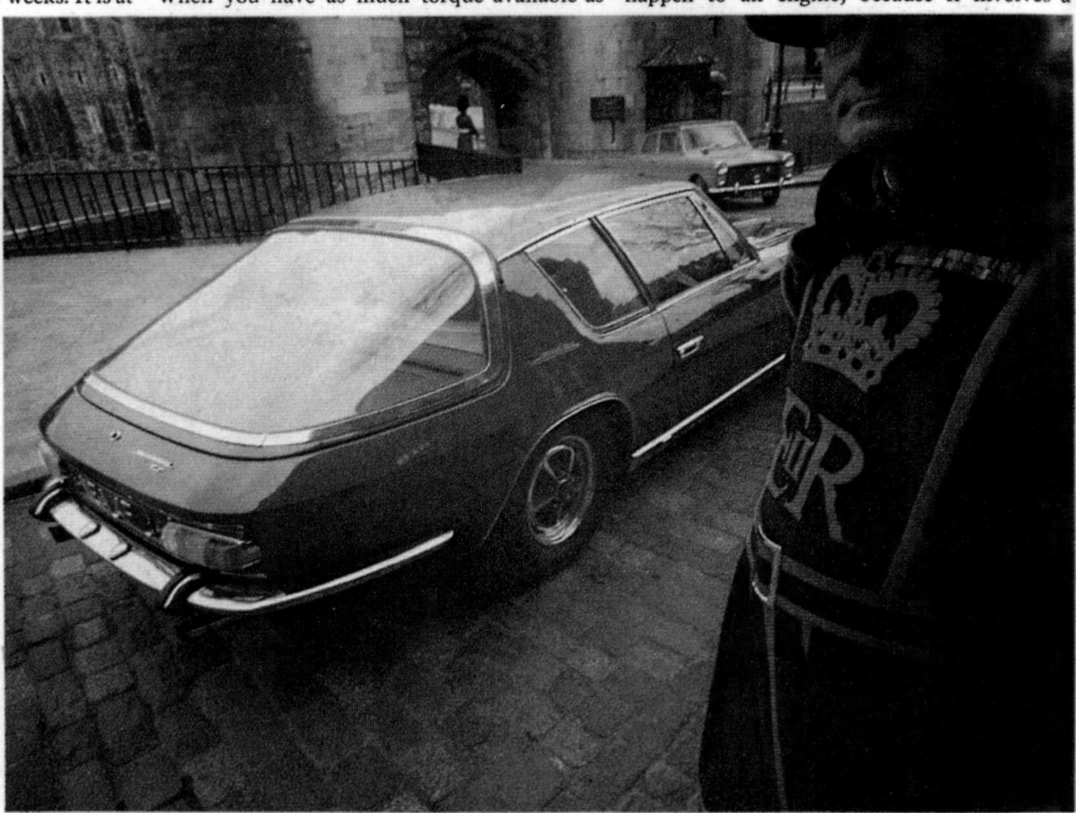

The observant will notice that this Jensen parked by one of the Tower of London's Beefeaters is the FF model which has been kept in deliberate low volume production until all the bugs have been ironed out. Jensen feel that it is fully developed now and production has risen from two per week to one a day. It is still only available in right-hand drive but left-hand drive cars should be coming through early next year

In other matters they have been a little bit more vociferous, and in some cases Jensen themselves have made the running. Sometimes they have been forced to by circumstances quite outside their control, such as the anti-pollution laws. These have led Chrysler into altering the specifications of virtually all their engines, not just the ones they use themselves, so the big V8s that come to West Bromwich are already detoxed, as it were. This is a nasty thing to happen to an engine, because it involves a deliberate weakening of the mixture in order that the exhaust gases be free of carbon monoxide—but the lean mixture makes the engine run hotter, especially at tickover when the engine definitely prefers richness and its compression could hardly be less adiabatic. The consequence of the alterations to the Chrysler engine is a 30percent increase in the rate of heat rejection from engine to coolant, and this has required a new heat exchanger (I have rather gone off calling them radiators), a crossflow apparatus of greater efficiency than its predecessors. In itself the operation profits Jensen not at all, for even with the detoxed engine they cannot sell their cars in America. This is because of another piece of American safety legislation, the bit dealing with projections on the facia, projections such as abound in the Jensen as in hardly any other cars I can think of save the now defunct Gordon Keeble. They are working on it, a variety of stylists including Trevor Fiore having been consulted.

More successful with the Jensen board has been another designer called Jon Bannenberg, whose principal claim to fame appears to be the interior design of much of the QE2. For Jensen he has produced the Director, a two-seater mobile office based on the Interceptor, with the rear passenger compartment replaced by a decked console containing a typewriter, overnight and attaché cases, an insulated food compartment, a portable dictaphone, a portable television set, a suspension filing cabinet and Air Call radio telephone. The idea is that this is what many of Jensen's busier customers require so that they can work while in transit. Most of the special equipment has been provided by Harrods, who can sell you the complete car if you would rather deal with them than with an ordinary Jensen distributor. The cost is £6581 9s 10d, including installation charges for the radio telephone equipment which is available only on a rental basis. It's all rather odd, but not so gimmicky that it should not attract customers. Perhaps the most surprising thing about it is that there is room only for the boss and his personal assistant—how many bosses insist that they should have a full four-seater at least? And will Rolls-Royce/Bentley retaliate with a two-seater Ghost T?

There seems no real reason why the Director package should not be available in the FF as well as in the Interceptor. Certainly any self-respecting self-aggrandising tycoon would consider that his reputation demanded the more expensive and possibly better car. Possibly? Is there any doubt but that the FF is far and away better than the Interceptor? On the whole, no. The FF would never do anything as indecorous as getting sideways during a full-bore getaway, allows you to use full power very early out of a corner if not all the way through it, and will generally run rings round the Interceptor in all those advanced manoeuvres which the average owner would never dream of investigating. And there's the rub, for the only advantage (apart from four-wheel traction on snow and ice, which is not going to bother many British customers) that might appeal to most owners is the lock resistance of the Maxaret-inhibited brakes. Now there's another thing I have rather gone off: practical experience of the two Jensens in rapid succession has led me to conclude that I prefer the uninhibited brakes of the Interceptor. There is no doubt but that the Maxaret, by interrupting the functioning of the brake system for such lengthy intervals whenever the wheels show signs of incipient locking, definitely impairs the braking performance of the FF. Without Dunlop's expensive toy getting in the way, the brakes of the Interceptor can be made to stop it very rapidly indeed, getting the wheels so near to the point of locking that maximum retardation can be realised. The Maxaret won't let you get that near, not unless you boot the pedal with such a force that the Maxaret is over-ridden—as it can be, its method being merely to reject the pressure of your foot firmly enough and with sufficient frequency to prevent the car from breaking traction altogether and sliding out of control.

Actually the Maxaret has not been without its troubles. One particular batch of cars had to be recalled for attention due to interior condensation and icing conditions leaving the braking system powerless. It was all most embarrassing, and although only a fairly small number of FFs was involved and all have been put right, there is some danger of the system getting a worse name than it deserves.

Even with the Interceptor there have been braking troubles that have caused a number of complaints, but these have been attributable mainly to the brake materials. They have been rather too temperature-sensitive, not only losing efficiency when overheated but also failing to generate anything like their proper stopping power when not heated enough. When the brakes are being kept warm by repeated applications on winding roads or in stop-and-go traffic, there is nothing to fear; but the prospects of being unable to slow the thing down promptly after a long session with the chill breeze of 130mph blowing in the Girling's kidneys is very intimidating indeed. The fact that they are Girling brakes should not pass unnoticed, for they used to be Dunlop, but the new brake has bigger pads and the next step is to replace the M33 pads by Ferodo's new F2430 series, one of the new range that has already won the lining firm some safety awards as well as not a few original equipment contracts. I have seen the mu/temperature curves for 2430, and though they are neither as long nor as flat as those of the more expensive and less compromising DS11 from the same stable, they are not at all bad.

What a lot of complications all these outside component suppliers create when you want to build a nice car out of their bits! Ferodo and Mintex, Girling and Dunlop, Chrysler and Harrods, Fortnum and Mason . . . I mean Armstrong. Their lever dampers at the front have been replaced by telescopics. I have also been given to understand from another source that their electrically remote-controlled Selectaride dampers are not much longer for this world, and if and when they go Jensen and one or two other manufacturers will have to look for some alternative rear dampers. This may be difficult, for with all its faults (which mainly arise only if the things are not used sufficiently but are allowed to get stuck in one position) the Selectaride is one of those rare things which is not only desirable but also unique. Of course it could be that Armstrong are developing something to replace it, but at present there is no effective substitute and I certainly felt that I could not always get the best out of the Jensens without them. With them, and secure in the knowledge that I had inflated the tyres to rather higher and less differentiated levels than the manufacturers recommend, the FF could be whistled across Salisbury Plain or oozed through Dorsetshire villages without any ride or handling qualms despite being laden to the gunwales with family and luggage. Similarly the Interceptor was very happy being hustled in intermediate gear through winding lanes in the New Forest, the very good power steering making up for any shortcomings of the suspension. Actually the power steering has been changed from the original Cam Gears design that Jensen first chose for the FF, and I am not entirely sure that the change has been for the better—it feels less direct—but judgement on this should perhaps be suspended for the time being pending completion of changes to the front suspension. This involves a resetting of the geometry so as actually to increase camber as the wheels move up to the full bump position, producing negative camber instead of the present positive camber of 1 degree. While they are about it they are increasing the progressiveness of the suspension by reducing the bump travel and increasing the rebound travel, remembering to modify the bump rubber appropriately.

Jensens and their customers alike are keen to convert both Interceptor and FF to radial-ply tyres. They have been agitating for this for a long time, but have been up against the slight formality of headlamp height regulations. Radial-ply tyres in sizes equivalent to the current 6.70.15 crossplies have greater static deflection and correspondingly smaller rolling radius, so if you shoe your Jensen with radials you might just find the headlamps below the statutory 24in minimum. Of course it is a chance worth taking, and you would be a fool to be deterred by such considerations, but Jensen simply dare not flout the law by selling cars in that condition. While they are working on the suspension they plan to raise the ride height slightly so as to accept radials, and it is to be hoped that they will get round to adopting wider wheels so as to allow a more realistic choice of tyre sizes. At present the biggest thing you can decently fit is a 185×15, which is all right—but only just.

In the meantime, why on earth do they fit RS5 tyres? To be sure, the high-speed crossply tyre is a splendid device to which I am often strongly attracted, but this ancient war-horse of Dunlop has very little to commend it save that Dunlop themselves are not very far away in Erdington. Avon's Turbospeed is a far better tyre, and so is Firestone's old Sports 130 except in the damp; but perhaps the best of them all is the India Autospeed which, like the RS5, is available from Dunlop, though Dunlop always seem to forget about it. With the SP Sport clearly looming in their future plans, Jensen are presumably not bothering to change the RS5 for something similar but better. A nice set of E70VR15 on wider wheels, like the new Jaguar's, would be a much more mouth-watering proposition and should get rid of the fearful tyre roar that intrudes on some surfaces at any speed in current Jensens and on any surface at 25mph in the Interceptor I drove.

So now we've added Armstrong and the Dunlop tyre division to the list of Jensen's suppliers. Are there any other bits left to be considered? Why yes, Jensen themselves actually make some of the parts. We don't have to worry about them, though, they are all right. Apart from the annoyance of things sliding off the rear parcels shelf when the boot lid cum rear window is opened, and a surprise at finding one or two little blisters of lifting paint on the otherwise superb exterior of the FF, I am bound to concede that both the current Jensens are very fine cars indeed. All my passengers swore to being supremely comfortable; that I wasn't is due probably to the fact that I am of funny shape and non-standard size. They are still superb cars in which to travel fast and get out of somebody's sight, or to travel ►

slowly and catch somebody else's eye. The FF in particular, with its recently strengthened hubs, modern tyres, and if possible with its Maxaret system doctored, would certainly find a place on my short list of cars I would actually like to have—and that is a *very* short list!

Even the ability to draw up a short list implies a somewhat eclectic attitude to cars, I suppose. In the context of an American-oriented (no, that can never be right; American-occidented?) issue, this may be out of place: for the American system is to level down and equalise—hence the SAA Colt. Still, the context demands that one further point be made, and it counts in the Jensen's favour. It is that the car is one of only two American-engined European cars to be really successful. For years it has been axiomatic that the way to build a good car was to take chassis and body from this side of the Atlantic, engine and gearbox from *that* side. There were the Graham-Paige, the Atalanta, the Brough Superior and the Railton, and they have gone. There were the Facel Vega and the Gordon Keeble and the Sunbeam Tiger, and they are likewise departed, though a few tears ought to be shed for the Gordon Keeble. There are the Iso and Mangusta and AC, and it is high time they went too. Then there will only remain (apart from that most American of our cars, the Rolls-Royce) the Bristol and the Jensen to show just what the real advantages of borrowing from the USA can be, and how they should best be exploited. Even the Bristol can be counted out on a technicality, for it has a modified *Canadian* Chrysler engine, you see—so the Jensen really is unique. Marshall Aid was never like this! •

now you've read all about the

improvements going into the Interceptor and FF, read MIKE TWITE's story of a long Continental drive in an earlier Interceptor

MOTOR MANUfacturers employ many different methods of introducing their new models to the press. Some just send you a specification sheet and a couple of pictures with leggy models obscuring the faulty curves in the bodywork of the new heap; they then write nasty letters when you print a paragraph about the car instead of the six page colour spread they were expecting. Others take you along to a stately home, fill you with wine and food then let you loose for an hour or two on the road; this is better than the first method but still inadequate. A third ploy is to take you to a racing circuit, fill you with ditto then let the sozzled press men on to the track; for obvious reasons this idea is gradually losing favour, as manufacturers find it difficult to replace bent machinery. The fourth method is to whisk you to some far flung corner of the world, give you the folklore bit, stress the dangers of the country and the colossal expense they have gone to in order to keep the new model away from prying eyes in Europe, then send you out on the road for varying distances. One manufacturer actually spent something approaching £20,000 to take the press abroad in order to give them some 50 miles each on the road! Others, like Ford and Renault, go to the other extreme at times and ask you to cram in 500 miles between breakfast and dinner. Exhausting but often rewarding and the number of column inches in the press on release date usually reflects the amount of driving that the press has been allowed to put in.

Jensen chose method three to introduce the Interceptor and FF. On a cold, damp day we members of the fourth estate gathered in morose bunches at Goodwood circuit waiting for something to happen. Eventually we were allowed to pile into the Interceptors and do two or three laps before being vigorously flagged in. One or two privileged people actually managed to handle an FF on the circuit and I sneaked a solitary lap before being flagged in like a naughty schoolboy. The scene then shifted to a grassy patch in the paddock where everyone was driving round like lunatics on the damp grass. We all pitched in and had the time of our lives, spinning furiously and attempting to prove that the FF accelerated much quicker on grass than its two-wheel drive mate. After a while I tired of this and asked one of the aloof, elegantly clad gentlemen from Jensen when the tomfoolery was going to stop and when were we going to find out something about the cars. There followed a furious back-pedalling session during which it became obvious that no one from the press was going to be allowed to get their grubby hands on the FF under any circumstances. When I told the aforementioned aloof, elegantly clad gentleman that I wasn't much addicted to driving cars, four wheel drive or otherwise, on grass and that the day had been more or less a waste of time he muttered darkly about ingratitude and what about the champagne and smoked salmon and come and have a drink old boy. I left early.

Ever since I have had a bit of a chip on my shoulder about Jensen, mainly because I haven't been able to lay hands on one for any length of time to find out how good it was. But at last an Interceptor arrived for a full week or so and I was despatched to the Continent on a race reporting trip to find out all I could. Much of the journey was completed two-up, with three passengers for the return trip from Belgium when another journalist hitched a lift. With three people and a fair amount of luggage on board we soon discovered that the Interceptor is hardly a four seater because our third passenger had to sit crosswise on his seat and also had to nurse some camera bags and odd items which would not fit into the boot. Quite why the 2+2 holds such a fascination for manufacturers I don't know but I would much rather choose between an honest to goodness four seater saloon and a two seater coupé than be stuck with a car which is trying to be a GT car in appearance while attempting to convince you that there is room for four adults. Jensen are not alone, for the Aston Martin DB6, the Porsche 911 and Lamborghini Islero amongst others are just as bad in this respect. In fact there are very few high performance four seaters in which I could feel comfortable in the rear seat; only the XJ6 springs to mind immediately and from there one has to descend the price range to the Austin 1800 to find another that suits me!

Fortunately I seldom have to act as passenger in any car, a prospect which terrifies me no matter how good is the driver, so it is more the actual driving of the Jensen which occupied most of my time. This was a pleasant chore in nearly every respect for there is only one sort of car that I like as much as one with a big lazy engine and that's another one of them. With 383 cubic inches of Chrysler V8 giving 325bhp at 4600rpm you cannot get much bigger or lazier and naturally the engine was mated with Chrysler's Torqueflite automatic transmission, although if you are addicted to manual labour there is a four-on-the-floor option at extra cost. Times change. Most of the time I just stuck the big tunnel-mounted lever in D and let the gearbox do the work although there is a slight gain in acceleration by using the manual holds on the lower gears. Perhaps the most useful aspect of the box is in being able to hold the middle gear when negotiating medium speed curves which helps in keeping the rear end sticking down well. The engine is virtually completely silent, starts first time and is unobtrusive in the extreme, showing no sign of overheating under provocations such as 130mph cruising for 100 miles and using no discernible amounts of oil. Its only drawback was a thirst as bad as that of an Irish labourer on a Saturday night. The Interceptor did about 13mpg in my tender care which is I suppose more than the Irish labourer would do. This problem of high fuel consumption is reaching ridiculous proportions in Europe, with the price of petrol heading for nine bob a gallon in some countries. It will soon be impossible to traverse France in cars like the Jensen without spending the entire £50 travel allowance on petrol. And I'm only half joking.

The learned Leonard has already explained the numerous subtle changes being made to the Interceptor's suspension so I will only comment that I thought the ride only average on poor Continental roads, with a good deal more transmission of road noise to the interior than I expected. I imagine that the change to radial-ply tyres mentioned by the good LJKS will tend to worsen this aspect. I was not as impressed with the Armstrong Selectaride as he appears to be for I assessed the ride as soft and choppy on the softest setting and hard and choppy on the hardest setting, but then I was driving on the worst that Belgium can offer which is about as bad as you can get; certainly much worse than the billiard tables of Devon. I somehow felt that if I had £5000 to spend on a car I would pick one with independent rear suspension. Even without this sophistication the Interceptor does handle very well indeed, having given me an enjoyable time hurling it back along twisting Belgian and French roads to meet the ferry for which we had inevitably left ourselves too little time to do too much mileage. Still I wouldn't qualify to work for CAR if I didn't put off till next month what I should have done yesterday or leave myself one hour in which to cover a distance which normally takes three. It was ever thus among us. One shortcoming with the Jensen which came to light during the headlong rush for the Channel was with the brakes; we started the journey with first class brakes but as the speed built up and the roads became twistier so the brakes began to wilt until on the final few miles one stop from 100mph left them completely useless if another stop was required within half a minute or so. Fortunately on the few occasions that the situation became fraught I was able to conjure up my incredible skill to induce some sideways motion from the rear end to scrub off the necessary speed. The brakes really did get a caning on that trip during which 130mph was seen on the speedometer so many times that it began to feel positively slow.

The Jensen showed its charm best when the pressure was off and you could whisper along at a gentle 100mph with the faintest rustle emanating from the engine compartment while the merest trace of a breeze fluttered by the thin screen pillars. It really was most relaxing, unlike Ferraris and Lamborghinis whose engines emit those metallic noises so beloved of the *cognoscenti*, but then the Ferraris and Lamborghinis have certain advantages over the Jensen.

Perhaps the main criticism that one could make of the Interceptor is that Jensen have tried to make it too cheaply. When it was first introduced its basic price was just over £3000, which with an imported engine and a costly pressed steel body meant that some cost cutting had to go into the other mechanicals. The basic price has risen in the intervening three years by nearly £1000, mostly because of Government action and not because the Interceptor has become £1000 better. We have a theory here at CAR that anyone who can afford a £5000 car can usually afford an £8000 or £10,000 one so I for one would have preferred to see a higher price and more engineering sophistication. ●

The engine of both Jensens (below left) is the Chrysler 6.2litre V8 which develops 325bhp at 4600rpm. Opinions differ on the styling of the Interceptor and FF (bottom), our road tester being of the opinion that it tries to be a saloon car disguised in a GT body with the result that the rear seats (below) offer insufficient leg room for long distance travel although the front seats are superbly comfortable

ENGINE Chrysler V8 90degree, pushrod operated overhead valves; bore 108mm, stroke 86mm, capacity 6276cc, compression ratio 10 to one; carburettor one Carter 4 choke; maximum power 325bhp at 4600rpm; maximum torque 425bhp at 4600rpm; water cooling
TRANSMISSION Chrysler Torque Flite automatic transmission, 3 speed with torque converter; gear ratios 1st 2.44–5.39, intermediate 1.44–3.19, top 1.0–2.2. Final drive hypoid bevel with Powr Lok limited-slip differential 3.07 to one
CHASSIS Tubular steel frame and steel body welded in unit
SUSPENSION Front independent by double wishbones, coil springs, lever arm dampers and anti-roll bar; rear rigid axle, leaf springs, Panhard rod, Armstrong Selectaride dampers
STEERING Rack and pinion
BRAKES Dunlop discs on all four wheels with vacuum servo, diameter front and rear 11.25in
WHEELS AND TYRES Pressed steel disc wheels with 4.5J rims fitted with Dunlop RS5 cross-ply 6.70/15in tyres
DIMENSIONS Wheelbase 8ft 9in, track front 4ft 8in, rear 4ft 9in; overall length 15ft 8in, overall width 5ft 9in, overall height 4ft 5in; ground clearance 5in; kerb weight 3651lbs
PRICE Interceptor £5198 inc tax, FF £7007 inc tax

so this is the People's Porsche

PHILIPPE DE BARSY

IT IS DIFFICULT FOR THE sports car enthusiast to understand why it took 21 years for Ferry Porsche to project and to build the successor to the first Porsche 356, which was an open two seater mid-engined roadster. In fact, this is not so surprising because since May 1948 both Porsche and Volkswagen have accomplished the necessary evolution to make the new car a really successful one. A short test of both the 914 and the 914/6 confirms that it has been worth waiting!

Ferry Porsche and his team are certainly not the only ones to be seduced by VW components and inspired to build a sports car around them. But Ferry has the unique luck to be the son of the great Ferdinand and to have been associated with the VW project since the beginning. He also inherited Porsche's design office which has, since September 1948, been adviser to Volkswagen. This assured Porsche of a regular income from the royalties paid by Volkswagen for each car leaving the VW factory and later the commercial support of the main VW importers all over the world.

This explains why Ferry Porsche was so careful in developing the 356 project which turned out to be a coupé with the VW engine at the back. The story of the VW-Porsche is fascinating because it started with the VW project itself before World War II. Ferdinand Porsche had just seen the first VW 3 prototypes on the road when he initiated the project of a 1500cc VW sports car.

The project never went further than the drawing board due to opposition from the leaders of the Deutsche Arbeitsfront. Later in 1939, he was able to produce the three Berlin-Rome streamlined single-seater VWs that should have been entered in the so-called race planned for 1940.

However, it is more logically the first 356, projected and built in Gmünd under the direction of Ferry Porsche, which may really be considered as the genuine predecessor of the VW-Porsche 914.

If that car had been built by any other person than Ferry Porsche, it would just have been another VW Special like so many since World War II . . . Just remember the Denzel for example—and all those American plastic bodied VWs!

But at Porsche, the VW components were carefully developed until, one after the other, new Porsche parts were made to produce finally a car with no VW parts left at all. On the other side, the VW cars were improved; the engine followed a complete evolution, of which the 411E engine is the latest development. One of the things that made the VW-Porsche settlement possible was that the 411E engine was to be available because the engine of the

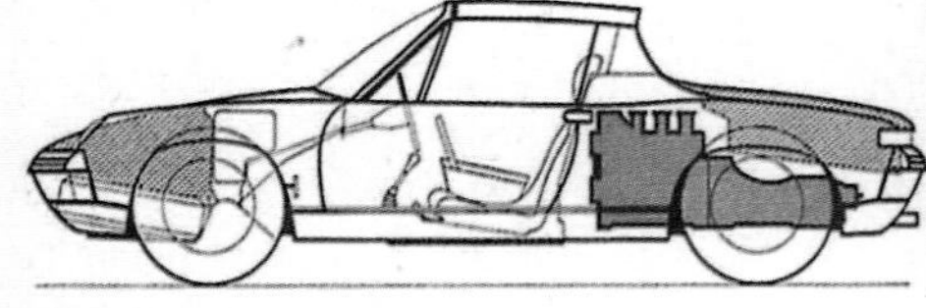

It may not be the most beautiful car you've ever seen but it doesn't half go, stop and handle. Price in England? Under £2000!

cheapest version of the new car had to be perfectly standard if the price was to be at all competitive.

Ferry Porsche did not put the mid engine 356 in production because at that time it looked very difficult to really reap all the benefit from the mid engine architecture with the VW parts.

If one looks at the 914 today, it is obvious that it is well balanced just because Porsche has developed a front suspension and a fuel tank that left enormous space for the luggage at the front. If the engines had not been air-cooled, the proposition would have been much less appealing for the Gran Turismo minded drivers who are very interested in the huge amount of room offered by the two luggage compartments.

This is only a small thing that contributes to the balance of the VW-Porsche and I choose to put it forward as evidence to explain that the 914 uses the best from both companies. It is a beautiful and rare example of how a small company can do good to a big one. One only needs to compare the story of Porsche and Volkswagen with the short and unsuccessful life of Cisitalia which presented the famous Pininfarina styled coupé in 1947, or the creative activities of Carlo Abarth, both working on Fiat parts.

The examination of the VW-Porsche 914 and 914/6 reveals that this car is mainly a new hull with all the main Porsche parts and, in the case of the 914, a stock 411E engine. There is nothing mechanical which could give trouble at the beginning of production. And one also feels this when one drives both cars for the first time.

The driving position is good, in fact excellent for tall people; perhaps the small steering wheel will be a little too low for some people, otherwise every lever, button or pedal is exactly where hands and feet like to find them.

Driver and passenger both feel very comfortable in the fully adjustable bucket seats and the layout of the rest of the cockpit is really efficient and well trimmed.

With the Volkswagen engine, the car is quick; the Porsche five-speed gearbox helps it to give its best from low speed and effortless cruising speed considering that only 80bhp (DIN) is available.

But what is really important is that the ride and the roadholding are so superb and the chassis so pleasantly rigid that it offers both the qualities of a GT car and a true sports car.

When you have the Porsche flat six behind you, the basic quality of the chassis is even more evident and just to convince you of the real virtue of the mid engine layout, the best thing to do is to have a short drive in a 911S!

On the Hockenheim circuit, the 'S' was not at its best on the very long straight which is not so straight towards the end; the front end really wandered under the influence of heavy braking, but with the 914/6, stability is just perfect and high-speed cornering is real fun. The behaviour is just perfectly neutral with the choice in the hands of the driver if he wants to induce some slight under or oversteer.

On the road, the steering is delightfully light and the arms can be comfortably supported by armrests on the straight. Noise level is surprisingly no worse than the 911. Only some slight wind noise could be heard in this prototype car, mainly because the side windows didn't shut completely. But even so, this is acceptable on what is after all a coupé/cabriolet. It's great to drive such a perfect motor car. It is so exceptional to find a car which meets all the requirements of its specification right from the outset.

Many Porsche enthusiasts will not resist the temptation of changing the T engine for a E or even a S and why an R for the racing driver?

With the S 1991cc engine, the power to weight ratio would be only 5.53kg/hp DIN. If lightened for racing purposes and fitted with 1991cc R engine, that ratio could be lowered to 3.5kg/hp DIN. Just think, the impressive C111 from Daimler-Benz has 3.9kg for each of its Wankel's horses!

That can't be bad, can it? ●

photography: Nigel Snowdon

Who's number one?

Mike Twite bravely picks the top drivers of 1969

THE YEAR 1969 BELONGS unequivocably to Jackie Stewart. He won six of the Championship races, just failing to equal Jim Clark's record of seven Championship wins in a season. His six wins were obtained in South Africa, Spain, Holland, France, England, and Italy. Of the other five he led the Monaco GP until retiring with a broken driveshaft, he led the German GP until gearbox troubles dropped him to second place, he led the Canadian GP until he was eliminated in a collision, he fought with Rindt for the lead in the American GP before retiring with a broken engine and in the Mexican GP he finished fourth. This is the sort of domination that only Fangio and Clark have been able to achieve before, but whereas they were often able to go out and win as they liked Stewart has had more opposition than he has cared to handle in several races this year. In Spain, only the unreliability of the opposition gave him victory as his car was running poorly; at Silverstone he had a great fight with Jochen Rindt which ended when Jochen's aerofoil began to disintegrate; at the Nurburgring Jackie Ickx caught him after a poor start and they had a big scrap until the Matra began refusing to select its gears properly and in the Canadian GP Ickx once again harried him unmercifully until the unfortunate accident which put the Matra out of the race. So he hasn't been entirely without opposition.

Where has he had the edge? As someone pointed out to me he is the only driver to be using a new design of car this year—everyone else is stuck with a 1968 car, which in effect means a 1967 design, and many of the drivers are actually driving the very same cars they used in 1968. Naturally they are well maintained but rivets start stretching, glue comes unglued and each tiny bit of extra movement means a less rigid car. This did happen to Lotus, whose 49Bs were handling poorly for no apparent reason at one stage in the season, and it was only when the cars were stripped completely that wear in the basic chassis could be traced.

Stewart quite candidly admits that the MS10 would never have won the Championship for him, so it was an astute move on someone's part to design a new 2wd car as well as an interim 4wd machine while everyone else was putting their eggs in the 4wd basket and keeping their old 2wd car as stand-by. Unfortunately, the 4wd layout proved to be anything but the magic elixir everyone hoped for, and there was much scrambling to update the 1968 cars. The situation was not improved at Monaco with the banning of aerofoils amidst much acrimony. However, everyone seems to have forgotten about the fuss, and the wings hardly seem to be missed any more. The MS80, with its dumpy fuselage, hardly looks a race winner but the centre of gravity is nice and low and it is not affected as much as some of the opposition by the weight transfer of fuel during a race. On occasions the Lotus 49B has been as quick as the Matra and the relatively simple Brabham BT26 has been slightly quicker when young Ickx has had ▶

▶the bit between his teeth, but Stewart has always had the edge on reliability and superb preparation from Ken Tyrrell and his men at the woodyard in East Horsley. Everyone was predicting a shattering performance from Jochen Rindt this year, but his bad crash at Barcelona in May seems to have affected his driving just as Jackie Stewart's crash at Spa in the BRM affected his. Probably neither of them would admit it openly but after their crashes they had just lost that fine edge. There was no real visible difference in Stewart's driving after his crash, but Rindt's is noticeably less lurid—he no longer takes that slight extra risk, no longer leaves his braking later than anyone else, no longer hangs the tail out on those sweeping fast bends and has developed a positive dislike for long circuits which need learning. Ickx is the opposite—he loves the long circuits as does Jackie Stewart, their natural ability and almost photographic memory putting them streets ahead of the opposition. Ickx had a bad crash in a Ferrari last year which left him with a broken leg, but it seems to have affected him very little and he is still very young and very ambitious—after all this is only his second Formula 1 season.

Stewart dedicated himself to winning the Championship with an almost monastic fervour. Despite his admitted interest in the 'bawbees' he gave up many lucrative offers of drives in the Tasman series, sports cars, Indianapolis and CanAm racing to concentrate full time on winning the Championship. He did endless series of tests with Dunlop to ensure their tyres were competitive, he visited nearly every circuit well before the race to carry out private testing and have the car properly set up before practice ever started and he weighed up the opposition very carefully during practice. He is also a master tactician. If you read Jackie's column last month you will recall how he worked out his gear ratios at Monza for the Italian GP so that he crossed the finishing line in fourth gear while everyone else had to change into fifth, thus losing that vital fraction of a second a gearchange takes. In fact he won the race from Jochen Rindt by a nose—just about the length of time it took Jochen to change into fifth.

Jackie has his critics. Many call him cocky, others dislike his extrovert long locks, still more vilify his campaign for safety in racing while his business acumen is the subject for much debate. Before Jackie, probably only Stirling Moss really capitalised on his ability, while other drivers thought it was ungentlemanly to ask for a lot of money in exchange for doing something they liked.

But a racing driver's life can be a short one, tragically short in so many cases, and who in all honesty can say that a top class driver is overpaid? If the market cannot stand it, then the money won't be paid. Jackie's earnings this year have been estimated by people (who cannot have the faintest idea) at over £100,000 but I don't think that's an unreasonable sum; after all a pop singer or a film star could knock that up in a week or two, their only brushes with danger being the possibility of a shock from their electric guitars. Over-exposure could be the danger, but Jackie's handler Mark McCormack has had a good deal of success in the field of promotion and won't let Jackie be seen too often. You can be sure, however, that his name is going to appear on all sorts of products, from driving gloves to tee shirts. Jackie gives his sponsors good value, for he is an amusing speaker and will sign endless autographs; he has also been known to prod some of his sponsors into getting a bit of publicity for themselves, as witness the recent sprucing up of Dunlop personnel with their yellow and black outfits.

I have gone into print saying that I thought the 1969 Formula 1 season has lacked excitement and interest from the spectator's point of view, but races since then have certainly gone a long way towards changing my mind. I still say, however, that small fields, one-engine domination and one or two drivers streets ahead of the others is no recipe for bringing in the crowds. With fields as low as 13 cars on five-mile-long circuits (as happened at Clermont Ferrand) there is not much to see, especially since the races seldom last longer than two hours. This forces organisers to lay on other attractions to give spectators value for their money, which in turn puts up the cost of promoting a meeting. Naturally, Cosworth cannot do anything about the uncompetitive state of their only two rivals, BRM and Ferrari, and in a way it does lead to closer racing since everyone has more or less the same amount of power. Neither can Stewart, Ickx and co help being better drivers than the others, but the fact remains that Grand Prix racing is not at its healthiest at present. You cannot force new people to join in, and even if they do there is no guarantee that they'll be competitive. At least one new car, the March, should be on the starting grids next season which will make a welcome change, but let's hope that Honda will come back, together with more international competition. I will openly admit that I gave several F1 races a miss this season and watched long-distance sports car races instead; to my delight I enjoyed them immensely, purely for the variety in the machinery and the opportunity to travel all round the circuit.

On the subject of safety Jackie Stewart has been cast as the villain of the piece, virtually being branded single-handed for stopping the Belgian Grand Prix. He happened to be the GPDA member who inspected the Spa circuit, but all the other drivers concurred with his decision, and since the organisers did not complete the necessary modifications in time the race had to be cancelled. Drivers who stand to earn more than £1000 in starting money if a race is held are hardly going to force its cancellation unless there's a very good reason. Now that the circuit has been modified there seems every chance that next year's race will be held. Nearly every driver has expressed his apprehension at the thought of averaging 150mph round the Spa circuit, which has claimed so many lives. The fact that it is now safer doesn't make the circuit itself any less demanding, but there is a peculiar bunch of people who think that unless the result of a mistake or a mechanical failure is a horrendous crash into the surrounding scenery then a driver is not proving his bravery, whereas the opposite is undoubtedly true.

What of the future? Motor racing changes so rapidly that it would be foolish to try to predict what will happen even in 1970. We can expect the old faithfuls like Lotus, BRM and Ferrari to remain on the scene, and McLaren, too, are already rumoured to have a new F1 car on the stocks. Jack Brabham has already said that the future of his team in Formula 1 is very uncertain and a very big question mark hangs over Matra, who could well be forced to sell their car subsidiary as it is becoming too big a financial burden on the aircraft side which makes the profits. Still, motor racing has survived many shocks before and will undoubtedly survive plenty more and still go on as long as red-blooded young men exist.

For my own amusement and yours I have graded the top drivers in the order of what I consider to be their ability. This is of course only my personal opinion and is as biased as anyone else's is likely to be and will no doubt anger the fans of certain drivers. It is more than likely that if some drivers had better cars they would be higher up the list, but there are probably some very good reasons why they don't have better cars. If you disagree with my choice let me know. I may even print your list! ●

Many drivers were jostling for tenth place, including Piers Courage (11th), John Surtees (12th), Jean-Pierre Beltoise (13th), Vic Elford (14th), Johnny Servoz-Gavin (15th), Pedro Rodriguez (16th), Jackie Oliver (17th), not to mention up-and-comers like John Miles, Brian Redman, Derek Bell, Henri Pascarolo, etc.

Photography: Nigel Snowdon/David Winter

1 Jackie Stewart

Almost total domination of the Formula 1 scene leaves Jackie Stewart as the only candidate for number one spot. His dedication to Formula 1 has never been equalled. ●●●●●

2 Jackie Ickx

Ickx has matured rapidly as a Formula 1 driver, challenging Stewart on more than one occasion in his Brabham, winning both the German and Canadian GPs. Next year Ferrari. ●●●●●

3 Mario Andretti

On the basis of Formula 1 success Andretti should not even be mentioned but he is another natural who can adapt himself to any type of racing. He may well enter F1 seriously soon. ●●●●●

4 Jochen Rindt

There was a time not so long ago when Jochen was the only possible contender to Stewart for the number one spot. His crash in Spain seems to have curbed his enthusiasm for the time being. ●●●●

5 Jack Brabham

Some people might seem surprised to see 'Black Jack' so high up, but after his injury earlier this year he came back and began going quicker than ever. Life certainly begins at 40. ●●●

6 Jo Siffert

I put Jo Siffert at No6 because he has really come back into the thick of things just when he looked to be on the way out. In sports car racing he's almost unbeatable. ●●●

7 Denny Hulme

Denny doesn't talk a very good race like some others but in a competitive car he's never far from the front. CanAm commitments have kept him busy but a new F1 car would help. ●●●

8 Chris Amon

Chris has often been labelled as the unluckiest driver in Grand Prix racing. True to a certain extent but he has to develop a more ruthless attitude and not play the gentleman. ●●●

9 Graham Hill

It almost seems like insulting the Queen to put Graham so low down the list, but he has not had the best of seasons with Lotus apart from his victory at Monaco. ●●●

10 Bruce McLaren

Bruce has so many dependants these days he daren't drive fast! But his list of good placings in F1 ensures him of a place in the top ten. ●●●

Porsches enGulfed

The factory Porsche team of type 917 sports cars will be run in 1970 by the John Wyer team which has previously raced Ford and Mirage cars. A two-car team will be entered in all the Championship races with a three-car effort at Le Mans. Sponsorship will come from the American Gulf Oil Corporation and the cars will be painted in Gulf's racing colours of blue and orange●

1

Easy living leisure wear in 'Bri-Nylon', 'Bri-Nova' and 'Crimplene'

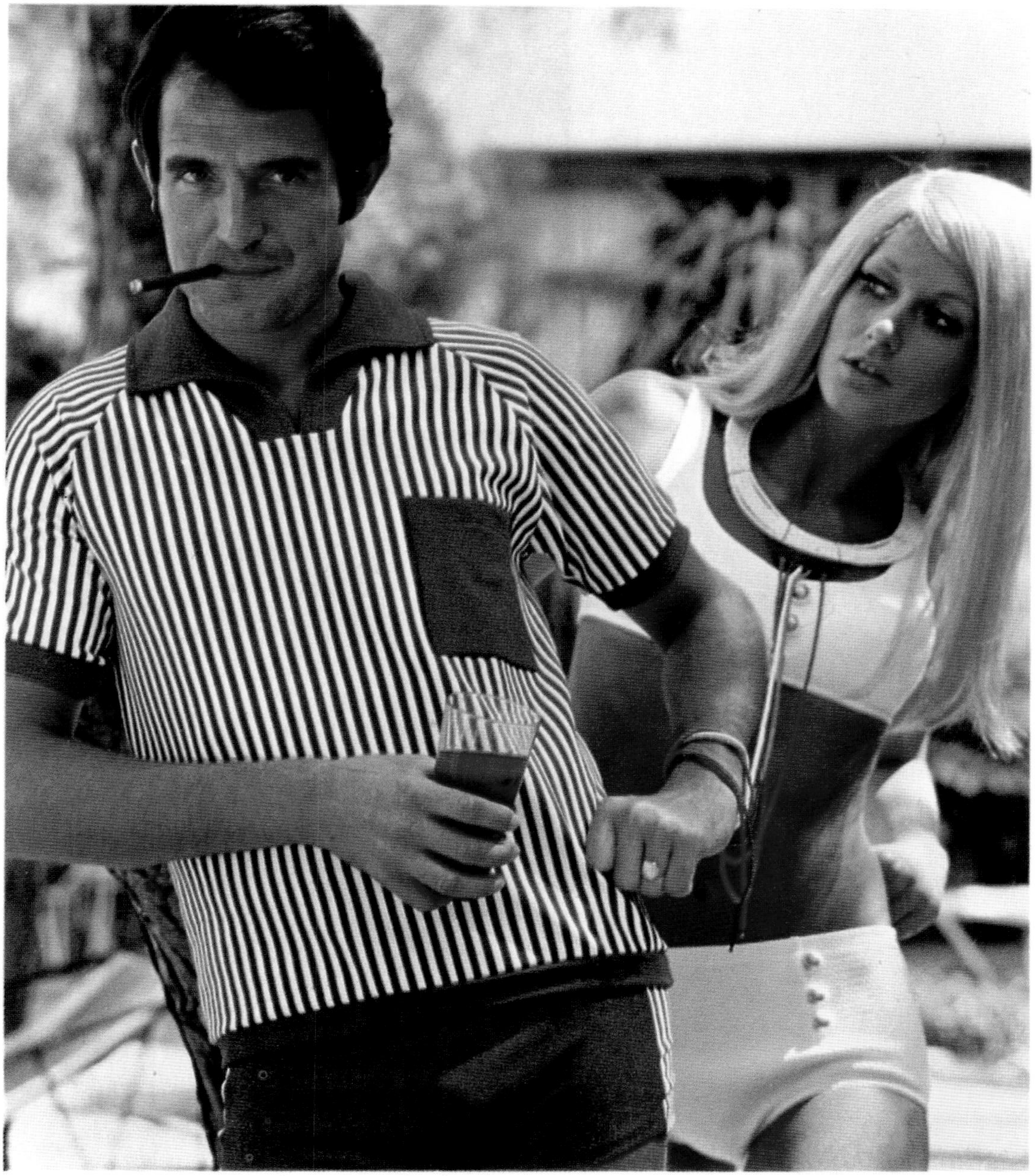

Beach-set in stretch 'Bri-Nylon'. Available as shown or in orange and white. Style 476. About 90/- the set. (Trunks available separately at about 30/-.) By Mentor Ltd., King Street West, Stockport, Cheshire.

The cast in approximate order of disappearance, reading down from the top of this column: Haflinger, Land-Rover, GP Beach Buggy, Ford Bronco. That's the Bronco again, doing the tiger bit on the right, and on the far side you'll see the Bugle Buggy in yellow with its funny four-seater hood and, beyond it, another GP offering on the full-length VW chassis

photography: John Perkins

If ocean cruising can be described as tearing up pound notes under a cold shower, that leaves us short of similes for the gentle art of —well, what the hell *do* you call it?

by MIKE (thanks for the buggy ride) TWITE

EVEN THOSE OF YOU LAYABOUTS who have been fortunate enough to escape conscription into Her Majesty's Armed Forces will have heard of the admonition passed on to all new recruits by the experienced hands never to volunteer for anything. I remember in my first few weeks in the RAF watching a particularly vicious-looking drill instructor asking for anyone with a knowledge of carpentry to take two paces forward; a few proud joiners stepped out of line to be met with a scream 'Now you 'orrible manky lot, git over to the cookhouse and chop up all that wood.' Alas I even fell for it myself when the billet corporal gently enquired if anyone was a horticulturist. 'Yes corporal' I simpered like a mug only too pleased to be able to show off my expertise, thinking that perhaps he wanted my advice on his *Ligustrum ovalifolium* (privet hedge to you), but I was soon regretting my rashness as I found myself outside crawling about on the grass trying to cut it with a knife and fork!

Unfortunately life is just as cruel even in civvy street, even within the hallowed portals of CAR magazine, no less. One day Editor Blain sat at his imposing desk, with his entire staff (me) standing around respectfully while the great man decided what was going into the January issue, his deliberations beginning to assume some urgency since most of the copy should have been written the previous week, while the art editor was gibbering in a corner about the fact that all the colour photography should have gone to the printer weeks ago. The imposition scheme, as the large piece of paper on which the contents are inscribed is called, was still very bare indeed and Blain, off the boil as usual, looked imploringly into my handsome, hirsute visage and pleaded 'Got any ideas, Mike?' 'Well' I said, 'why don't we do a piece about funny cars, you know, cars you can drive off the road?' 'Hmmphhh' he grunted 'as far as I can see you drive all the bloody cars off the road.' But seeing the tears spring to my dark brown eyes he relented: 'Good idea, when can you get it finished?' You notice that, gentle reader? 'When can *you* get it finished?' Not 'Let's get working on it,' or 'Can you organise it?' but 'When can *you* get it finished?' I shuffled my feet, feeling the hole in my size 10s and mentally reminding myself about that raise I've been plucking up courage to ask for, and offered, in a voice which was querulously pitched an octave too high, 'About six months?' 'Yes, well' he muttered, furiously pencilling page after page into the imposition scheme and ignoring my comment, 'Get it done by next Thursday—that gives you at least four days.' 'Yes, but I've already got to drive 27 tuned cars, write the whole of Competition News, and go to my grandmother's funeral, and I've still got two weeks of my holiday to come.' 'Nonsense, who needs holidays?' quoth he. 'Well, you do for one' volunteered I bravely, 'since you've just come back from your third fortnight this year.' I realised I had gone too far this time—his National Health gnashers were set in a grim snarl and if the expensive chandelier was not reflecting in his National Health specs I'm sure I would have seen that steely glint in his eye. 'Get it done by Thursday' he spelled out, and I backed out into the tea lady, tipping the precious fluid on to his Axminster carpet and provoking a hail of stolen instruction manuals kept as missiles.

Safe at last in my draughty attic office I sat down to ponder on the unfairness of life, furiously vowing never to volunteer for, or even say anything in future, at the same time

The Haflinger looks a little lost among all the boondocks in wildest Surrey but is in fact capable of looking after itself in the most outrageous situations —short, that is, of hauling a Land-Rover out of an even deeper bog than it happens to be standing in at the time

idly flicking through the Situations Vacant columns of *Advertisers' Weekly, UK Press Gazette* and *Campaign*. Since nobody seemed to want anyone with my lack of qualifications I set to thinking about what cars I could include in the feature. Having written Land-Rover on my pad I sat back for half an hour or so trying to think of some more, but having failed I ordered my secretary 'Get as many funny cars as you can by Tuesday.' 'Can you give me a list?' she enquired, pencil poised over pad. 'Must I do everything around here?' I hollered, savouring my tiny piece of authority.

Somehow she managed to rustle up some vehicles and amazingly we ended up with a list of nine possibles, seven probables and six arrivals, which is not a bad average the way things go with test cars these days. Naturally, the Land-Rover headed the list, this being probably the best known and most versatile of cross-country vehicles. Next came a Steyr-Puch Haflinger, famed for having caused Ronald Barker to write that immortal heading 'You Steyr and I'll Puch'. The third of our funnies was a Ford Bronco, with more affinity to horses than toilet rolls and certainly the most powerful of our fleet. The balance was made up with Beach Buggies of varying shapes and sizes, including the new long wheelbase one from GP Speed Shop, a Porsche engined Bugle Buggy and a fairly standard VW engined device. There should have been a Volksrod Buggy but it broke down on its way to us and was never seen again. This is not the sum total of cross-country vehicles available of course but such machines as the Toyota Land Cruiser, Willys Jeep and the like are just not available in England while BLMC's Moke, Champ and Gypsy are all out of production. We almost laid hands on an Amphicat which, you may remember, appeared on the Crayford stand at the Motor Show but unfortunately it was not registered for road use and we did not have a big enough vehicle to get it to our test track in the short time available.

We had decided to use the rough road course at the Bagshot Heath test track for our little outing, and on the appointed day a strange convoy straggled out of London down the A30 to that spot where all the rally teams do their destruction testing. Our convoy was limited by the 47mph top speed of the Haflinger but eventually we arrived at Bagshot where the track controller surveyed our motley collection and remarked dolefully 'The Land-Rover's the only one that'll get round the Alpine course, although the Haflinger should get a fair way and the Buggies will break in half before you've gone a mile.' Faced with this sordid news we asked him if he would chauffeur us round the course in his Land-Rover so that we could pick out the least dangerous parts of the track. This was a mistake because our hero hurtled off down the first hill at full chat, sucking away at his pipe, while we clung on the grab rails as if we were on the Big Dipper. Nothing upset our man as he hurtled into off-camber, downhill hairpins covered in huge pools of muddy slime, nonchalantly catching enormous tail slides with consummate ease, flicking levers and pulling knobs as he ground up near-vertical inclines while we grimly hung on, mirthless smiles etched into our faces. It was pretty obvious, as we motored slowly back to the paddock, that the circuit had been churned up so badly by tanks and other military vehicles that no normal road car would last very long at any speed, so we decided just to take some photographs at a quiet part of the circuit and move on elsewhere to drive the cars. Unfortunately, we were thwarted in this attempt by the controller, who had received word from up above that we were driving foreign cars on the hallowed track, which meant instant expulsion. The terms of the agreement we have with the Fighting Vehicles Research and Development Establishment are that no foreign vehicles will be tested. The reason for this, as one military man explained to me, was that we might praise the foreign cars as a result of our tests and the army ought not to assist in promoting the sales of imported goods! I pointed out that the army test many foreign vehicles and probably purchase quite a lot of foreign military equipment, but he was unmoved.

So we went off and found a much more suitable spot near by which was normal sandy heathland, with a few hills and yumps on which to test the machinery. The Bugle Buggy which I was driving was already covered in mud and, due to the lack of sidescreens, so was I. This was merely the result of driving slowly through a few puddles, but the wide tyres, which protrude illegally beyond the mudguards, flicked the mud all over the place. Since the day was cold the pleasures of Buggy driving were fading fast along with the light, especially as the ignition system had an obscure fault which resulted in a refusal to start eight times out of 10. After an hour or so of driving and photographing the light had faded far enough for us to call it a day and wend our weary way back to the Smoke, but we were all determined to come back on the morrow and have another bash. In this we were thwarted by both the Buggy people, GP Speed Shop finding that theirs was suffering from a sick clutch while the Bugle people had promised theirs to someone else. We were fortunate enough to be able to borrow a privately owned GP Buggy from Stuart Baker (who is trying to sell it—free advt) and as the Bronco had by now arrived we set off with another four-car convoy for deepest Surrey, this time to that area known as Chobham Clump, quite close to the famous treacle mines which the army have devastated by simply driving all over everything with their tanks. After many trials and tribulations, including retrieving the Land-Rover from the Police Pound and jury rigging the ignition of the Buggy as the ignition key had been stolen, we arrived at Chobham and began to discover the delights of off-the-road motoring, and after a few hours of hurtling round the hills and coping with several other dramas, such as near total ignition failure on the Buggy, a jammed starter motor on the Land-Rover and so on we all returned to London, worn out but reasonably happy.

What follows is an individual appraisal of each vehicle by the driver who handled it most during the tests. MLT

FORD BRONCO The Bronco which was loaned to us by Ford's Competition Department prior to being sold to Sales Link, the Players Autocross publicists, is a product of the latest American craze, started by Beach Buggies, for off-the-road racing. The sport is now fully organised in California and Mexico, with huge prizes being offered in long-distance races over some of the most inhospitable country in the world. A Bronco won the Mexico 1000 race which was held in the Baja peninsula, and various other races have fallen to the tough Fords. They start life as pickup trucks but when the Holman Moody and Stroppe tuning firm have finished with them they look and go very differently. The cab is cut off, the doors are thrown away, as is much of the rear bodywork. Two huge padded rollover bars are mounted on the chassis and a strip of canvas stretched between them serves as a roof, while a couple of miniscule aero screens keep out a little of the wind and rain. On the rear platform is mounted a huge welded steel fuel tank, which allegedly holds 40 gallons and which is filled by twin fillers, one each side of the vehicle. The only other 'extras' fitted are a spare wheel, a big refreshment bottle, a spade and a jack. Underneath, the machine looks incredibly rugged, the huge axles being supported by so many springs and dampers that it would not be surprising if their suspension was solid. Big wheels shod with chunky Goodyear cross-country tyres look after road grip and naturally the vehicle has 4wd. In the lefthand-drive cockpit the driver, who sits in a tight fitting bucket seat, is faced with the sparse instrumentation and a pair of levers sprouting from the floor, one being the Hurst shifter for the 4speed box, the other looking after the transfer gears which give a higher ratio; we never fully mastered this and motored around most of the time in low gear which gave a top speed of about 60mph, although since the Bronco is powered by a tuned 4.7litre V8 it should be able to top 100mph with ease.

The Bronco was undoubtedly the fastest thing we've ever tried on rough stuff because of its sheer power and speed; it would just rocket up any gradient in any gear with no trouble at all, with a great throaty roar from the big V8. In fact Art Editor Bodecott was rash enough to promise to drive it back to London if I could persuade it to climb a particularly steep and badly potholed track. Taking a run at it I was over the top, still changing up and going about 50mph while poor Bodecott was already winding his scarf round his face ready for the drive home! For picking your way over really rough and muddy going at low speeds the Bronco would probably have to give best to the Land-Rover but if there is any sort of an opportunity to build up speed then the Bronco will be there before the Land-Rover's in second gear.

If you attend any of the Players Autocross meetings next season you should have an opportunity to study it at close quarters. It's quite a machine! MLT

BUGLE BUGGY The Bugle Buggy is built by the grandiosely named Bugle Automotive Traction and Manufacturing Company of London Ltd, who purchase glassfibre bodies from Pierre du Plessis's GP Speed Shop and build complete cars, using secondhand VW parts. The Mk1 with 1200 VW engine costs £750, which is of course considerably more than you would pay if you built it yourself but it does come sprayed in your ▶

choice of colour and is finished very professionally, with full carpeting, rear seat, leather steering wheel, bucket seats, wide wheels with radial-ply tyres, chromed exhaust system, pvc hood and chrome trims on the body edges. The test car, in Sahara yellow, was fitted with a Porsche Super 90 engine using Carrera cams, which was extremely powerful to say the least—too powerful for the chassis on the road, because the big wide tyres pick up every undulation, cat's eye and white line, making control a real problem. Bugle Director Roland Sharman claims a top speed of 120mph for this one but we never exceeded a safe 70 and felt quite brave at that. Off the road the Bugle was more in its element so long as the really rough stuff was avoided, and we spent an amusing time hurtling through the sandy hills on the heathland for ace photographer John Perkins's benefit. And that's where the Buggy is in its element—off the road, so long as it's not too rough. If you have to use your Buggy as normal day to day transport then you begin to discover the snags. MLT

LAND-ROVER

What can we say about the Land-Rover that hasn't been said so often before? It is still the world's most versatile go-anywhere vehicle; our comfy 12seater version would cruise comfortably, if a trifle noisily, at a steady 60mph and as our man at the test track proved it will climb practically anything. Even if it won't climb a hill or pull itself out of a bog under its own steam you can fit the winch, which enables it to tow itself out by hitching up to a tree, or if you're in the desert you just bury the spare wheel and winch yourself out that way. Of course everything rattles and bangs, the ride is board hard and the driving position is so bolt upright and close to the wheel that I was suffering severe claustrophobia inside an hour. Whatever criticism you care to make it is an inescapable fact that the Land-Rover was the only one of our bunch capable of climbing the side of a house from a dead start halfway up. Long may it live.

We hear rumour of a V8 Land-Rover more attuned to road driving but still equipped with all the 4wd attributes. If true this could be another winner for Rover's clever design department. MLT

STEYR-PUCH HAFLINGER

If beach buggies are all brute force and ignorance, the Austrian-built Haflinger cross-country vehicle is by comparison a tiny technical masterpiece.

It has to be called a vehicle since by no stretch of the imagination does it come anywhere near being a car. Neither is it in the jeep category, for the cab only has room for two people. Anyone else has to ride in the hooded payload space behind.

As befits an Austrian-made vehicle, the power unit is a tiny 643cc Steyr-Puch air-cooled twin, tucked away beneath the high floor astern. Despite its minuscular size it still puts out a highly respectable 30bhp at 4800rpm. You might think an engine as small as that better suited to a motorcycle than a mud-plugger. The Haflinger men don't. For a start, they have kept the all-up weight of the machine down to 1400lb so that the power to weight ratio is actually reasonably high. And, more importantly, there is a weird and wonderful transmission system to ensure that not a drop of the power is wasted.

For road use there is ordinary rear-wheel drive. Four-wheel drive can be brought in when conditions get slippery and if that can't cope there is a lever for locking the rear differential. If *that* isn't enough then the driver still has a trump card up his sleeve in the form of another lever-controlled lock to put the front diff out of action. In this extreme form the wheels, all geared together, are churning remorselessly round—one of them, at some corner or other, must find enough grip.

To make assurance doubly sure, the gearbox has five forward speeds. The gate is arranged to give second, third, fourth and fifth in the normal H pattern, with first around the corner to emphasise its function as an emergency ratio for mountain ascents. The Haflinger is so slow in first—and the engine buzzes away so furiously—that you think the clutch is slipping. Under no circumstances will fifth gear exceed 50mph even downhill.

Our first encounter with one of these devices was on the grassy slopes of Box Hill, Surrey. Box Hill on a weekday afternoon is more normally the haunt of tweeded and brogued matrons walking their plump pets. We were duly sorry to disturb the even passage of their lives by bursting unheralded out of the bushes and chugging up increasingly steeper gradients. Even with the negligible traction afforded by Surrey turf the Haflinger never missed its footing. The limiting factor, at least under these conditions, is the driver's nerve. Sitting at what feels a great height in a forward control cab and remembering that the Haflinger has so much ground clearance that it looks hopelessly top heavy, you expect it to fall over at the slightest provocation. In fact, it doesn't. Our nerve finally extended to a gingerly made traverse of a 30degree bank.

Moving across Surrey to find harder going, low gearing made the Haflinger a tiresome road performer. Using rear-wheel drive only, the swing axle rear end permitted so much oversteer that we, precariously placed up front almost at the scene of the impending accident, felt like Tazio Nuvolari having it out with the prewar Auto Union.

A turn off on to the mud and slush of some freshly deluged heathland restored the Haflinger to its element. Again, with all wheels working together, it managed manfully to cope, the light weight ensuring that the wheels didn't just dig themselves a grave and sink, but when the Land-Rover's starter motor jammed it could not tow it out of the bog—all four wheels just spun, and dug, and spun.

There are snags with the Haflinger, the main one being that—at a price of £1102 as tested—we can't quite see what anyone would want it for. And there are peculiarities, like a throttle pedal hinged beneath the seat and projecting forward. And a steering system laid bare for all to see in the cab, where it is ideally placed to catch a foot making for the brake pedal, which is so high off the floor that one of our men missed it altogether and bumped the back of the Land-Rover.

Still, it could qualify for a role as a sort of miniature Land-Rover. What's more, a 5speed gearbox, backbone chassis all round independent suspension and 4wd can't help but sound impressive at the saloon bar . . . IW

GP SUPER BUGGY

The Super Buggy is built by the GP Speed Shop, of Hanworth Air Park, Feltham, Middlesex. GP were one of the first British Buggy-builders and have come a long way in a short time, to be exact from a dilapidated shed near the Grand Union Canal at Brentford to a respectable building in that hive of West London motoring activity where Aston Martin used to live (neighbours include the Daf people, engine builder Racing Services and chassis man Chas Beattie). Production is running at a Buggy kit a day and the only problem seems to be keeping up with demand. The impression that GP Speed Shop is actually becoming a motor manufacturer of sorts is heightened by the fact that partners Pierre du Plessis and John Jobber have brought out a New Model—once upon a time they just made changes. The New Model is the Super Buggy and what is really new about it is the fact that it fits straight on to a VW Beetle floor pan. On what now becomes the short wheelbase Buggy—the original GP—you have first to cut 15 inches out of the punt and rejoin it, a laborious business.

GP's Super demonstrator has an old Porsche 1600 engine straight out of a decrepit Super 90 and we were adjured to spare its life during the test. Frankly, we were *glad* to spare it, because you have to be braver than Biggles to travel at any speed on the road.

A legal 70mph was the most we saw, though even with the exhausted state of the engine there was power enough in hand for countless mph more. After all, it only had to propel a flat steel floor, four wheels and a body like an *art nouveau* bathtub. At 60, let alone 70, the noise is deafening, the hood sides are coming unbuttoned and, worst of all, the Buggy is exhibiting about as much directional stability as a March hare. Handling is something else again. The VW floor pan is braced by nothing more than the bolted-on plastic body and is flexing away like mad, to judge by the scuttle shake. Front suspension is, naturally, by VW flailing arms and the rear by swing axles. The saving grace is that the demo car had £59 12s-worth of 7in rims and 185 SP tyres which look less impressive but are more predictable than the huge rims and second-hand racing covers favoured by most Buggy-owners (buggiers? bugsters?).

All in all, it's very much like a prewar sports car and after an hour or so any driver is glad to turn off on to the rough stuff. This is where the Buggy comes into its own. The ride—diabolical on the road—feels no worse because the long-travel torsion bars can beat the dampers to sop up the bumps. With the engine hanging out the back—but protected by glassfibre shrouding from water—the grip of the rear wheels is fantastic. So fantastic, in fact, that attempted power-sliding turns can catch out the almost weightless front and send one understeering ignominiously out of sight. With so little weight to stop, the ordinary VW brakes are fine. Indeed, the limiting factor in how fast you travel through the countryside is your ability to ignore the horrendous crashes on landing after taking off on a yump. The Buggy itself appears robust enough to go on forever like this—and has the autocross wins to prove it—but sooner or later the exposed exhaust system suffers from the pounding. The other object of suffering is the driver's right side which, unless hood and sidescreens are erect, disappears beneath a torrent of mud. The vestigial wings do nothing to stop it and the cure, for private owners, would be to fit the kind of horizontal splash plates that Maserati used to put on the 250F.

These drawbacks are more than outweighed by the sheer fun of belting about in the rough. And the fact that it can be done in a vehicle that was originally intended for soaring over California sand dunes says a lot for the basic design, both the VW bit and GP Speed Shop's.

Anyone who wants to follow suit will have to start by buying a wrecked Beetle with body damage only, or—much more expensively—by buying all the mechanical bits from a dealer. The GP men themselves sell only the body kit, though they have eight agents dotted around the country who may be prepared to supply a complete Buggy in bits. The Super body comes with the parts necessary for mounting at £158, which is £18 more than the standard shell but saves construction time and cost, as well as giving a rear seat with more legroom than anyone could want. GP lists a variety of more or less desirable extras. Of these, hood and sidescreens at £41 10s are worth having, as is a rollbar at £10 5s and decent bucket seats (there's little else to stop people falling out) at £25 a pair, and a small-diameter steering wheel is almost essential.

You could put one together for around £300, avoiding purchase tax because the car counts as kit-built, but £400 would be closer to it for something that would cut a dash in the King's Road *concours* as well as among Farmer Brown's turnips. IW

An alternative version of the Haflinger (above) showing the canvas rear door which gives access to the platform. The world's most impractical pick-up truck (left) showing the back of the Bronco which has a 40gallon tank and a spare wheel taking up all the space. You get wet in a Buggy if you drive through puddles. This is a Bugle Buggy (below). The Bronco could well be the fast four wheel drive vehicle on and off the road. Our hero tenses himself waiting for the crash (bottom)

Geneva Show

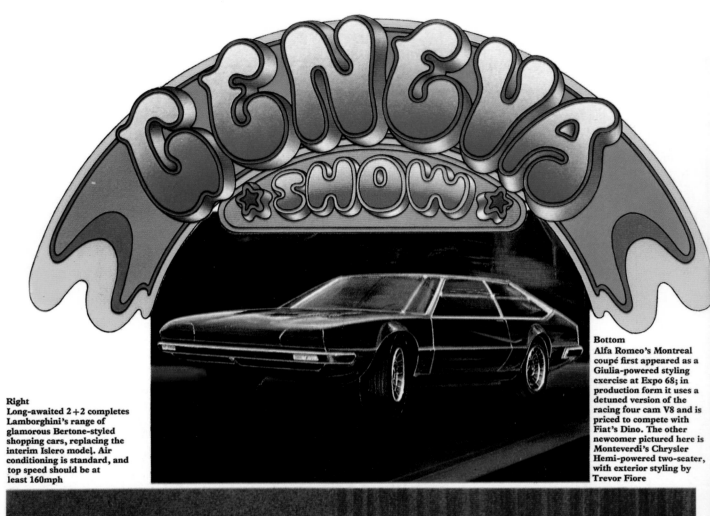

Right
Long-awaited 2+2 completes Lamborghini's range of glamorous Bertone-styled shopping cars, replacing the interim Islero model. Air conditioning is standard, and top speed should be at least 160mph

Bottom
Alfa Romeo's Montreal coupé first appeared as a Giulia-powered styling exercise at Expo 68; in production form it uses a detuned version of the racing four cam V8 and is priced to compete with Fiat's Dino. The other newcomer pictured here is Monteverdi's Chrysler Hemi-powered two-seater, with exterior styling by Trevor Fiore

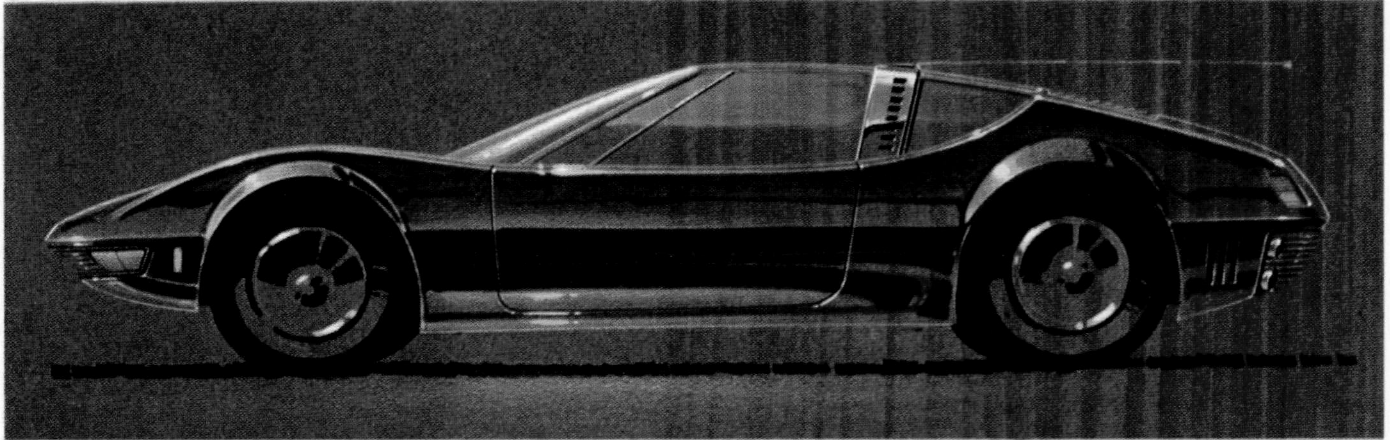

MORE THAN EVER, GENEVA IS Europe's luxury show. This year there wasn't a single new popular family model, unless you count the Rootes Group's Avenger (called a Sunbeam in Switzerland and looking as smart as its metallic paint could make it) which was making its public debut outside Britain and bringing in plenty of serious enquiries, too. Oh, and there was an addition to Opel-Suisse's Ranger range, with standard Rekord saloon/coupé bodyshell and a Vauxhall Victor front end; its sales are to be restricted to the Swiss market, although a similar car exists in South Africa.

Most of the real excitement was concentrated on the popular priced car, but one or two manufacturers slipped in modified versions of established models just outside the luxury class. Opel, for example, had their Commodore GS/E coupé, which is based on the normal and very successful Commodore GS which LJKS assessed a couple of months ago. This is in effect a Rekord with the high camshaft 2.8litre fuel injected six cylinder engine from the big Admiral 2800E installed under a groaning and suitably decalled decked bonnet. It should be a real flyer, for the much bulkier Admiral is itself an effortless 120mph car, but how the Commodore's sorely tried handling will stand up to the boost is very much up to the suspension engineers and the tyre people. Further exercises in the same vein came from Ford of Britain, who showed an Executive version of the 3litre Capri, with separate seats and matt black trim, and of course from the American Motors group who were launching their ultra compact Gremlin saloon on the European market at a reasonably competitive price. The Gremlin is a very clever piece of production engineering using the front end of the compact Hornet and a new tail section incorporating a Reliant GTE style opening window and a couple of occasional seats which fold to make room for luggage. Racing cars, real and imaginary, were also in evidence, starting with a hot BDA Escort and a 160bhp Cologne Capri and graduating via the revised Seven to the latest two-litre Lola.

BMW and Mercedes usually have something to say about this time of year, but both were keeping quiet apart from the latter's justifiable pride in its latest 4rotor Wankel C111 (which we shall come to in a minute). Fiat were celebrating the first anniversary of the luxury 130 saloon, still a rare sight even on Italian roads, with a 20bhp power boost which may do something to overcome our reservations about the model's ability to compete with the better German and British opposition.

These, however, were mere preludes to the big news of the Show, which was the positive explosion of activity among the builders of luxury 3litre coupés. Quite why this has come about we couldn't really say, but it certainly seems that what the sporting driver in Europe was expected to want more than anything else in 1970 was a fast and glamorous 2seater or 2+2 in which to show off his mistress while resting between conferences in some of the more fashionable watering places, ski resorts or coastal carnality camps. Porsche had of course set the pace in exploiting this very noticeable gap between the more expensive, mass produced competitors to the V12 exotica, and the wonder was that others (with the exception of Fiat and its successful Dino range) had been so slow to follow suit. Anyway Geneva saw both Alfa and Citroën on parade with their long awaited challengers and only the New Year strikes prevented Lamborghini from joining them with the transverse engined V8 which they are now planning to launch in midsummer.

The Citroën SM is as sensational in its way as the original DS was; its Maserati V6 engine gives 170bhp and the top speed should be around 130mph. The interior is lavishly endowed with thick leather padding

Citroën's SM (the S continues the series designation with the DS, while the M stands for Maserati; any connection with Stirling Moss is coincidental, although he did apparently do some testing work for Citroën on an earlier flat 6 project) is as unorthodox as one would expect. Even the 4cam V6 engine, designed by Alfieri, who was on hand to see it launched, is full of original thinking, devoted, one imagines, to keeping bulk to the minimum in order to allow space for the occupants' legs at either side. Camshaft drive is by Duplex chain, but only the primary drive is located at the front (in this case the back, of course, because the engine is installed to drive forward); a stout jackshaft runs between the 90deg cylinder banks and secondary sets of Duplex chains take the drive out to the camshafts from between cylinders one and two on the left bank and cylinders two and three on the right. This eliminates the bulky chain boxes which might otherwise have meant an unwelcome increase in the car's already long 116in wheelbase. The engine's capacity is 2670cc and it's claimed to give 170bhp (DIN) at a gratifyingly modest 5500rpm with 170lbft (DIN) at a suspiciously high 4000rpm. It breathes through three twin-choke downdraught Webers and drives forward to a five-speed gearbox in which both fourth and fifth are overdrive.

Suspension is by a developed version of the familiar Hydropneumatic system, but the steering incorporates a fascinating variable assistance arrangement.

The SM body is the work of Citroën's own design department under the direction of Monsieur R Opron, who succeeded the intriguing sculptor turned designer Monsieur Bertoni (sic) after the latter's death. The new shape lacks the integrity of the original DS although it is equally well proportioned, with a strong forward visual bias which emphasises the car's front drive and probably aids directional stability. The sculpture is clean, too, but there is confusion around the windows and at both ends. An all glass front end makes practical sense by meeting the needs of the aerodynamicists and the lighting technicians (the SM has two sets of three quartz iodine lamps, the central pencil beam swivelling hydraulically with the front wheels) but it is not really a satisfying solution aesthetically, while the tail treatment with its high mounted number plate recess and full width tail lamps is a disappointment.

Inside, thick leather padding abounds together with the usual organic Citroën shapes and confusion of minor controls. The two hammock-like front seats with articulated backrests are exceedingly comfortable and visibility is excellent; we wanted to try the rear compartment, but it is obviously intended only for occasional use. Price in France is NF42,000 (£3200) which suggests a figure close to £4500 for Great Britain. Planned production is 1000 units a year, starting in July.

Alfa's contender in the same field, the Montreal, looks like being even more expensive, for the importers, in Geneva, were talking about charging £5500 for it. As its name suggests, this is a development of the Giulia-engined coupé of which a handful were built by Bertone for showing at the Montreal Expo '68. But whereas the Expo car was essentially a styling exercise the new Montreal is a Grand Tourer in the great Italian tradition, its bolder and chunkier although essentially similar styling exemplifying (as the handout aptly put it) 'a promise of power and safety.'

The power part comes from a detuned version of the racing Tipo 33 V8, an undoubtedly more flexible but inevitably less lusty unit which retains the sophistication of its competition counterpart (including the four overhead camshafts and the dry sump) as well as, apparently, a good deal of the sound output. Although slightly smaller than the Maserati V6 used in the Citroën, at 2593cc it is considerably more powerful. The rated DIN output is ▶

▶200bhp at unstated revs and maximum torque is 200lbft by the same measurement—an odd coincidence that power and torque figures for both engines should be numerically the same. The cylinder banks are set at 90deg and Alfa are particularly proud of their crankshaft, which uses sintered tungsten alloy counterweights for optimum compactness. Valves, as in the Citroën, are driven directly by inverted cups and the exhaust valves are sodium cooled as in most Alfa engines. Sparking plugs are located at the tops of the combustion chambers instead of being offset as in the SM. Fuel injection is standard—a mechanical system developed by Spica, the Alfa owned firm which was responsible for the injection setup used in 1750s for sale in the USA.

The new engine is set well forward in a monocoque steel body/chassis structure of undoubted strength. Another surprise comes from the rear suspension, which is by live axle located in the usual Alfa way, albeit with a self locking differential. The official justification for this is twofold; one, that the weight of modern tyres, wheels, brakes (the Montreal uses dual circuit, compensated perforated discs with internal drums for the handbrake) and halfshafts makes the difference in unsprung mass between a rigid axle and an efficient independent setup more or less negligible; and two, that their traditional solution allows them to take fullest advantage of the very wide (195/70 VR 14) tyres fitted to the standard wide base magnesium wheels. Obviously, time will show, but these arguments sound very much like Fiat's at the launch of the original Dino—and the Fiat rigid axle gave way to a much more efficient irs layout within two years!

Moving on a bit, the other two show stoppers belong well and truly in the exotics class. Lamborghini's Jarama is intended as a replacement for the Islero but is not by any means just a new set of clothes. Instead of using the familiar tubular frame it is a pure sheet steel monocoque structure like the much bigger Espada four seater; in fact it is an Espada with a drastically shortened wheelbase—nearly 10in shorter than the Islero—and uses the same suspension, steering, brakes and running gear as well as the same extremely neat and compact underbonnet layout with the familiar 4litre V12 engine set, as in the Alfa, well forward.

The Bertone body styling breaks new ground not only by reason of its uncommonly high wheelbase to length ratio but also because of its very low belt line and abnormally small glass area. It has some unhappy angles, and the wheel arches are a trifle clumsily handled, but the proportions are excellent and the detailed treatment clean. The interior, too, deserves praise for its pioneering use of horizontal tumbler switches set in front of the neat, very plain instruments. The seats are comfortable but headroom is limited. The boot is small.

We now come to the stand of Peter Monteverdi, where the gentle were assaulted on press day by the sight of the long awaited centre engined 450SS coupé decked out in the most horrendous shade of mauve yet conceived by man or nature. The car is a good looker however, although the body builders, Fissore of Savigliano, have misinterpreted some of the subtler touches apparent in Trevor Fiore's original drawings and quarter scale model. The interior, which Fiore did not design, is dominated by an enormous black box which covers the mighty 7litre Chrysler Hemi V8, prompting a friend of ours to query: 'Anyone we knew?' His remark could prove prophetic for the newcomer's chassis, despite the novelty of a de Dion rear end with a kink to clear the transaxle, is as unsubtle as its predecessors' and the performance with that engine (an alleged 450bhp probably translates as 350, which is quite enough) in an ensemble which, although not as light as it looks, is hardly a heavyweight at about 32cwt, should be formidable indeed. The asking price in Switzerland is about £10,000 and Monteverdi is not expecting many orders.

Among the one-off cars, Mercedes had probably the most interesting display with their revamped C111 in orange on a high mounted turntable. The 1970 car of course uses the fourth rotor which was promised originally with Mercedes' Wankel engine, giving 350bhp (DIN) from the equivalent of 4.8litres. The bodywork has been revised, with a very much bigger windscreen and improved ducting at front and rear. We had a short run in the only existing prototype on the tight Monthoux gokart track but were not allowed to drive the car; we will try and rectify matters within the next few weeks and let you know how it handles. Meanwhile Mercedes are going ahead with a limited series of at least eight more cars and it

photography: Charles Pocklington

looks as if some of them will be available to private owners.

Among the coachbuilders, only Bertone had anything significant to contribute, and even that was lacking in inspiration. His BMW 2002, latest in a series indicating a determined flirtation with the Munich firm, is a saloon after the style of last year's Fiat 128, all glass and sharp corners, nicely proportioned and beautifully finished but with some disappointing excess of detail which takes it into the extrovert class—most notably a lozenge shaped distortion of the traditional BMW grille and a rather bizarre interior incorporating many of the ideas which were shown in the Lamborghini but with none of the latter's subtlety of execution.

Even the BMW, however, paled beside the extrovert Pininfarina Ferrari—a wayout two seater in matt black and white, centre engined, with a continuous slope running from the snout to the top of the screen, the usual vast glass area, a forward sliding roof pod, and cutouts in the wheel arches exposing the tops of the tyres to no obvious purpose. It all seemed rather pointless to us, but was certainly attracting the crowd which no doubt was the main objective in its creator's eyes.

Ghia had nothing new, preferring to keep their latest Ford based exercise for the New York show a few weeks later, and Vignale of course are now defunct. Michelotti chose to emphasise his decline with an unhappy Fiat 125S coupé, while Frua showed business awareness with a 'productionised' derivative of Opel's experimental CD V8. ●

American Motors Corporation's new Gremlin baby saloon looks awkward in profile but features a neat, GTE-type tail panel

The Pininfarina mid-engined Ferrari (far left) looks different, which is about all one could say in its favour. Bertone's BMW 2002 (left) looks sensible if rather staid, but the traditional BMW grille has been desecrated. Despite all the criticism, notably from *Motocar*, the Mercedes C111 (above) continues to progress towards production state. Latest version has 4rotor Wankel and cleaned up styling

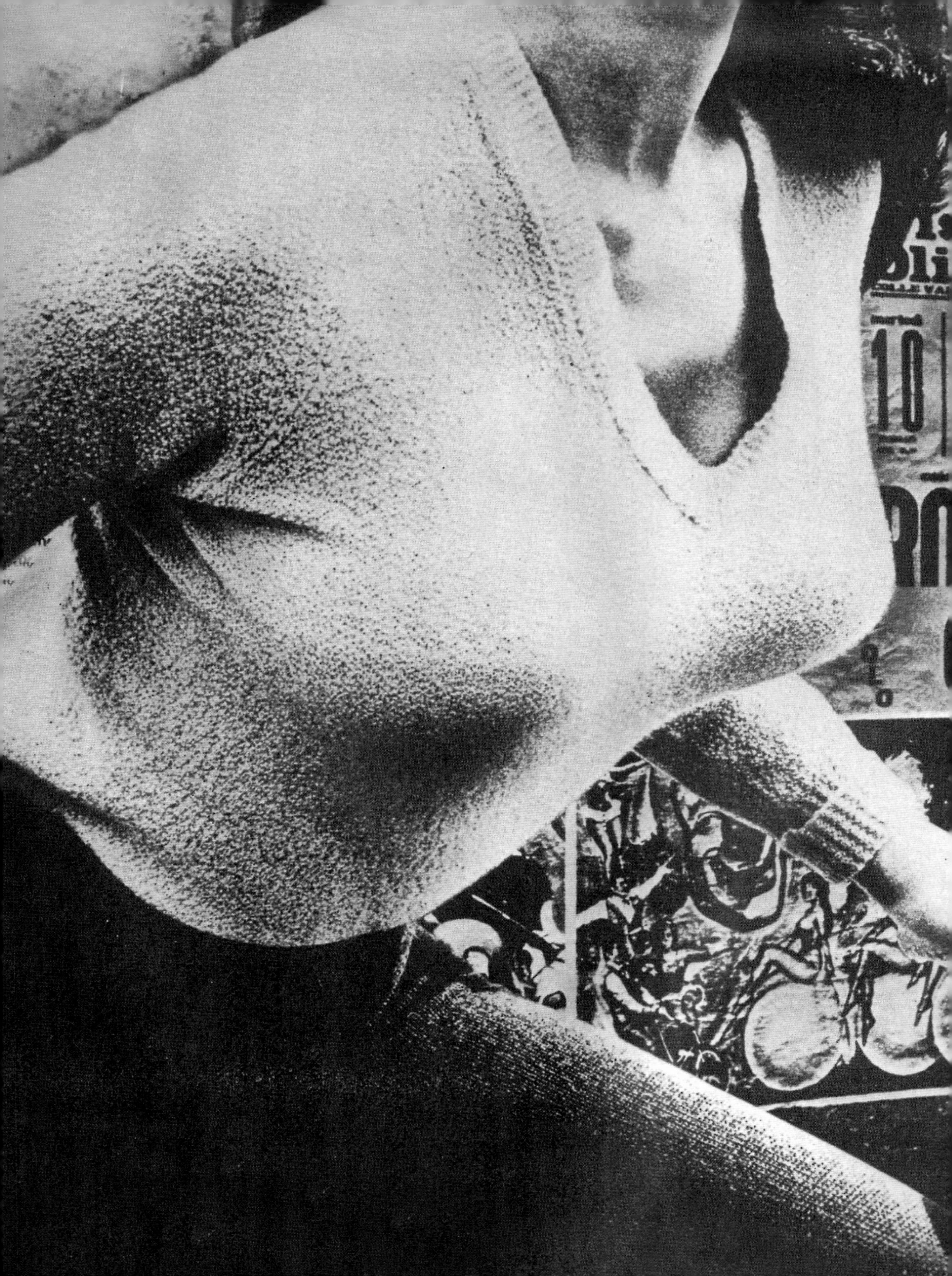

Derek Forsyth Partnership

Of all the hazards facing Italian drivers, two in particular stick out.

The Italians' desire for speed is only matched by the Italians' desire.
The combination of the two makes driving in Italy a truly hair-raising experience. Every pretty girl gets attention. Quite often she gets it from a passing motorist (probably passing at 100 mph). And while she's getting attention, the road isn't.
So several years ago, we did something to help. We introduced our radial-ply tyre: the Cinturato. (Which is just as well, considering that more Italians drive on our tyres than on any others).
And we haven't stopped there.
We have factories here in Britain. So you can get the same superlative Pirelli Cinturato here, too, at a realistic price.
You'll probably never need them as much as the Italians do, but it's nice to know you're that much safer with a set of Cints under you.

PIRELLI CINTURATO

If they can keep the Italians out of trouble, think what they can do for you.

THE BIG TWO IN BRITAIN, Ford and BLMC, have widely differing marketing policies for no reason that is readily apparent. BLMC introduce a new model and keep it going for year after year, long after it has, to all intents and purposes, become obsolete. The odd facelift and performance increase resuscitate moribund models from time to time to justify continued production, which is why such devices as the Morris Minor and Oxford still exist—even an occasional Austin A50 van trundles down the line at Longbridge, and that design dates from the early '50s. The Mini is entering its 12th year of production and showing no sign of dying, while the Ford Anglia, introduced at the same time, has been out of production for two years. Ford's policy seems to be following that of their American parent very closely these days, with almost annual model changes of some sort or other even though the existing model is wildly successful.

Quite who is right would only become evident after a very close study of car sales and balance sheets, but despite its much-publicised industrial troubles the Austin/Morris division of BLMC is currently outselling Ford in this country by a healthy margin. In the first six months of 1970 Austin/Morris sold 306,620 cars in Britain against Ford's 273,147. Also in BLMC's favour is the fact that tooling costs on most models have been amortised long ago, whereas Ford's frequent model changes must be extremely costly. However, in the Americans' favour is the fact that most new models they have produced in recent years (the Escort, Capri and now the Mark Three Cortina) are also produced in Germany, with shared development costs, while the latest overhead cam engine is also being sold in large quantities to Dearborn for the ultra-compact Pinto.

So, while Austin/Morris enter the 1971 model year with nothing radically new to sell, Ford are producing their third version of the Cortina since the model was first announced in 1962. With the Mark Three variant Ford have not deviated one iota from their policy of building conventional, technically unexciting cars and have again concentrated on styling as the big selling point. Disappointing as this must be to critics who would dearly love to see a really advanced car from Ford, it must be admitted that their cars usually incorporate a good deal of enthusiast appeal despite the anachronisms of rigid back axles and the like; they are of course cheap to develop, easy to service and occasionally more reliable than their more advanced competitors. Still, we can but hope.

The latest Cortina follows the successful formula of the Capri, with a number of basic models plus endless options, so that in theory the customer can sit at home and 'design' his own car. It worked with the Capri and it will undoubtedly work with the Cortina.

The basis of the new car is a brand new, unit construction body/chassis unit which was very much a cooperative effort between British and German teams—hence the somewhat Taunus-like look about the front end. The whole of the body shows unmistakable committee influence, with the coke bottle look favoured in the past by Vauxhall combined with a semi-fast back roofline to give a rear three-quarter view that is at least more attractive than that of the Capri. As one journalist whispered after he was ushered in to see the car at a private preview: 'Would you believe Vauxhall would let Ford build the Victor under licence?'

The basic range of Mark Threes is almost too complicated to describe because of the almost limitless variations. Starting at the bottom, there is the standard Cortina, available in two or four door variants and as an estate car, with a choice of 1300, 1600 and 2000cc engines. Next comes the L model, which replaces the Mark Two de luxe series and is available with the same body and engine options but with more interior luxury items. The XL replaces the Mark Two Super and is again available with the same body and engine options. The new GT is next in line, being available only in two and four door saloon form with no estate car option, and with only the new ohc 1600GT and two-litre engines. Top of the line is the GXL which replaces the 1600E; like the GT, this one is available only with the ohc engine in 1.6 and two-litre forms and as a two or four door saloon without an estate version. The Corsair range has been dropped completely.

The 1300 and 1600 pushrod engines are the same as used in earlier Cortinas, although improvements to camshaft timing, manifolding, inlet valving and carburation, together with an improved combustion chamber shape, have been incorporated recently. The 1300 now gives 57bhp at 5500rpm and the 1600 68bhp at 5200rpm, while the new 1600 ohc engine gives 88bhp at 5700rpm, the output going up to 98bhp at 5500 in two-litre form. Ford claim top speeds of 85 (1300), 91 (1600), 101 (1.6 GT) and 103 (2.0 GT) together with respective 0–60mph acceleration times of 18.5, 14.8, 11.9 and 10.2sec. The estate cars are naturally slower in acceleration but Ford claim a top speed of 105mph for the two-litre estate, presumably reflecting superior aerodynamics. These figures are of course taken with the standard four speed gearbox; a three-speed automatic is an option for all models except the lowly 1300s.

There have been some changes to the running gear of the new Cortina, the principal one being the replacement of the MacPherson strut front suspension by unequal-length double wishbones and coil spring damper units. The new suspension is mounted on a subframe to suppress road noise. Rack and pinion steering is fitted for the first time to a Cortina. The rigid rear axle is hung on coil spring/damper units and located by four pressed steel leading arms, two on each side. The very fact of abandoning cart springs is a pretty radical move for Ford.

Braking is by 9.6in diameter discs on the front wheels, 8[illegible] diameter rear drums on the 13[illegible] and 1600cc models and 9in diameter on the 1600GT and 2000GT versions. The two latter models have vacuum assistance as standard, but it is optional on the less powerful cars.

Ford were not as advanced as they usually are when the press were invited to try the new model at their Boreham test track in August, as they had only been able to hand build half-a-dozen cars before the annual holiday. There were a number of detail faults in these, plus assorted differences from the production models, so it is not possible or indeed fair to give a critical assessment based on a mere 30 or 40 laps of the flat, featureless Boreham track. For more detailed comment you'll have to wait till next month.

On the basis of worst first, we went out in the standard 1600 first of all but after half-a-dozen laps we were no wiser than before and when we pulled off the track to be met by a Ford man who asked 'What do you think of it?' we found ourselves at a loss for comment. In the end we mumbled that 'It's very nice, isn't it' but in fact the car has so little character that it is impossible to pass an opinion. It accelerates adequately, it corners adequately, it brakes adequately and handles adequately but there is nothing that one can enthuse about. Feeling rather depressed, we switched to a GXL with the new two-litre

FORD HAVE A BETTER IDEA

IT'S THE THIRD NEW CORTINA IN EIGHT YEARS

Ford are seldom among the trendsetters in styling. Now, just when Vauxhall are beginning to abandon the kicked up coke bottle rear contour, Ford have introduced it on the Mark Three Cortina. Committee styling is evident in the Taunus-like front end. One plus point is the interior which has acquired better seats and more legroom for back seat drivers

ngine. This naturally felt a much velier car, while the more lavish nstrumentation and interior gave much greater feeling of opuence. The reclining seats, which re standard on the GXL, are ofter yet more figure-hugging nd have a height adjustment for he leading edge of the cushion. .fter a few laps in the GXL we elt better, for this version went p to 90mph quite comfortably, elt smoother and quieter than the 600, and accelerated quickly, lthough one or two pressmen hought they detected a trace of oughness and a flat spot in the cceleration. However, it would ppear that the rear axle might be oo well located, for a side trip n to a concrete road with a roken surface showed quite a lot of axle hop and a tendency for the rear end to help with the steering. All the corners at Boreham are pretty smooth so it was impossible to check handling on bumpy surfaces, but the car did give an uncomfortable lurch when being cornered hard.

Ford buyers are obviously not desperately interested in advanced engineering, and the company's share of the market indicates that plenty of ordinary motorists want simple, easily serviced, reliable transport. This the Mark Three Cortina will undoubtedly provide, although we must withhold detailed comment until we have tried the car on the road over a longer distance—something we intend to do in Belgium for the next issue. ●

WILL THE REAL LE MANS STAND UP?

85% of MG Midget owners are men.

Which means lots of girls will be relaxing in our new, thick contoured rake adjusting seats.

A scene we're sure will appeal to both driver and passenger.

As will the trendy new look. There's a new matt black recessed grille with chrome surround. New light clusters. Split rear bumpers. Black and silver Rostyle rally wheels. And round the sides you'll find black side-winders. For a long, lean look.

The MG Midget comes in four wild new colours. Glacier White, Blue Royale, Flame Red, and Bronze Yellow. And of course, you can still get Pale Primrose and British Racing Green.

Get switched on – and immediately you'll know why this is the enthusiasts' car. The famous race and rally proven twin-carb. engine performs brilliantly.

The MG Midget will give you dynamic acceleration. Magnificent high speed cruising. And economical fuel consumption.

We've given you all this (rake adjusting seats included) for £838*. The girl you'll have to get for yourself.

*Recommended price including P.T. Extra is charged for delivery, seat belts, number plates, radio and aerial.

Sport the real thing. MG Midget.

BRITISH LEYLAND

MG

IT WAS MY FIRST TIME ON A FILM set, although the 'set' was very familiar ground to me as it was the pit area at Le Mans. As all the world knows, Steve McQueen is shooting his epic which is titled simply *The 24 Hours of Le Mans* and I was anxious to see if film sets and the people who work on them were as I had imagined. Did a wizened old man hobble out in front of the cameras with a clapper board? Did the director shout 'Roll' and 'Cut' and 'Print it'? Were there canvas seats with the stars' names stencilled on them? Did the female lead prance and posture even when she wasn't on set? Yes! It's all absolutely true, I'm delighted to say. My illusions for once were not shattered. Director Lee Katzin smokes constantly, even while eating his lunch, and smokes cigarettes, pipes, cigars without noticing what's in his mouth. On one traumatic occasion he rushed from the set to his little canvas seat with his name stencilled on it and out of a side pocket produced a bottle filled with a blue liquid; he gulped it down and tore back to the pits to grapple with the problem in hand. In contrast, Steve McQueen is quiet, self effacing, melts into the background, rides away on one of his fleet of motorcycles with his wife on the pillion and keeps himself to himself.

McQueen's motorised activities on celluloid have been eulogised too many times to bear repeating here, but suffice it to say that his exploits in *Bullitt* did as much for his image as his entire screen career before that. He has nurtured an ambition to make a realistic film about motor racing for many years but it was not considered 'box office' by the film moguls even though mundane screen epics like *Grand Prix* and *Winning* did well enough at the box office to change that view. He was all set to make a motor racing film called *The Champion* three years ago but an illness put paid to that, then *Grand Prix* came along and the project was shelved. The ambition did not die and although he kept his hand in on such films as *The Thomas Crown Affair* (remember the beach buggy antics?) and *Bullitt*, followed by *The Reivers*, which is now on release, the idea of a motor racing film never moved far from his mind. The opportunity to do a film of Le Mans came up and now that he had his own production company he was less in the hands of film moguls, although the backers did kick up when he announced that he would drive with Jackie Stewart in this year's race. They had their way eventually and for three weeks McQueen was unapproachable, but he came round and probably now realises that it would have been expensive and awkward if he had been injured during the race.

McQueen felt that a good film could be made by filming a major motor race 'straight', without any serious attempt at providing a script. This horrified everyone connected with the film, who couldn't see the general public sitting through a 1½hr film about pure motor racing with no 'love interest' or story of any kind. So McQueen was persuaded to accept a screenplay, but in the early days of shooting he fell out with the first director John Sturgess over several things, but mainly the script. Sturgess finally quit the picture and a new director, Lee Katzin, was appointed. Katzin is mainly noted for his direction of TV series like *Mission Impossible* and *It Takes a Thief*, but he has done film direction—his major success being *Whatever Happened to Aunt Alice?* He was on his way to San Francisco to do a TV movie when the call to Le Mans came, but he quickly adapted to the new film, and is respected by the crew.

As a cynical and suspicious motoring journalist I approached the film set ready to pick holes in everything, but I came away impressed beyond measure. Everyone connected with the film is concerned in making it accurate in every possible way, even if the difference between doing it right and nearly right is thousands of dollars. Unlike *Grand Prix* in which F3 cars with ghastly looking simulated F1 bodies trundled round to the annoyance of enthusiasts, *Le Mans* uses 25 of the cars which took part in this year's race plus most of their drivers. The only serious faking that was done was to dress up a couple of Lolas to look like a 512S Ferrari and a Porsche 917 for the crash scenes, because even Solar Productions blanched at the thought of shunting a pair of £14,000 cars. But I defy you to say when you see the film (hopefully June 1971 is the release date, just prior to next year's Le Mans race) that you can tell the difference between a real Ferrari and the 'Lolari'. I had to have a good look round the 'Lolari' before I spotted the differences, and so lifelike is the dummy driver who occupies the driving seat during the shunt that I absentmindedly wandered up to have a chat to him!

There are two major crash sequences in the film. I was fortunate enough to be present when the 'Lolari' was crashed and afterwards I saw the rushes (that film jargon again!) of both that crash and the Porsche one. I can categorically state that they provide the finest racing car crash sequences I have ever seen. When the rushes were shown to the crew everyone burst into applause at the superb camerawork. Extensive use is made of slow motion film, which shows the 'Lolari' disintegrating in minute detail from every possible direction since 11 cameras were used to film the sequence. As no stunt driver could be expected to hurtle into trees at 100mph, the 'Lolari' was expensively fitted with radio control equipment for steering, throttle and clutch operation together with a cine camera inside the car to record the crash from the driver's viewpoint. British club driver Malcolm Sear assisted in setting up the cars for these shunts and can tell of many hairy moments as the guinea pig in the driving seat while being guided by radio control. The first two attempts to crash the 'Lolari' went wrong because the car veered off course and shunted the guard rails, but on the third attempt it hurtled down at full throttle in first gear (the car had a bog standard Chevy engine with hydraulic valve lifters so it couldn't come to much harm through over-revving) hit the sandbank at nearly 100mph and soared into the air, knocking down a Martini sign, brushing through the tree tops, and crashing back to earth with an almighty thump which broke all the suspension. Since there was a camera crew only 50 yards ahead, Malcolm Sear cut the engine as soon as the car hit the bank, a fortuitous move because there would have been several dead or injured cameramen if he hadn't. The car had originally been intended to pass through the trees and knock them down, but it went so high that it passed over most of them. The crew had carefully sawn through the trunks of the trees so that they would snap off more spectacularly, but a high wind blew up a day or two before the crash was to be staged and blew several ►

This is going to hurt you more than it hurts me! Malcolm Sear in the driver's seat of the Lola (née Ferrari) is about to be sent off on a test run with all the controls being worked by the man on the right. This car was later crashed spectacularly. The steering of the Lola was operated by a bicycle chain drive from a radio-controlled electric motor

of them down! Miraculously, for the purposes of the film, the driver survives the crash and runs away just as the car blows up. Of course this sequence was shot several days later and dynamite was used to disintegrate the Lola. Amazingly, someone actually bought the tatty remains—so beware if you are in the market for a T70 Lola—if the vendor says it has blown up he really means it!

One unintentional disaster was when the 512S Ferrari Derek Bell was driving caught fire and burnt out while returning from a filming sequence. Derek received some nasty face burns and the Ferrari was totalled, although someone bought *that* soggy heap, too! Professional to the last, one of the cameramen groaned 'Hell, and we didn't have a single camera there.' Poor David Piper also shunted his 917 Porsche when returning from a filming session, and he was unlucky enough to put himself out of action for some time with a badly broken leg.

The other intentional crash is that of another Lola dressed up to look like the Gulf-Porsche that Steve McQueen drives in the film. This time the car is made to brush the guard rail near Maison Blanche, then thunder across the road to crunch the opposite barrier. The rushes of this sequence are again quite superb because the car is shown to disintegrate in slow motion, while the telephoto shots are some of the most superb action shots I have ever seen. McQueen (alias Mike Delaney in the film) survives the crash, returns to the pits and takes over another Gulf Porsche. An amusing part of the crash which probably won't be seen in the final edited version is that the radio control equipment was damaged in the crash and there was no way of stopping the engine running at full throttle. The car wedged itself against a barrier and sat there with the rear wheels spinning until first the tyres then the mag wheels were ground away. Eventually a brave soul ventured into the smoke and switched it off.

The film actually started way back in early 1969 when a film crew went to Le Mans to film the race and take mountains of notes about the circuit, the crowd, the cars, drivers, pit crews, girl friends, and all the million-and-one items which make up a motor race. Orders had to be placed for hundreds of items of clothing, like anoraks, umbrellas, caps plus mountains of other equipment. The drivers' Nomex equipment had to be spot-on, down to such minutiae as names and blood groups being stitched on to the overalls, the decals on the cars had to be authentic, even the drivers' wrist watches had to be correct. Before the 1970 race all the owners of advertising signs were asked if they would leave their hoardings in position for the film—not that any of them were likely to refuse such free advertising! But it all had to be taken down and stored because souvenir hunters would have nicked it. All the owners of trade caravans were asked if they could bring their vehicles back for the paddock scenes to give the authentic touch. The attention to detail ran to such items as making the drivers' suits dirtier as the race wore on—a difficult job as sometimes early scenes were shot after late ones. The cars had to get dirtier as the race progressed and even worse, mechanics, drivers, spectators, photographers all had to sprout stubbly chins for the early morning scenes. The shooting schedule reminded everyone not to shave in the mornings before shooting started, and if anyone forgot, they had to be made up to look black bearded. Where possible the crew used real people to do the jobs they did at the actual race, so many marshals, gendarmes, mechanics and so on played the same part as they played in the real race. They even imported some real motor racing photographers to play themselves because the extras who were given the job originally did not look authentic. Your humble servant was even given the job of playing a cine cameraman, although he was a complete novice!

The cost of setting up the operation runs into many millions of dollars—no one is quite certain just how much—but Solar Productions reckons to have spent four million dollars in the Le Mans area alone. The main problem was getting the use of the circuit, which uses a lot of normal public roads and runs past many houses, restaurants, factories, etc. The avaricious Automobile Club de L'Ouest and the Departement de la Sarthe were convinced that it would be a good idea to hire out the track, especially when Solar offered a 30,000 dollar fee! Another 30,000 dollars was spent on building the Solar village inside the circuit; this consists of a huge dining hall, offices, workshops, toilets, dormitories and caravans, together with practically every facility that might be needed by the crew. Anything between 150 to 300 people are working on the film at any one time, plus up to 1000 extras in the crowd scenes. The huge 75mm Panavision cameras are hired from a London firm at astronomical cost and consume film at a horrifying rate, especially during the slow motion sequences.

Perhaps the most expensive undertaking was to assemble the 25-car selection of sports cars and their drivers. There were four Ferraris, five Porsche 917s, three Porsche 908s, two Lolas, two Chevrons, four Porsche 911s, a Matra, a 312 Ferrari, a GT40, a Porsche 914 and an Alfa Romeo 33. These were all assembled by ex-Lotus team manager Andrew Ferguson and kept running under appalling conditions by a team of mechanics who were housed in a huge garage owned by a caravan firm. The cars, most of which had got through the real Le Mans, had to do day after day of stop-start motoring over a three-month period. Surprisingly there were few breakdowns. The real drivers commuted back and forth from their various racing commitments, but the cars usually stayed at Le Mans, their owners suitably compensated

continued on page 75 ▶

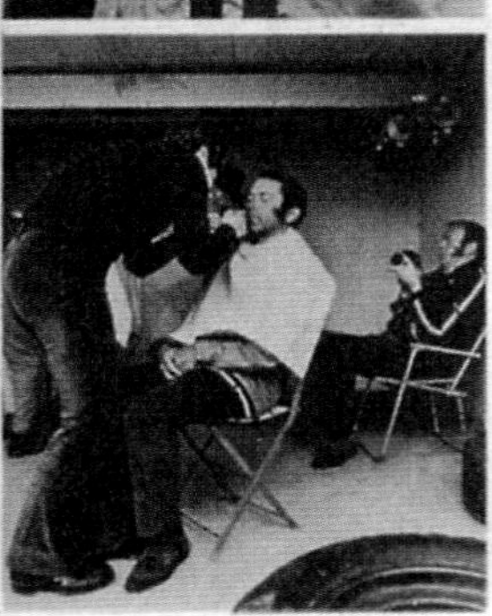

When the Lola (née Ferrari) was crashed deliberately, injudicious placing of a camera nearly got it and its crew written off. The car stopped about a yard short (top left). Filming is expensive as the shots of these burnt-out hulks (one a Ferrari, one a Lola) prove (bottom left). Steve McQueen asks for two more cups of coffee—we think! Real life motor racing photographer Michael Cooper gets made up for his part in the film in which he plays, guess—a motor racing photographer. Behind him Dunlop PR man Ian Norris inspects his cameras

for the loss of racing miles. The drivers, who were paid a minimum of 200 dollars (£80) a day, varied their time between hurtling down the Mulsanne straight at 180mph and sitting in their caravan playing chess, reading and getting thoroughly bored. In fact the big problem in film making is the time taken to set up each scene, which involves only a few people in the lighting, sound and camera departments. Everyone else stands around feeling completely useless. Two of the drivers actually get small parts in the film; Jonathan Williams plays Jonathan Burton, co-driver of Ferrari No 5, and Erich Glavitza, the Austrian rally and racing driver, plays Joseph Hauser, co-driver of Ferrari No 8.

Apart from McQueen few people will have heard of any of the other actors in the film, who seem to have been deliberately chosen for their anonymity. The only well known British actor is Ronald Leigh-Hunt, who plays the part of J W's team manager. Being a real professional he earned the accolade from one mechanic 'He's more like David Yorke than David Yorke is!' So dedicated is he to his part that he even eats with the mechanics at his hotel in Le Mans. One or two of the actors over-act like mad both on and off the set, which I hope does not show through in the film. Gino Cassani, who plays the Ferrari team manager, seemed most unconvincing to my inexpert eye but at least he showed a fine turn of speed when an airline blew off its pipe in the pits. While everyone else stared curiously, Cassani was hotfooting it down the pit lane. What was that joke about the book of Italian war heroes?

Everyone in the crew has some story or other to tell of his exploits. British sound engineer John Mitchell had to sit in the passenger seat of a 917 next to Rob Slotemaker while he hurtled down the Mulsanne straight to record the noise of a Porsche on full song, and worst of all he had to record Slotemaker spinning the Porsche on a wet track. The cameramen who have had to sit in the jump seat of the special cut down GT40, and in cradles outrigged behind 917s, all have their tales to tell, but I can't repeat them as most of the camera crew are French, the chief cameraman being Rene Guissart, who filmed *Grand Prix*.

I won't spoil things by telling you the story of the film—it might change between now and next June anyway! However, Steve McQueen *doesn't* win the race after all and he *doesn't* get to kiss the leading lady. All I can say is that this will undoubtedly be the finest movie about motor racing yet seen. The shots taken from the Porsche 908 which took part in the race driven by Jonathan Williams and Herbert Linge are quite fantastic. Amazingly, had this car been eligible for the race it would have finished eighth overall despite its enormous load of two cameras. They didn't make pit stops for fuel, just new reels of film! The other action photography is also some of the best I have seen. You just can't afford to miss it. ●

The man sitting in the hot seat of this cut-down GT40 had to film at 180mph on the Mulsanne straight (far left). This could almost be a real Ferrari pit stop (second from left) if it wasn't for the sound boom hanging down. There's a cameraman under that tarpaulin in front. This is the 'film' ending of Le Mans (third from left). Steve McQueen doesn't win! A cameraman actually sat in this outrigged space frame behind a Porsche and filmed at high velocity (below)

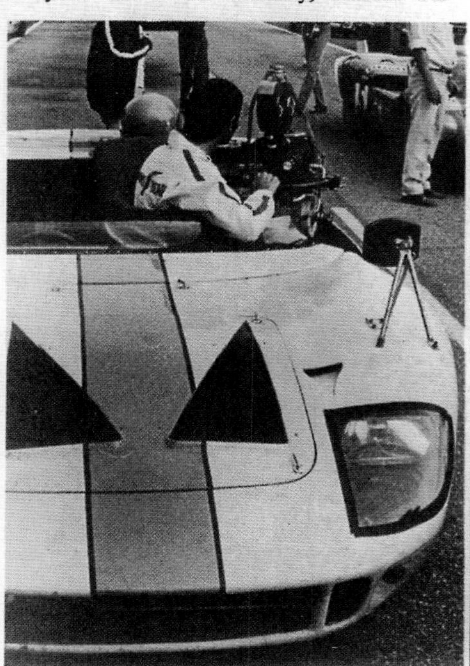

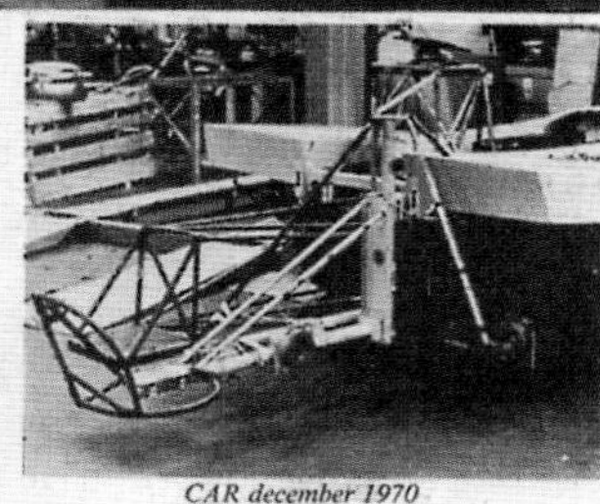

CAR december 1970

"Paying 6/- for a spark plug is strictly for the birds"

"Not if you're World Champion."

You don't win World Championships by cutting costs. Graham Hill insisted on Autolite spark plugs because only Autolite could deliver the performance and total reliability he needed to win the biggest prize in motor racing.

(In an incredibly successful year's racing Autolite-equipped cars also won the World Manufacturers' Sports Car Championship and the British Saloon Car Championship).

If you take your driving as seriously as Graham Hill, you'll also insist on Autolite.

They cost around 6/– each.

You'll probably see other plugs offered at lower prices. But you won't see Graham Hill buying them.

Autolite

AUTOLITE MOTOR PRODUCTS LIMITED, ENFIELD, MIDDLESEX.

The new Marina is twice as beautiful as any car in its class.

One thing we've always noticed about alternative body styles. They aren't.

In fact, up to now, a four-door version of a two-door car meant just that.

With the new Marina things are different. We've designed two different bodies, which is one up on the competition.

Our four-door Marina shares all the advantages of the two-door.

The great road-holding, the ride, the comfort, the performance.

And the anti-pollution system, which ensures that while you're clocking up the miles, you're not fouling up the atmosphere.

It shares the same thorough anti-rust treatment and underbody protection. So your car will keep its value, and its looks, over the years.

And the choice of three engine options, and three different interior trims.

And it shares standard features like two-speed wipers with a column-mounted flick-switch for giving the screen a single wipe. And electric washers.

Perhaps most important of all, it shares the same pedigree, with Morris reliability and British Leyland know-how.

But because what looks right with two doors looks wrong with four, we designed a different body for it. Which has certain significant advantages, apart from its looks. Like easier access to the back, more headroom, and a bigger boot. And, of course, two more doors.

Which is a simply beautiful solution to what's been an ugly problem.

Prices range from £923* for the 1·3 litre De Luxe Coupé to £1177* for the 1·8 TC four-door Saloon.

You can test drive the new Marina at your nearest Morris dealer.

**Ex-works price including P.T. (Automatic transmission, seat belts, delivery charges and number plates extra.)*

The new Morris Marina beauty with brains behind it.

A product of British Leyland

Roving the ranges

Through uncharted southern Spain, across the storm-lashed Straits and into the wolf-infested wastes of Africa: Doug Blain continues our saga

SP Sport Radial. Engineered by Dunlop. For action. Focus right in: the low-crouched silhouette and the meaty, wrap-around tread. Unmistakably SP Sport! But beneath the pretty face, sir, a rally-proved appetite for action. Example? Take SP Sport's special cunning in the wet:

Here is a radial tyre engineered to pump (actually pump dry!) the road beneath. Water is sucked up and shot clear by the extra deep centre channel (or twin channels in some sizes). More water is pumped through under-rubber ducts to nozzles circling tread – spitting water clear.

And the whole cunning system bales, at 50 mph, a full gallon every second! Now dry tyre bites dry road. And the system's <u>all</u> ours.

So now you're free for <u>real</u> driving. Real action in the wet or <u>the</u> dry. The rough and the smooth. SP Sport allows you more real driving and more, many more miles. Up to 80% greater mileage – SP Sport over standard crossply tyres. This is fact: up to 80% greater mileage with Dunlop SP Sport. **Dunlop SP Sport is the radial engineered for <u>action.</u>**

DUNLOP SP SPORT RADIAL

UNDERSTANDABLY, FOR OUR NOTE-keeping was not perfect, Steady Barker got a bit out of sequence towards the end of last month's first instalment of this our Range Rover saga. He left us on the way out of Jaen—a disappointing agglomeration, incidentally, apart from its old quarter around the classical cathedral, but boasting a Parador or state-run tourist hotel in a superbly restored castle on a nearby mountain top. Here we had been refused accommodation but had dined spectacularly, if rather poorly, by candlelight in what might have been the refectory had they had not had most of the floor up for attention to the central heating—a circumstance which had caused one of the somewhat sulky waitresses to measure her length on the hard tiles and simultaneously to offer the contents of four piled plates as an impromptu contribution to the décor. Our supply of maps was at this point restricted to Monsieur Bibendum for Spain, adequate for main roads but hardly up to Ordnance Survey standards, so it was probably foolish of us to set out, after an unadventurous night in an unexceptionable modern hotel in the town, across country in the hope of forging a short-cut through to Algeciras, in which we had decided lay our best hope of getting quickly and cheaply across to Africa. At all events, the inevitable happened, and we got quite hopelessly lost.

The area in which this occurred was one of undulating, tightly packed and swampy olive groves. The road was of clay, rutted beyond belief, full of corners and deep hollows and glutinous, axle-deep mud. Traffic, of which there was a great deal, consisted solely of donkeys—dozens upon dozens of them, laden to the ears with market produce and each capped (although one would have thought they could carry no more) by a compact and swarthy peasant in a wide sombrero. What a challenge! Impossible roads in an uncharted territory, with a tight schedule to keep and a Range Rover on our side. Obviously, we triumphed. The big car was in its element, pounding imperturbably over the potholes at an uninterrupted 60mph, slithering around slimy corners on what often felt like full opposite lock, all four knobbly Michelins churning mightily, the lazy V8 silent as ever, the truck-like but reassuringly robust gearbox whining lustily (we were no longer alarmed, as we had been during day one, by a tendency for the higher ratio to become elusive if one rushed one's upward changes). It was one of those gratifying occasions on which one is conscious that, if one had not brought *exactly* the vehicle one had, one probably wouldn't have made it at all.

Mud gave way after a time to bitumen, swamp to rolling green sward, and we found ourselves in recognisably Spanish hill-territory again with the sun (for it was early yet) illuminating a honey-coloured castle above a sea of morning mist. Between here and the coast it was to be hairpin bends and sudden descents punctuated by increasingly Moorish-looking, white-painted villages, all crooked streets, precipitous ravines and gaily clad people lolling on the narrow pavements. Potholes abounded, and we were full of admiration for the Range Rover's supple suspension as, firmly wedged in with cushions and fortified by careful preliminary diet against the ill-effect of this never ending switchback, we hurtled on. Body roll, we soon discovered, was definitely present, but within strict limits, so that after a time one barely noticed it. The elevated driving position and perfect visibility through wide, deep windows made it safe to maintain what might otherwise have been absurdly high averages, and one felt doubly secure in the knowledge that, should the unexpected occur, one could take to the verges with almost guaranteed impunity.

Up till now we had managed a steady 20mpg on the cheapest Spanish petrol (Range Rovers are tuned to run happily on as little as 85 octane). But hour upon hour of second and third gear work had brought this down to 14 or so. Lunch in the sun off red mullet and sharp white wine fortified us for an afternoon of similarly active motoring, with the difference that the road surface had once again deteriorated and was now composed largely of deep ruts linked by short stretches of tarmac. Navigation was difficult, one of the hazards being a tendency for the route to come to an apparently complete final halt, as for example at a small country railway station where it transpired that we were to take a dusty cart track leading at right angles down beside the line before crossing, then turning, and at last resuming our previous route. There was a single stop during the afternoon for photography—a group of jolly peasant women, splashing and laughing over a communal washtub (a handy waterfall), had caught Henri Cartier Barker's colour-conscious eye—and another in the early evening for tea in a bar boasting what the Americans would call a comfort station but which that the local builder, choosing perhaps from some *fin de siècle* Birmingham sundriesman's catalogue, had chosen to dub in so many very English words a Water Closet. We were obliged to ask the barman for the key to this, and one of the customers at the far end of the Men Only bar showed us the way up the dingy stairs through a painted first floor saloon which hadn't been used since 1934. Blain was reminded of Ireland, Barker of an early film.

Algeciras, famous for its rats, welcomed us with pungent effusiveness as we headed for the only Michelin-recommended hostelry in town (the Spanish edition is a combination of red and green Guide, with paragraphs of commentary and a potted history of each major venue). Deciding it looked expensive we retreated to the sea front where, as we parked, a pair of bellhops, one in red, the other in blue, rushed up pleading the attractions of their rival establishments. Blain's instinct for faded opulence triumphed, as usual, and we opted for the decadent splendours of the Hotel Anglo Hispano with its yellow tiles, cast-iron balustrades and metre upon metre of moth-eaten red ▶

plush. To our surprise the plumbing worked, but dinner, a sorry mess of brown Windsor (thus labelled, believe it or not) and what tasted like reworked mountain goat, generated an air of gloom that was only dispelled by what we interpreted as a sporting offer on the part of the hall porter to buy our ferry tickets for us in the morning.

This, it turned out, was a favourite local industry, the touts making a sizeable commission on the deal, but as the customer did not appear to lose it made good sense and obviously kept countless local bellies pretty full.

The ferry itself, which we have already described (CAR February) was another antiquarian device, gleaming mahogany, polished brass, yellow canvas deck chairs and all, with a superb view of the Rock in the background as we slid across towards Tangiers, lunching indifferently but where else?

We had heard about the hippy invasion of North Africa, but were unprepared for the cluster of pedlars who made us their target immediately after driving ashore, crawling round us in the port buildings and besieging short of foreign currency, and has an elaborate but not particularly strict system of exchange control) and setting off for the centre of Tangier.

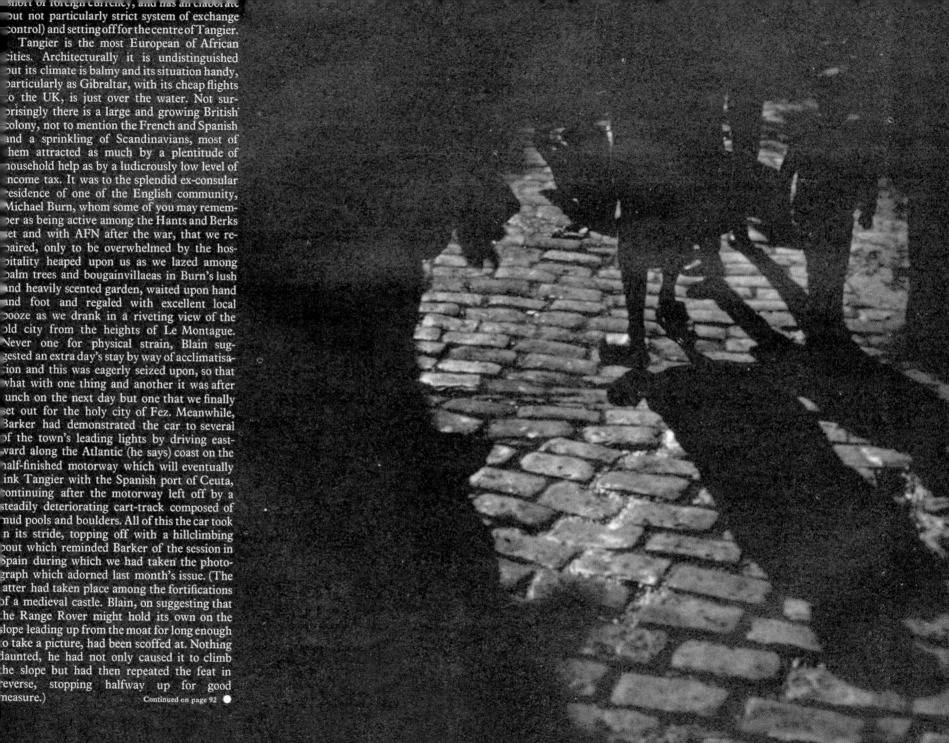

Tangier is the most European of African cities. Architecturally it is undistinguished but its climate is balmy and its situation handy, particularly as Gibraltar, with its cheap flights to the UK, is just over the water. Not surprisingly there is a large and growing British colony, not to mention the French and Spanish and a sprinkling of Scandinavians, most of them attracted as much by a plentitude of household help as by a ludicrously low level of income tax. It was to the splendid ex-consular residence of one of the English community, Michael Burn, whom some of you may remember as being active among the Hants and Berks set and with AFN after the war, that we repaired, only to be overwhelmed by the hospitality heaped upon us as we lazed among palm trees and bougainvillaeas in Burn's lush and heavily scented garden, waited upon hand and foot and regaled with excellent local booze as we drank in a riveting view of the old city from the heights of Le Montague. Never one for physical strain, Blain suggested an extra day's stay by way of acclimatisation and this was eagerly seized upon, so that what with one thing and another it was after lunch on the next day but one that we finally set out for the holy city of Fez. Meanwhile, Barker had demonstrated the car to several of the town's leading lights by driving eastward along the Atlantic (he says) coast on the half-finished motorway which will eventually link Tangier with the Spanish port of Ceuta, continuing after the motorway left off by a steadily deteriorating cart-track composed of mud pools and boulders. All of this the car took in its stride, topping off with a hillclimbing bout which reminded Barker of the session in Spain during which we had taken the photograph which adorned last month's issue. (The latter had taken place among the fortifications of a medieval castle. Blain, on suggesting that the Range Rover might hold its own on the slope leading up from the moat for long enough to take a picture, had been scoffed at. Nothing daunted, he had not only caused it to climb the slope but had then repeated the feat in reverse, stopping halfway up for good measure.)

Continued on page 92

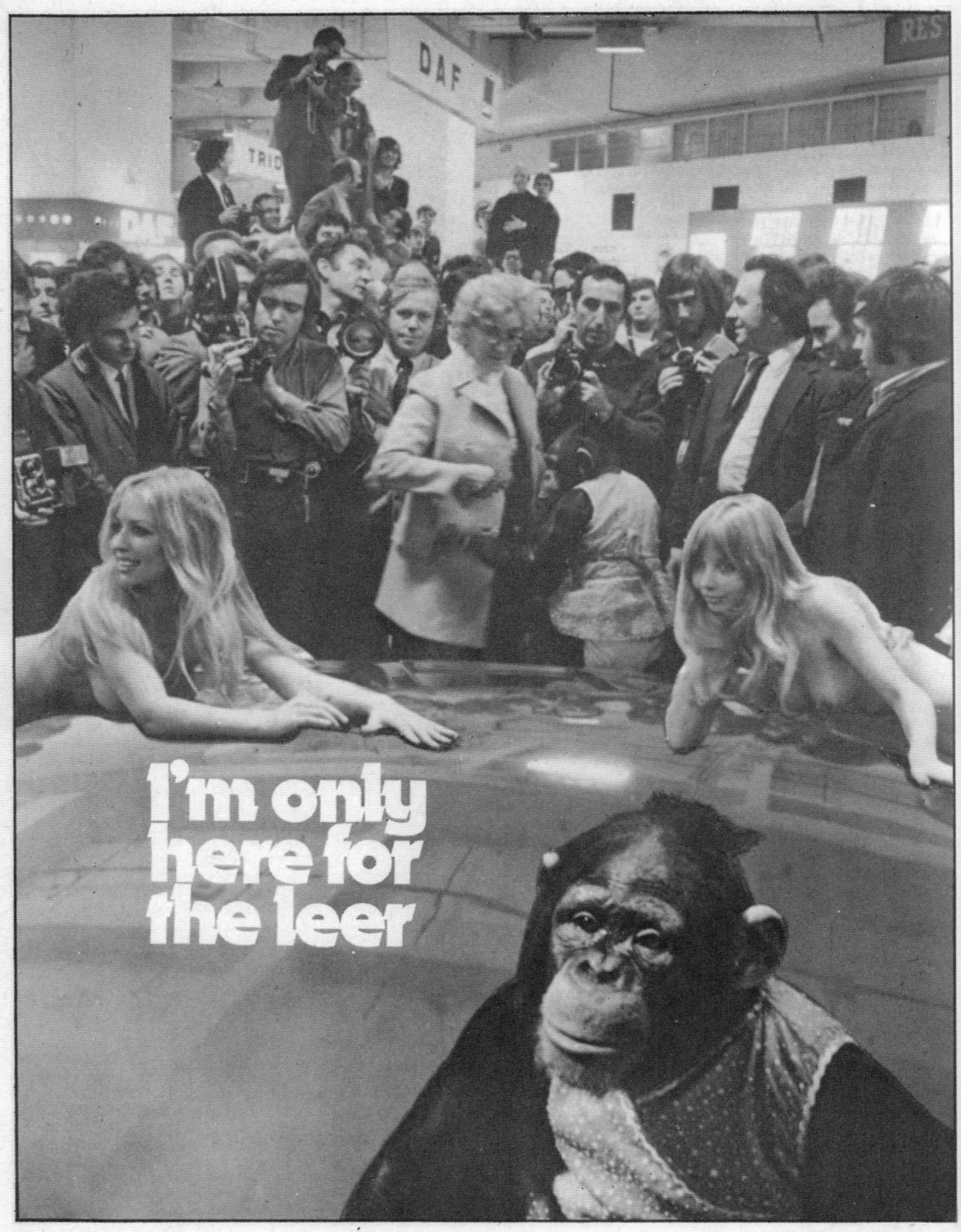
DAF
TRIO
I'm only here for the leer

REVIEW

WHAT THE HELL IS THIS, THEN? A MOTOR show, a strip club or a zoo? Whatever you may have thought of Andrea Lloyd, the hippy little blonde on the Skoda stand (Uncle Doug even takes their names!), or of the lion cub, the three flamingoes paddling quietly among the Lamborghinis or the hirsute chimp gambolling between the bosoms and buttocks on the TVR stand, Earls Court '71 was undeniably one lousy attempt at a motor show.

More and more, it is the smaller, specialist makers who provide the interest at these junkets anyway. And as everyone knows Mr Nader and his pals are slowly squeezing even the most hardy specialists to the point where they daren't change a specification that has cost them the best part of three years' development budget to get through the 1972 impact norms, let alone those of '73 or '74. With Marcos, Piper and the Adams brothers gone from the scene in the past 12 months, Rolls-Royce Motors (1971) Ltd scrambling to disentangle itself from the parent company's disastrous nosedive, Aston Martin embroiled in a most insalubrious public airing of Sir D Brown's financial linen, Lotus overhung by ever-thickening merger clouds (the new V8 engine plant is allegedly siren in chief, with the bulky 2+2 in which it is to be launched next autumn said to be shaping well) and one or two of the lesser fry up to their necks in water of varying temperature, it was indeed a sorry scene.

It was hardly helped by the general reluctance of the equipment suppliers (most notably the tyre manufacturers who, with one exception, abstained), foreign car importers (Renault in particular were cynical enough to deny Britons a sight of their costly but newsworthy 15 and 17 coupes) and even motor caravan manufacturers (a handful made the scene but not CI, whose Carl Olsen-designed Ford pick-a-back I had looked forward to admiring) to come to the aid of their back-slapping brethren who make up that jolly bunch known as the Society of Motor Manufacturers and Traders.

Of those who did fork out for space, hardly any succeeded in finding a genuine novelty for display to the bedraggled and weary multitude, the Big Four having either let off such ordnance as they possessed in order to lure the last of the summer customers or else elected to hold their fire until next spring in hopes of doing even better. In the case of **Triumph**, Lord Snooks's current lame duck, matters had got out of hand, with the workers demanding such horrendous piecework rates that the overhead cam Dolomite had suffered yet another setback, management preferring to wait until December by which time they hoped to have negotiated a new system of payment. **Vauxhall** and **Ford** meanwhile had also decided to save their big guns, the former contenting itself with a token concession in the form of a tarted-up Viva estate car with plastic wood trim, the latter with yet another of its interminable pseudo-sports cars, the Escort Sport, in effect a 1600 Escort GT with bright paint, stark trim, a wicked price tag and a long list of options plus a minor and rather pointless facelift for the Capri. **Jaguar** had witheld the forthcoming XJ6 V12, having decided to build a Daimler as well and save it for next year, **Rover** of course showed the manual 3500 V8 with some further and even more pathetic styling revisions (this had already made its bow at Paris, as had the tarted-up Land Rover) and **Austin** had the mildly altered 1300 (just displaced by the Mini as Britain's best-seller) to pit against their stablemate **Morris's** Marina, the latter complete with revised front-end geometry as discussed in my column this time.

Getting back to the little people, **Lotus** had made an effort to display the intelligently reworked Europa Twin Cam to advantage, and surprisingly successful it looked, with almost every previous drawback removed apart from the fierce price and the poorly spaced gearbox ratios. **Jensen**, still sitting on the dull-sounding Healey sports car which we are now to see early in '72, scored a minor hit with their big-engined Interceptor (early reports suggest it is down on power) while **Bristol** were making their usual quaint boasts for the engaging 411. **Aston Martin**, still reeling from the indignity of having their road test V8 driven backwards into a betting shop by a Top Person who should have known better, had replied to earlier criticism by installing American-made air conditioning as standard. **Morgan**, having reputedly made the very sensible decision to let the Americans go hang by pulling out of that lucrative market (they had celebrated by introducing a new set of tail lights) and concentrating their efforts elsewhere, made the mistake of showing everybody why by displaying, on someone else's stand, quite the most flimsy chassis in current production—a gesture which **Gilbern** were unwise enough to emulate by showing their own particular bit of blacksmithery alongside an unchanged Invader, thus allowing the curious to demonstrate that even a Brunellian mass of triangulated pipework will not prevent one corner of so unscientific a structure from yielding to the pull of quite modest muscle-power while leaving the other three wheels in firm contact with the carpet.

The distinction of launching virtually the only new production car in the whole show fell to young Martin Lilley, whose shrewd and unassuming management of **TVR** ought to serve as an object lesson to the playboys of the industry. His latest effort demonstrates the wisdom of the company's founders all those years ago in selecting a chassis design which concentrated all the stresses within a very bulky central tunnel, for with today's fashion for low, wide and more or less handsome bodywork Lilley has been able to commission a new glassfibre shell which is at the same time very roomy and very, very close to the ground. This is a confidently styled and competently sculpted design, square-snouted in the manner of Coggiola's current Saab Sonnett, high-tailed, sitting firmly on a set of Midland Metallics diecast alloy wheels, with a letter-box rear window, after the fashion of the cheeky Honda Z, which opens to reveal a shallow but spacious luggage platform. Its shape is perhaps a little rectangular in plan, and there is an unhappiness about the triangular rear quarter windows, but altogether I was struck by the professionalism of the design both inside and out—so much so that I pressed Lilley hard in an effort to find out who was responsible. 'A friend' was all he would say, implying that the friend actually worked for a rival manufacturer. He did reveal however, that the moulds were made by Specialised Mouldings, the Huntingdon firm which was also responsible for building Harris Mann's one-off Leyland Zonda prototype two years ago. Now I come to think of it . . .

Be that as it may, the new TVR is scheduled for production, initially as a supplement to the present range, powered by the fuel injected Triumph six-cylinder engine and selling fully built-up for about the price of an Elan Plus Two. Meanwhile the old body has had both ends restyled yet again for its Triumph application, which is slowly replacing the Ford V6 version as TVR's staple seller. Vaguely related, in that their ageing Fiore body design started life as a TVR commission, were the **Trident** coupes just across the hall—the Venturer, Ford V6 powered, the Tycoon(!) with Triumph injection and the new Clipper V8 with a 300bhp Chrysler V8 situated in, of all things, a TR6 chassis . . .

One-off fuoriserie coachwork is getting scarcer at Earls Court with the demise of the traditional British industry, but this year the *Telegraph Magazine* had joined forces with the Institute of British Carriage and Automobile Manufacturers to foster British design as best they could by mounting a stand on which would be displayed one of the winning designs from IBCAM's annual styling competition plus a specially commissioned one-off centrepiece in the *Tele-*

GILBERN
WARTBUR
ŠKODA
ŠKODA
MAZ
SKODA S 110 GT
SUPERSPORT
GRAND TOURING CAR
DESIGN EXCERCISE
CURRENT S. TYPE
SM TVR
4 doors or 2 doors

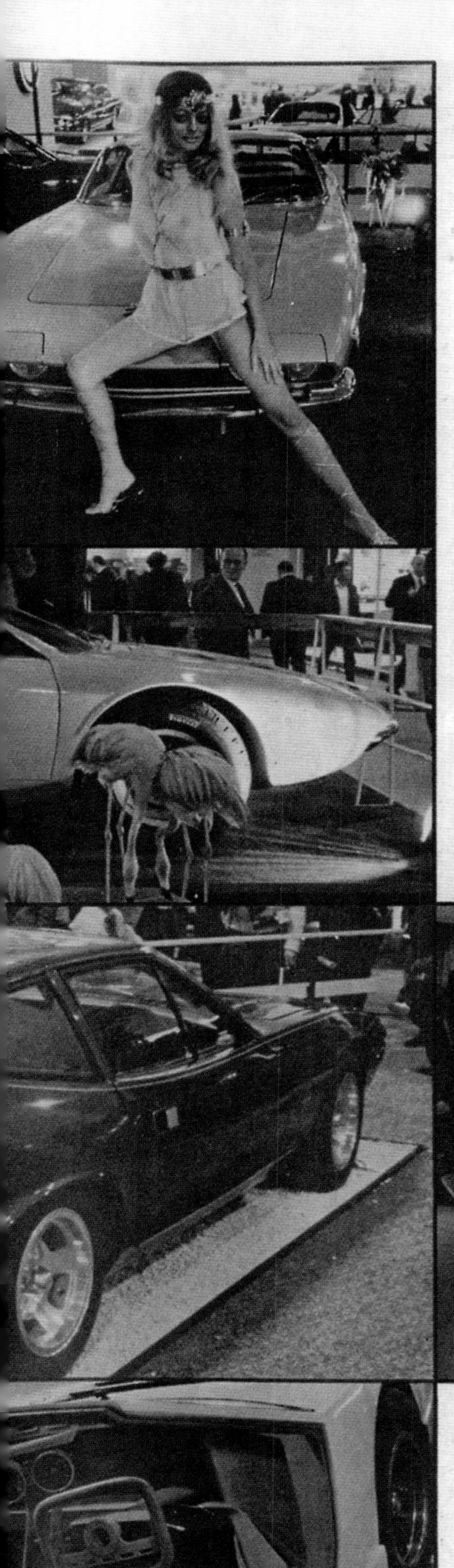

graph's established tradition.

Now the **Voodoo,** an Imp-based two-seater with enclosed two-place aerodynamic bodywork in the best traditions of small-capacity circuit racing, clean, compact and obviously very light, was a pleasant enough thing in its way, though quite meaningless as a styling exercise as it had all been done before. But the real showpiece, the Aston Martin V8-powered **Siva,** was a major disappointment to us.

Siva, you will recall, is the trade name of young Neville Trickett, the West Country hot-rodder who was at one time associated with Geoff Thomas of Rob Walker and now Marcos fame in the abortive Minisprint and Opus projects. Neville is a nice unassuming sort of chap who bristles with clever ideas, some serious such as the first Siva streamliner which he introduced at the last Racing Car Show, others frankly jokey such as the Ford Popular-based veteran which he is selling in considerable numbers to Carol Brown's trendy buddies. The trouble is, though, that he has no relevant design training and really ought not to get involved in body design at this level. The Siva Aston, though far better finished than I thought it was going to be, is merely a development of the earlier effort and looks like it, full of awkward angles and inept detail which only serves to draw attention to the amateurishness of the basic concept. For this machine is far too bulky ever to make a racer, yet too cramped for a road car; it has no luggage space, no crash protection and no visibility to the rear quarters and it obviously suffers from an unsatisfactory rearward weight bias, the massive four cam engine being bolted direct to a ZF gearbox a la Monteverdi Hai. Not that I want to knock Trickett, who after all is a tryer and a valuable ideas man. The trouble is simply that he ought to have hired a professional designer to translate his ideas into something valid aesthetically, and the *Telegraph* should have paid him to do so instead of allowing an embarrassed world to think that this is the best that Britain can do. Ogle, Olsen, Town, Fiore . . . Heaven knows, this country is rich enough in talent, all of it crying out for a shop window.

It was all birds, breasts and bums on press day at Earls Court with TVR showing a very popular chassis (top left) and below that Skoda revealing some interesting coachwork on a prototype coupe. The Honda Z nestles appropriately sideways between them and the young lady obscuring the Iso but the Lamborghini hunting budgies (oops sorry) flamingoes hardly seemed necessary on a stand overloaded with pretty things. Once the nudes had disappeared you could admire the lines of the TVR SM which once upon a time would have been called a 'bread van coupe'. A mess both inside and outside is what we would call the Siva shown below the TVR while the gentleman above is making one of himself trying to enter the Bertone Stratos

Having said which, it remains for me just to mop up the odds and ends before signing off. Let's see now, there was **Crayford's** stand, more of a mess even than usual with a veritable traffic jam of ill-assorted vehicles, mostly production saloons (one of them a Cortina Mk III, another Japanese—two new departures) which they had either cut down as convertibles or tarted up with stick-on vinyl roofing, but with a sprinkling of more interesting stuff such as the latest in eight-wheeled all-terrain vehicles and a very smart estate car conversion on the small Mercedes chassis. Balancing this, on the other side of the stand and covered for some reason in gigantic suitcases, was a prime candidate for Blain's Ugliest Car in the Show award—a Leyland 1800 on the back of which Crayford had tacked a sort of shed made of tin and glass, capping the whole with a massive roof rack for the use of cameramen and to the order, apparently, of the RRL.

Most of the Italian supercar people took space, but neither **Bertone** nor **Pininfarina** deigned to produce anything new. **Monteverdi,** who has his share of problems at present, having lost Fissore as a body builder and fallen instead into the hands of Lucky Reisner's Italsuisse concern, showed several of his less attractive variations while **Iso** were on hand with the familiar Lele (named after boss man Rivolta's wife) and the worthy 5.3litre Grifo with its attenuated snout as introduced at Turin last year.

Which reminds me that I owe Rivolta an apology for having closed him down prematurely the other month; it is quite true that he has sold his old factory to Olivetti, but only in order to move into a brand new one where he is building his own bodies in order to escape the chronic strike delays at Bertone.

What else ? Only an inept but encouraging centre engined one-off from **Skoda,** a flip-top two-seater far too big for its puny engine which at least shows that the Czechs are making an effort to keep up with outside trends, plus the usual gimmickery including a moon car mock-up on the **General Motors** stand and That Man's championship Tyrrell across the way at **Ford.** The SMMT used to be pretty snotty nosed about allowing in exhibits that weren't intended for production and purchase. Now I'm beginning to wonder if they weren't being wondrous wise. *DEB*

OGLE ASTON

It is always a big moment for a design studio when a newly bodied car is pushed out into the daylight for the first time. At last there is space enough to stand back and check that features which looked so good on the drawing board actually work in three dimensions. Although handsome, curvaceous and purposeful looking, Ogle's Aston says little that is new. The greenhouse roof of the design guarantees a light and airy interior while the functionalism of uncovered interior support tubing adds to the cleanliness. Covers hide the lamps and their cleaning equipment, while the sequential braking and indicating lights give maximum information to following drivers

COMMON-MARKET NEGOTIATIONS and French-speaking reactionaries in Quebec notwithstanding, some Canadians still love us ! Montreal Motor Show-organising Canadians specially, for that group has taken upon itself to sponsor an all-British, Ogle-styled, star-car for their 1972 exhibition this month. Based on a DBS V8 chassis and running gear the Ogle could be the last time an Aston Martin is the star of anything unless the financial troubles are cured mighty soon.

It was the esteemed Tom Karen of Ogle who was responsible for the design—the same Tom Karen who did for Reliant the Scimitar and the Bug—but we are not too sure that the Italians, for instance, would have the same ultimately practical approach to a show car. There are no new solutions or even anything adventuresome in the shape of the Ogle Aston, although electronic novelties and gadgets abound.

Pro-British feeling around Montreal was the real reason for the car coming into being in the first place. The show organisers wanted an elaborate attraction and decided to get a British design group to attack an all British high-performance chassis : the Aston Martin was the logical choice. Inevitably, it took time to get the project off the ground but then British motor industry started being helpful with promises of co-operation in the more specialised fields where there is no indigenous backstop such as there is in Italy. Nevertheless, Triplex rose to the occasion, as did Lucas, Smiths, Lennig and others who will benefit from the rub-off publicity that the car will undoubtedly generate in North America. The car was started in the middle of last year and was finished in December.

But the real question is : does the Ogle Aston have the people of Montreal shouting "stop the show, I want to get in" ? And the answer, really, is No ! The basic reason is that little new and fresh has been said in the overall design. The greenhouse roof arrangement is nothing startling when one considers that the Queen has been riding around in a glasshouse for some time now. Triplex Sundym glass is used, its heat absorbing properties working in conjunction with Koolair air-conditioning to provide civilized living quarters for the occupants. Being wedge shaped, the styling is biased towards the tail so that the stainless steel motif of the sills extends from the front of the car to the massive rear assembly and continues—Porsche Targa like—into a roll-bar capping which separates the roof proper from the multiple-curvature rear window. The glass panels of the superstructure are carried on load-bearing Reynolds tubing which features flanged faces onto which the Sundym panels are sealed. The beautifully curved body panels and bonnet were made up in glass fibre by Fibreglass Limited.

The green-painted, uncapped tubing motif is carried into the interior so that the tubes form the surround for the instrument console and for the seats. A three placer (the third seat is mounted sideways in the back) the interior of the Aston's cabin is trimmed in a green-buttoned corduroy material ; specially-designed instrument faces are being made up to match the colour scheme. An aircraft-type "head-up" information display system is used. It consists of warning lights for major malfunctions which are projected onto the windscreen just below the driver's line of sight alerting him to that particular problem.

Each panel of the body has been lovingly painted (by Valentines) to Rolls-Royce standards. The four Lucas quartz halogen headlamps hide behind pneumatically operated shutters until needed, and are fitted with a Lucas washer/wiper system of the type offered by Saab but steadfastly ignored by British mass producers.

The massive tail of the Ogle Aston looks like a particularly succulent piece of Gruyere cheese. Its perforated area provides recesses for no less than 22 lamps. The four amber turn indicators are sited on either side of the centre line and they flash sequentially. The stop-light assembly has 10 lamps set across the width of the vehicle, three of which on either side light up more brightly to indicate heavy braking.

Set on fat, seven-inch wide rims shod with 15in Pirelli radials, the low, wide posture of the car and the gradual thickening of the mass from the sharp nose to the upswept tail make the Ogle Aston look directionally stable and capable of acquiting itself well on the road. But is that the name of this particular piece of gamesmanship ? Plans for the car, which cost around £25,000, include some kind of sponsorship deal in the Americas and then a showing at the Geneva and Earls Court Motor Shows, but memories of the Countach, the Carabo and the Stratos make the Ogle Aston appear sober and conventional by comparison. ●

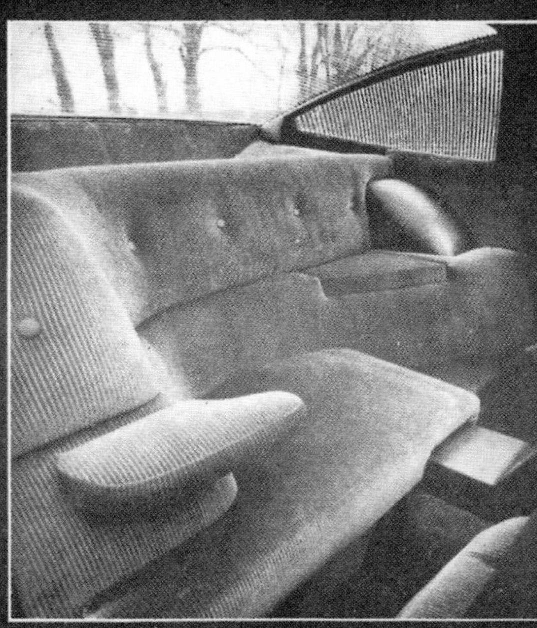

Interior (left) is tidy but not wayout; important feature of the instrumentation is a "head-up" display, similar to that used in aircraft. Sideways seat (right) in back of Ogle Aston provides space for third person. Trim is in corded velvet material

C111 REVISITED:

How long now before you can buy one? asks Doug Blain

THERE is a strong possibility that the world's largest producer of luxury cars will swing soon to Wankel power.

Engineers at Daimler-Benz in Stuttgart have solved many of the problems that plagued early rotary engines. Meanwhile, the company's business heads are attracted by the Wankel unit's possibilities in the face of stiffer-than-ever American pollution legislation.

On a recent visit to the Daimler-Benz headquarters, CAR's international fact-finding team met a wall of silence where formerly the company had been particularly forthcoming. This indicates that Wankel engines are no longer a curious novelty. Said one Mercedes executive: 'This is a bad time to talk about rotaries. Major decisions are being taken right now, and everybody is particularly sensitive.'

If Daimler-Benz decides to invest heavily in the tooling needed to produce Wankel engines in quantity, it will probably herald the move by building a limited series of the exciting C111 prototype. These cars, offered at a subsidised price to perhaps 100 carefully chosen 'influential' motorists in Germany and abroad, will pave the way to public acceptability of the rotary engine as a luxury power unit. At the same time they will help to pinpoint any last-minute bugs that the engineers may have missed.

Assuming that such a test-marketing exercise went well, the company might then go on to produce a rotary-powered variant of one of its normal saloons—probably a relatively low volume model such as the 300SEL. The cars in this larger range are in any case, according to rumour, due for replacement perhaps even later this year. It would be relatively easy for Mercedes to plan for a supplementary model to be slotted in after a couple of years.

What is the reason for this sudden renewed interest in a power source that, after all, has been around for years? Initially, the Wankel concept attracted wide attention for its extreme smoothness, lightness and relative compactness by comparison with comparable reciprocating designs. But already there were misgivings about its high fuel consumption. Then came the first signs of an emissions scare in California, and engineers despaired of meeting the new regulations because of the Wankel's relative inefficiency and the consequent incompleteness of its combustion process. At the same time there were doubts about whether, by the time the necessary auxiliaries were added, it really saved much underbonnet space.

Now, the wheel or rather the epitrochoid has turned full circle. The very much tougher 1975 American anti-smog requirements have put a far higher premium on space and weight saving, so that even the Wankel's small advantage here has become important. At the same time the need to reduce the lead content of petrol and the noxious content of exhaust gases has led to rougher running in conventional engines, so that the Wankel's extra smoothness is an even bigger attraction than before. And, most significant of all, the new laws are so stringent that even for the 'cleanest' conventional engine it seems that a catalytic exhaust afterburner will be needed by the end of the decade. Such afterburners, as well as being costly to buy and to service, require a separate fuel supply to sustain heat inside them, thus putting up petrol consumption. An inherently 'dirty' engine such as the Wankel is therefore at an immediate advantage because the high unburnt fuel content of its exhaust makes this separate supply unnecessary, and the reciprocating engine's previous economy lead is eliminated.

It is safe to assume that Daimler-Benz's decision on whether to 'go rotary' will depend on America's determination to go ahead and implement the proposed legislation. This in turn may well depend on the American industry's indication, or otherwise, to campaign vigorously against it. At present, the signs are that General Motors in particular are keen to capitalise on their enormous investment in the Wankel. Nobody knows how far they have got with their research, because a clause in their annual contract with the Wankel licensing organisation excuses them from the obligation to share the fruits of their labours. But already there are rumours of orders being placed for machinery to build rotary engines in large numbers and knowledgable observers are predicting that Wankel power for certain 'prestige' General Motors products is imminent.

The spur to much of this American interest has nothing to do with emissions. It is a matter of money. The Wankel engine lends itself much more readily than other types to fully automated assembly. In a labour-intensive and labour-sensitive industry like motor cars this is important—especially when, like GM, you are using the world's costliest labour to build, relatively speaking, some of the world's cheapest cars.

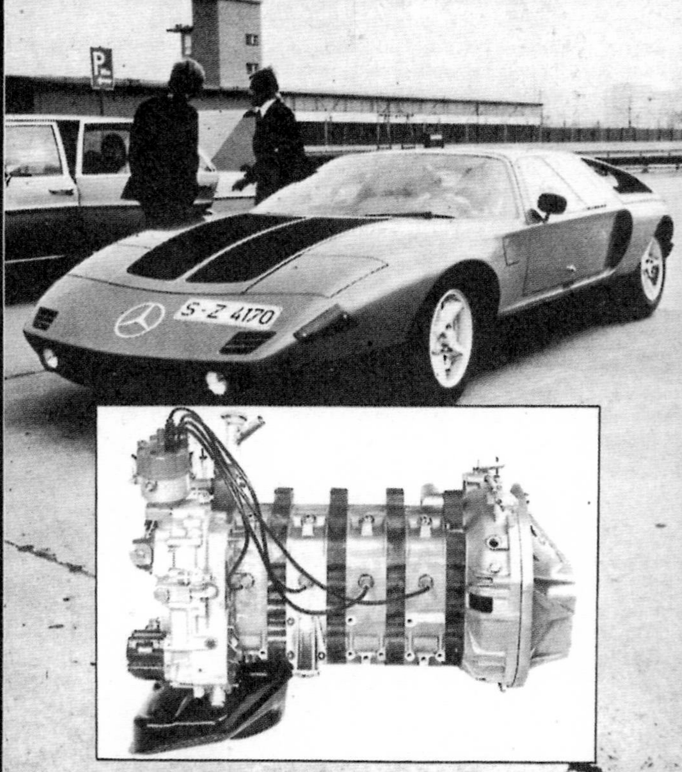

Daimler-Benz, despite the legendary excellence of their Swabian workforce, have shown themselves in the past to be keenly interested in labour-saving production methods. Already their Sindelfingen small-car plant is highly automated, using largely American machinery and methods. On these grounds, as well as in terms of smoothness, silence and adaptability to smog-reduction techniques, the Wankel probably has as much appeal to them at present as to any European manufacturer.

While we were in Stuttgart, we jumped at the chance of another drive in the C111 itself. We had already tried it in its original three-rotor form and as a four-rotor design with revised bodywork, each time in circuit trim with hard suspension settings and racing tyres. This time it was on roadgoing Michelins and production alloy wheels. It had undergone further body modifications, too, including the addition of small ventilation ducts in the nose and enlargement of the radiator air outlets in the top of the bonnet. But the biggest surprise came when we found that it had of all things automatic transmission!

Dr Hans Liebold, Merc's sun-tanned senior test engineer now that Rudi Uhlenhaut has officially retired, explained that fitting the automatic had meant detuning the engine considerably. Otherwise, the standard production components in the slush-pump would have been stressed so far beyond their design tolerances that constant breakages would have been the result. As it was, the selection mechanism was playing up when we drove the car on the hair-raising Daimler-Benz test track with its vertical wall of death (Dr Liebold told us one engineer had already been killed there—in a VW!).

Even so, we were struck by the 'soft' feel of the car by comparison with the original boy-racer version. A lot of work had obviously gone into the suspension, so that the original strongly under-steering, hard-riding, noisy semi-racer had been transformed into something much closer to a roadgoing luxury coupe. The automatic, although by no means perfectly mated to the engine, ironed out all of the Wankel's characteristic low-speed hunting and gave a clean, constant power delivery without the need for constant attention to the revolution counter.

The original C111 may well have been a plaything, designed as much for publicity as anything else. But nobody takes 40bhp out of an experimental engine and hooks it up to a production lemon-squeezer without a good reason, does he? ●

MERCEDES C111

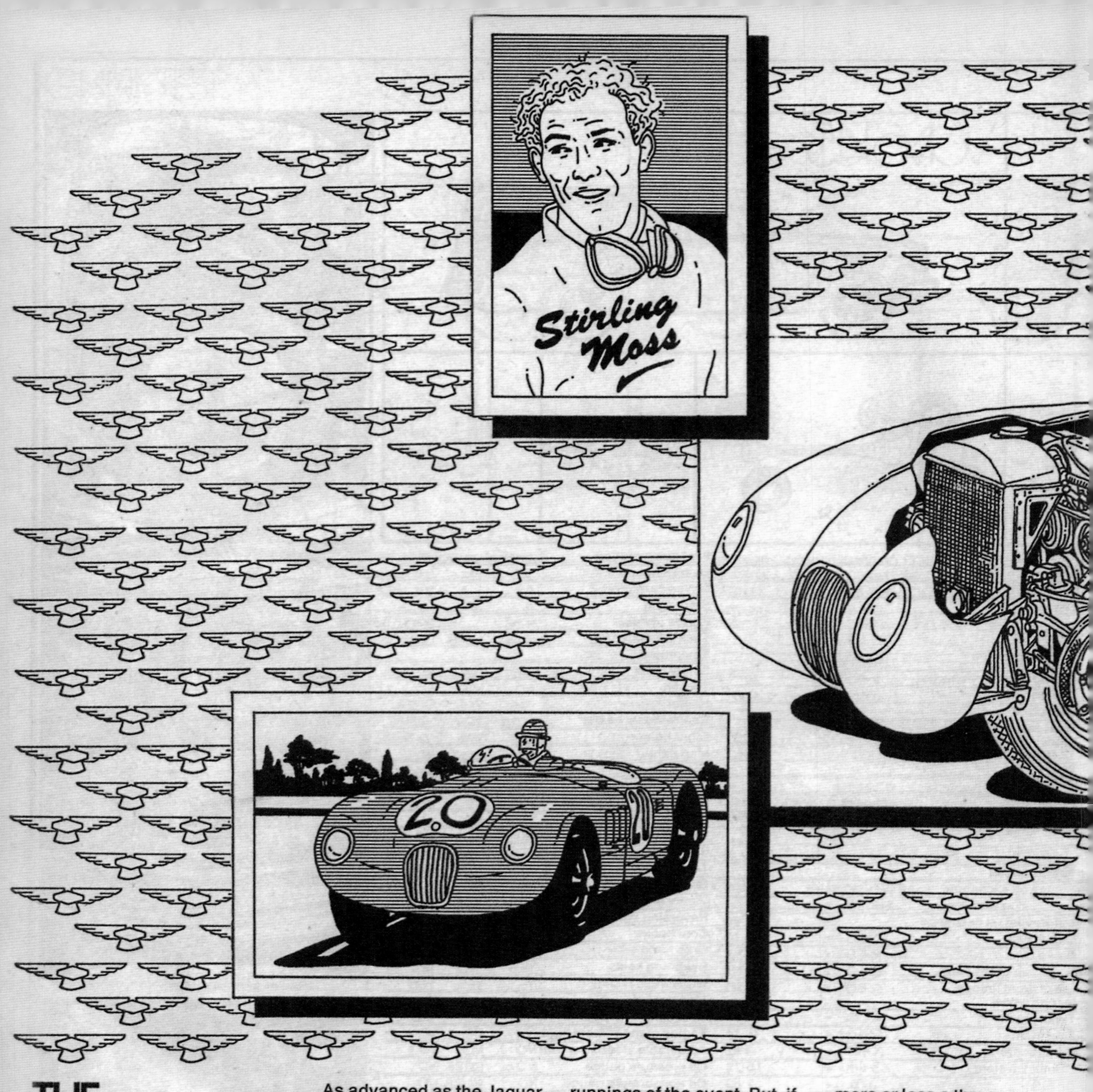

THE LEGENDARY C-TYPE

Wally Wyss unearths a flawless survival in unenlightened California

As advanced as the Jaguar XK-120 was at its introduction back in 1948, with its streamlined fuselage, DOHC six cylinder engine and 120mph performance, it was not a long-distance racing car, but a tourer.

Jaguar's founder, Sir William Lyons, and his chief engineer, Bill Heynes, attended the 24 Hours of Le Mans in 1950 and were impressed with the amount of world attention that focussed on the event. They decided that Jaguar should sponsor a factory team in subsequent runnings of the event. But, if they were to be competitive, they would need virtually a new car.

Analysing the weak points of privately owned XK-120s that had competed at Le Mans, Jaguar engineers saw that the primary requirement was a substantial reduction in weight. A more sophisticated suspension system, designed to cope with speeds up to 160mph, would be a help too.

The chassis of the new car was a space frame of the robust and relatively simple type favoured at the time, more or less a three-dimensional monkey bar structure of welded steel tubing designed to provide almost super-abundant strength without super-abundant weight. The tubing varied in diameter, with the thickest tubes carrying the most weight, and the only welded-in panel sections were bulkheads ahead of and behind the driver's compartment. A squat, spare, clean-limbed and aerodynamically efficient aluminium body was designed to fit over this sturdy chassis,

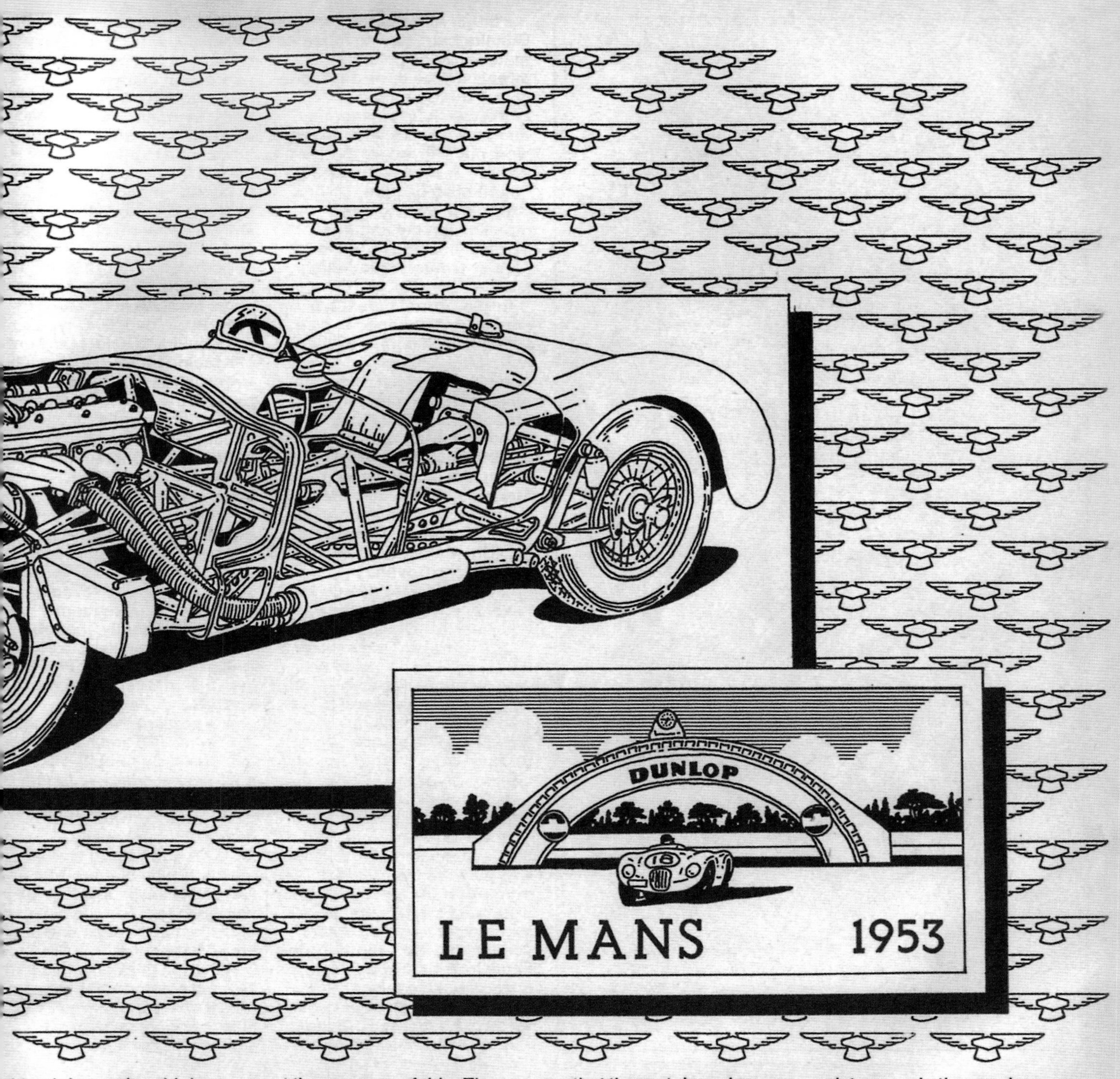

with minimum drag higher on the list of priorities than in most rival camps, so that even with the same engine as a standard 120 the XK-120C, or C-type as it came to be called, could go 20 per cent faster because of its lower wind resistance.

The suspension was made up largely of production XK-120 bits and pieces, the front retaining the standard unequal-length wishbones, longitudinal torsion bars and big Newton shock absorbers, but a stout anti-roll bar was added to minimise body roll at the expense of ride. The rear suspension was more original, with a single torsion bar mounted parallel to the axle. The bar was anchored in the centre and had a trailing link running from each end to the axle casing

Of course, the standard engine, powerful as it was, had to be tweaked up for racing, and who better to attend to the task than Mr Harry Weslake, of Sussex, the engine designer who joked about 'selling air', which he did in a way by designing experimental heads of wood to improve the airflow so that the metal versions would be so much more efficient? Weslake had the ports modified, and specified bigger valves. The cam profiles were also redesigned for more lift. Larger twin SU carburettors were fitted, later, in '53, to be supplanted by triple Webers on the factory team cars. Of course, the C-type benefitted from the research done in the development of the XK-120M in 1951, a supplementary model which offered a high-lift camshaft, lightweight flywheel, high-compression pistons and other mods sufficient to take it well over the 120 mark in road trim and considerably more, sans hood and screen. The XK-120M, surprisingly, cost very little more than the standard XK-120.

In June, 1951, Sir Lyons and his henchman were again at Le Mans. This time they could gaze proudly out on the grid and see three C-type Jaguars defending Britain's honour. The competition wasn't too ferocious, however, consisting mostly of Talbots and Aston-Martins, Ferrari and

the brash American, Cunningham, having failed to materialize as genuine threats. Of the three Jags, one, driven by Whitehead and Walker, won by an enormous margin while the other two went out with the same malady—lost oil, due to failure of an oil pipe support. In Ireland three months later the Jaguars took first, second and fourth in the Tourist Trophy, with Stirling Moss in the lead.

In 1952, the C-type team cars were developed to give 204bhp at 5500rpm. For the Mille Miglia, Italy's immortal long-distance road race, then at the height of its prestige, disc brakes were fitted to one car, but other trouble forced it to retire, letting the exciting new Mercedes 300SL take the race.

Jaguar's return to Le Mans in '52 was hardly a repeat of '51. The Mercedes looked so fast that the Coventry engineers tried to design even lower and leaner bodies for even less form drag. Several overheating problems were the result. The re-styled cars were then abandoned for subsequent races, and Moss won at Rheims and Ian Stewart took first in the Jersey Road Race in C-types with the original body shape.

Jaguar fielded three 'lightweight' C-types at Le Mans in 1953 and finished first, second and fourth. This was perhaps the greatest triumph for the car.

Ecurie Ecosse went on running the original cars for years afterward, engraving the name forever in sports car history. But the factory engineers had already begun work on a successor. In the winter of 1953 they wheeled out the D-type, which looked vaguely similar to the C-type but was in fact completely new and in many ways revolutionary. A monocoque body, in magnesium instead of aluminium, and dry sump lubrication to allow a lower bonnet line—these were the important departures that helped to outmode the C-type still at the height of its power and destined to go on racing successfully until 1955. In fact one of them beat the D-types to come in fourth at Le Mans in 1954. In all, over 50 C-types were built and sold. Many are still racing today in local club events all over the world, and particularly in Britain, where the Griffith formula caters for ageing but worthy sports-racing thoroughbreds.

The car in the colour photograph is now owned by a Californian called Jim Kirk. It was one of the first C-types to be exported to the West Coast, having been sold in Los Angeles in November, 1952. It was subsequently raced consistently, though without spectacular success. It was once driven by Phil Hill in a race at Brergstrom Air Force Base, Texas.

The present owner bought the car in 1970 and has painstakingly re-built it from the frame outward. A Jaguar fan in the good old American tradition, Kirk owns a half dozen of them, mostly XK-120s and 140s. 'I started my thing with Jaguars with an E-type' he says, 'and worked my way back. The C-type is my oldest at the moment, but I'm still shopping.'

Although this car will still do 140mph comfortably, he only fires it up once in a while to take to concours events. For shame, sir. For shame!

Sports cars up to £1600

This class is something of a desert. The Clan is the only bright spot, and a costly one at that, although we have been very impressed with the rigidity and quality of the device.

However, the era of the cheap two-seater sports car is over, thank you, despite the few that still hang on.

Sports cars £1600 to £2750

The enormous performance of the Lotus Europa attracts us like mad, for it really is a great little car. However, the Alfa GTV is infinitely more practical and not that much slower from point-to-point. Is beginning to look a bit dated, though.

Shortage of anything else that's better for the price allows the Jensen-Healey to creep in here, but we are not greatly impressed with it.

Sports cars £2750 to £6000

Think what you may about the E-type, but you have got to admit that its enormous performance and low price make an unbeatable combination, specially if smoothness and flexibility enter into it, too.

This is the class where the Ferrari Dino would score, but it's being phased out to make room for a V8 two-plus-two to compete with the Urraco and Merak. Meantime, there's the Porsche—superbly made—and the lusty but not terribly efficient Montreal.

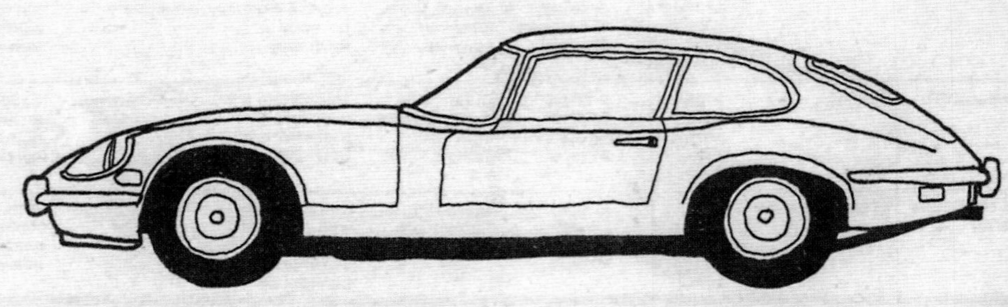

Sports cars over £6000

When you start spending a lot of money, the possibilities are endless, as is evidenced by the equipment listed herein. However, it's the Urraco that takes the cake by a big, big margin, for it has enough performance and more roadholding than most people would use.

The Pantera is close to the Lambo in price but is not as refined. Hard to say that a £10,000 two seater can be a good buy, but the Bora is in a class by itself. Most luxurious of the group, it's also a flyer. ●

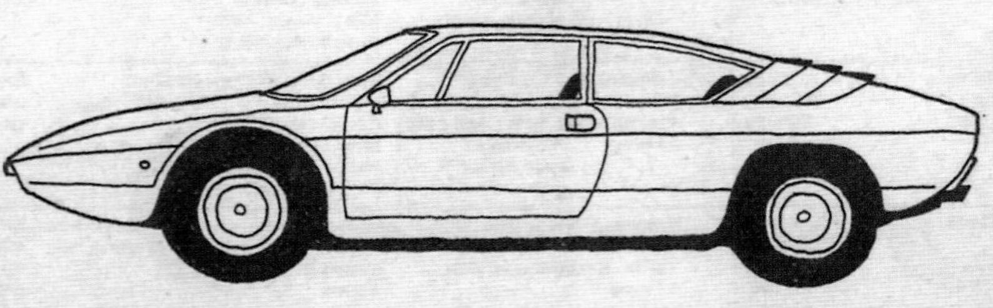

Make and Model	Price	Seats/Doors	Engine	Performance	Styling	Handling and Roadholding	Brakes	Comfort	Comments
Clan Crusader	£1396	2.2	875 cc, 50 bhp at 5800 rpm, 4 cyl, sohc	0-50 mph in 9.5 secs, 100 mph top, 37 mpg	Nothing wonderful.	Limit set by Imp bits, but still very good, as rally successes indicate.	Drums all round, cope well with light Clan.	Choppy ride although tight-fitting seats successful.	All fibreglass sports car that has proved itself in hot-blooded competition. We are developing a soft-spot for it, despite high price.
Triumph Spitfire	£1053	2.2	1296 cc, 63 bhp at 6000 rpm, 4 cyl, pushrods	0-50 mph in 9 secs, 95 mph top, 30 mpg	Nothing to get excited about.	Swing axles have been sorted out reasonably satisfactorily.	Disc/drum No problems.	Firm, old fashioned sports-car ride. Too noisy, though.	Sloppy body, too much scuttle shake and all that sort of thing. Like Midget, it's quite hopelessly outdated.
Ginetta G15	£1175	2.2	875 cc, 50 bhp at 5800 rpm, 4 cyl, sohc	0-50 mph in 9.2 secs, 100 mph top, 39 mpg	Neat but not spectacular.	Points very well indeed.	Disc/drum full marks.	Very harsh ride, although seats help compensate.	Limited volume and sales potential, but notably sporting coupe with few compromises. Like Clan Crusader, engine hangs out behind back axle.
Alfa Romeo 2000 GTV	£2587	+2.2	1962 cc, 131 bhp at 5500 rpm, 4 cyl, dohc	0-50 mph in 6.5 secs, 123 mph, 22 mpg	Early Bertone, although still perfectly respectable.	Rolls a bit, but hangs on like mad. Steering is heavy at speeds, poor lock.	All disc Full marks.	Well controlled suspension gives fine ride, good front seats.	A two-plus-two concept that provides useful amount of versatility. Gradual development has refined the GTV to a fine edge.
Lotus Europa	£2369	2.2	1558 cc, 126 bhp at 6500 rpm, 4 cyl, dohc	0-50 mph in 6 secs, 120 mph top, 21 mpg	Latest mods have made Europa more practical at cost of appearance.	Sticks like blonde hairs on your coat.	Disc/drum, effective!	Really good suspension, tight-fitting cabin.	Mid-engines are the thing, and with the twin-cam unit installed the Europa is a great car. If the new X1/9 Fiat does cost about £2000 (see this issue) the Europa's a bargain!
Jensen-Healey	£1959	2.2	1973 cc, 140 bhp at 6500 rpm, 4 cyl, dohc	0-50 mph in 6.4 secs, 120 mph top, 23 mpg	Conventional and ugly.	Not bad for live axle car, but not good either.	Disc/drum, no moans.	Ride's soft, seats fair. Not too bad overall.	Gets in our list because of price more than anything else, but it's still far too costly for a car that's only a small improvement on MG-B.
Jaguar E-type	£3367	2.2	5343 cc, 272 bhp at 5850 rpm, V12 cyl, sohc	0-50 mph in 4.8 secs, 148 mph top, 14.5 mpg	Too many bulges and humps.	Big on cornering, but power steering is edgy at speed.	All disc, full marks.	Firm and well controlled ride, reasonable seats.	Performance for money must put the old E right at the top of the list, but it's a strange device by current standards for high performance.
Porsche 911S	£5675	+2.2	2341 cc, 190 bhp at 6500 rpm, 6 cyl, sohc	0-50 mph in 4.9 secs, 144 mph top, 16 mpg	Very smooth shape that is still attractive.	Corners very well without being tail happy.	All disc, work well.	Choppy ride, well designed, and cosy interior.	Very well-made car that has been developed to the point that engine placement does not matter in reality. Cheaper models with less performance also available, fit better into Sporty Saloon and Coupe classification.
Alfa Romeo Montreal	£5549	2.2	2583 cc, 200 bhp at 6500 rpm, V8 cyl, dohc	0-50 mph in 6.1 secs, 137 mph 15 mpg	Bertone again. Very handsome car.	Rolls quite a lot but hangs on securely enough with some understeer. Very heavy steering at low speeds.	All disc, no problems.	Good ride but a bit soggy at times. Nice seats.	Smooth, steady performance but not as agile as smaller mid-engined cars like Ferrari Dino. Feels cumbersome on tight roads, but excellent motorway cruiser.
Lamborghini Urraco	£6545	2.2	2463 cc, 220 bhp at 7500 rpm, V8 cyl, sohc	0-50 mph in 4.8 secs, 145 mph top, 18 mpg	Compact and beautifully balanced.	Staggeringly good by any standard you would care to name.	All disc, same applies.	Quiet, pliable suspension. Good front seats. Little noise.	Price keeps going up, but the Urraco is worth the bread for sure. Is the best handling car we have ever driven. See CAR January 1973.
De Tomaso Pantera	£6696	2.2	5763 cc, 350 bhp at 5000 rpm, V8 cyl, pushrods	0-50 mph in 4 secs, 160 mph top, 12 mpg	Clean, handsome car that looks as burly as it is.	Lots of initial understeer, then lots of road-holding when aided by oodles of throttle.	All disc, some fade when you are really getting into it.	Comfortable, absorbent ride so-so seats.	Unsophisticated Ford V8 engine amidships helps keep the price down and the performance way up. It's not a refined or luxurious sports car, but it's a real machine.
Maserati Bora	£9970	2.2	4719 cc, 290 bhp at 5500 rpm, V8 cyl, dohc	0-50 mph in 5 secs, 170 mph top, 13 mpg	Looks heavy (it is) and well balanced.	Soft suspension but very secure handling.	All disc, using Citroen high-pressure hydraulics.	Agreeable ride, little noise, luxuriously-fitted cabin.	Is a sort of replacement for the Lambo Miura in the very high price sector of the market, although not as chuckable. Interior appointments help justify the enormous cost.

WOULD YOU GO TO WAR TO KEEP YOUR CAR?

And, er, incidentally: did you know it takes 100,000 gallons of water to build a single vehicle?

Here's IAN BREACH on what really happens when the resources run out

ALL THINGS, AS SIR Bernard Docker once said, are relative, so if the British motorist fetches up driving a Velosolex some time in the next few months he probably won't feel a lot different from the American who stores his Parisienne and ventures out in his youngest son's Volkswagen. The world at large oscillates between two far wider extremes. The developed countries—principally the United States, Europe, and Japan—have staked their life styles on the assumption of infinite reserves and continuing deliveries of cheap raw materials. These countries are almost completely dependent on foreign sources for two dozen of the 74 non-energy commodities essential for a modern industrial society.

At the other extreme lies all that defines our concept of 'cheap': low wages, malnutrition, weak or vulnerable political systems, illiteracy, and general environmental poverty. And where there are raw materials in abundance, some or all of these afflictions are present. Look at any of the world's great extractive industries and basic metalworking settlements and you will find—unless you take a stupid and romantic view of these things—a picture of man degraded and nature befouled. It is true within the industrialised nations themselves: you need pay only a short visit to South Wales, Pennsylvania, the Ruhr, or Kobe to see the nature of the modern economics at work. In return for demand, the supplier has to give not only goods—a strangely inappropriate word more often than not—but a bit of his health, his real standards of living, and his local heritage.

However, it is the allegedly underdeveloped countries who have begun to challenge the arrangements that have sustained Western man for so long. With more or less of a fuss, they have started to resist the idea that their oils and ores can be ripped from the land and carted away at the buyer's price. For years we have laughed at the story of Manhattan being purchased for a dollar, while accepting that pretty much the same thing has been happening in our times. We may yet be strangled with the beads we gave for sovereign mineral rights in one part of the world after another, for these exploited countries (forget about rich Sheikhs: they're irrelevant) are now asking at what rate they want to see these resources depleted. And they are coming up with a variety of answers that should interest anyone who still wonders about the future of the private car. The shortage or denial of oil is but a trailer for the other scarcities which now face us.

Without a comprehensive analysis of world economics and the price chemistry as affected by shortage, we can do no more than examine the *likely* physical causes and effects. No longer, for instance, can we take known or projected reserves of any commodity and divide it by existing and projected demand to come up with a yield in years. As price goes up, a threshold is reached at which demand is lowered: this can operate at either a national level—where balance-of-payments problems limit imports of non-essential materials (the definition of which is a whole different ball game)—or at an individual one, where the cost simply becomes too great to bear.

That would be one reason for treating the conventional equations with caution. The other would be that the supplying nations decide to restrict the export of commodities that bring back nothing but trouble and low-value currencies. The most familiar example has been the Organisation of Petroleum Exporting Countries (OPEC), who ought to be seen as behaving out of more than simple spite, greed, or hatred of Israel. As Lester Brown recently put it: 'What should determine the rate at which Venezuela's remaining oil reserves are exploited—its own longer-term foreign-exchange needs or the short-term consumption needs of the United States? The former may argue for a much *lower* level of petroleum production and export than the latter.'

Exporters of other raw ▷

How long will it last?

OIL
1987

All along, I have adopted a worst-case programme, which seems reasonable at a time when population growth shows no sign of diminution and international understanding is at an all time low. Suppose we consider an hypothetical situation in which nothing is changed and none of the factors I have so far brought into the discussion are to be included. What would be left for the motor industry? If we draw on Gerald Leach's study, conducted on behalf of OECD at the end of 1972 and not materially out-of-date now, we see that oil reserves lie within a range of 1350-2500 x 10^9 barrels, with estimated peak production in the 1990s and 2010s respectively: '. . . most of the ultimate reserves have yet to be found, while today's proved reserves will last until about 1987, given present growth rates of oil consumption'. If the highest estimates prove to be correct, then we shall have little problem in matching supply to demand for oil this century *all other things being equal* (ie, we assume that the West will draw freely and more heavily on the global supply of oil). Serious crisis would not occur before the late 21st century.

If, however, present trends continue, if growth of road vehicles in service follows official projection, if fuel consumption patterns remain as now, if refinery outputs are not altered to favour cars at the expense of other sectors, and if ultimate oil reserves are anywhere near the lower estimate, then the car will precipitate a major oil-supply crisis all by itself, and cars now in the showrooms will be in serviceable use when the crisis is felt. The possible responses, as Gerald Leach points out, are many and complex. If, for example, as a recent BBC vox pop suggested, there are many motorists who would be happy to pay £2 or more a gallon for petrol, then the laws of supply and demand might as well be thrown out of the window.

At the end of 1973, the size of the world's car population stood at roughly 250 million (rising at 10 million per year net). Given the weights of various materials averaged out between American cars and those produced elsewhere, this represented some 210 million tons of iron and steel, 10.9 million tons of aluminium, copper, lead, and zinc, and 27.1 million tons of other non-ferrous metals, glass, natural, synthetic, and reclaimed rubber, glassfibre, and cotton. Iron and steel in all forms have been used in decreasing proportions over the past seven years, though they still account for huge proportions of total industrial use. A Senate Subcommittee Hearing in 1970 was given the following estimate of what the car takes from the common industrial pool: 20percent of all steel, 10percent of all aluminium, seven percent of copper, 13percent of nickel, 35percent of zinc, 50percent of lead, and 60percent of natural rubber.

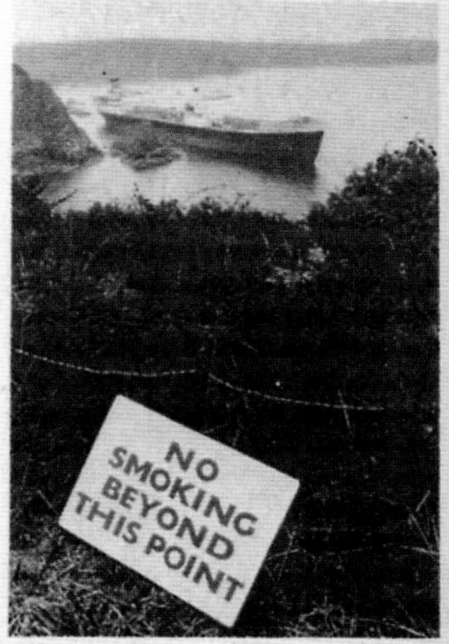

How long will they last?

IRON
2174

The demand on fresh raw materials is considerably lower. A half of steel production is scrap; for aluminium, a fifth to a quarter; for copper, one sixth to a quarter; and for zinc, a fifth. There need be few worries as far as iron and steel are concerned, for with colossal deposits still to be exploited and reclamation rates as high, the supplies demanded by the motor industry could be met—in theory—for a couple of hundred years more. With all the other basic metals, though, a less promising outlook is suggested.

ALUMINIUM
19-?

Aluminium, being used more and more as a replacement for iron and steel, comes from very large, accessible reserves of bauxite, and if transport and processing costs could be further cut, it would play an even greater part as a substitute—not just for ferrous metals, but also for copper, brass, and other alloys.

MAGNESIUM
19-?

The same arguments apply to magnesium, which ocean-mining could turn into a metal of the first importance throughout industry. The three remaining metals in widespread use are likely to be in short supply well before the end of the century unless extraction rates or usage patterns are radically altered.

LEAD
1980

Lead is reasonably well reclaimed from the primary form in which it is used—batteries—but even a recovery rate of 75percent is not going to protect it against the possibly increased demand in larger conventional cars with heavy-duty electrical systems or, if it happens, in the development of lead-acid batteries for motive power. Estimates vary between 1980 and 2020 for severe shortage.

materials so desperately craved in the developed world are emulating OPEC's example. One odd case is that of the US itself, which is trying to arrange a quota for Japan on the quantity of timber that country can import from North America. More obviously, Brazil cut beef exports by 30percent in 1973, Thailand banned rice exports altogether, and the four major copper-exporting countries are getting together their own pressure group. Similar moves are being made where bauxite is mined. It is hardly surprising when you see, for instance, that Zambia's entire production of copper is swallowed by the USSR, or that Jamaica and Surinam, together the prime producers of bauxite, fall nearly 50percent short of supplying the US. Obviously these are not direct export-import examples, but they illustrate the gross disparity to which the mineral supply situation is host. If those three countries want manufactured goods in copper and aluminium, they must pay three times over—in foreign currency, in the loss of their own resources, and in the rape of their environments.

There are two further factors we should keep sight of before looking at the resources themselves. First is the fact that scarcity breeds scarcity. A shortage of oil, if prolonged, would bring about a shortage in the supply of clean water that could be pumped to homes and factories: water is already under siege, and is constraining development all over the world. It is the first resource to come under strain as populations burst their natural boundaries. As necessary for steelmaking as it is for agriculture, its sequestration by the powerful and prosperous is a political issue in both national and international contexts. Traditionally, a country's economic strength has been measured as a vector of population size, steel output, and electrical power consumption, but this has invariably assumed unrestricted supplies of cheap or free water. All that is over—and the implications for the motorist and the car industry are salutary. It takes 100,000 gallons of water at present rates to produce a single vehicle.

The last factor is the knock-on effect in those countries half way between being undeveloped and developed. India, for example, would suffer massively—already is—from a price hike in petroleum and cereal products. With little, or comparatively little, to barter for these and manufactured or semi-manufactured goods, countries like Bangladesh, India, or Colombia will be losing a battle for foreign assistance with nations that are resource-rich, like Indonesia, Algeria, and Brazil. They will be supplying not water, iron ore, or oil to produce the West's consumer goods, but *wheat, rice, potatoes* and *corn*. Having been asked to determine what resources we depend upon for the production and use of cars, I say what I said at the outset: we rely on a vast number of other people's tolerance to poverty and hunger. Of these are made our cars, our homes, our medicine, *our* way of life.

Where shall we stop in considering the material resources necessary to build and run the world's cars? Shall the paper on which these words are printed be taken into account? Shall the energy requirements for the road-construction industry be included—and the building materials for Transport Ministries and filling stations? Clearly they ought to be, even though, as Gerald Leach notes, the list is endless 'and covers the whole spectrum of an industrial society's material consumption'. A computation of the energy used to power cars, produce motor spirit, manufacture and sell cars is one thing; to calculate that used for repairs and maintenance, replacement parts, accessories, oil swaps, insurance, parking and tolls, and the construction (and planning even) of highways, only the most approximate methods can be adopted. Eric Hirst, in his mammoth study of transportation energy costs, concluded that these functions consumed some 20percent of the total raw energy allocated to the car in America, itself almost 25percent of total US energy consumption. US energy consumption—for six percent of the earth's population—currently runs at roughly 35percent of the world's.

Hirst's was one of the best pieces of applied research to come out of the US in recent years, but it was incomplete in itself and only a beginning of what must now be a mandatory scrutiny of energy costs in every single process-intensive industry—with everything counted, from the prospecting for an ore to the delivery, use, and maintenance of the finished product. (The same,

COPPER & ZINC 1990

Copper and zinc are both at an increasing premium and substitution is being introduced apace. Both could dry up this century, with copper being replaced in the car before the end of the '70s and zinc being usurped by plated plastics a little later.

PLASTICS 1984

For plastics, however, we are back with oil. Already there is a worldwide scarcity of polymers, and it is being left largely to arbitrary forces to decide which particular sectors should have the greatest claim on outstanding supplies of plastic feedstock. The competition is an unequal and a bizarre one, with hospitals ranged against the packaging trades, the building industry vying with the car manufacturers.

We are likely to see the difficulties I have outlined brought to a head and thus resolved very much more quickly than any the world has previously faced. It must have been plain to most people that we were not going to continue until we exhausted every natural resource in support of the motor car, but most pitched the time for change well on the comfortable side of their individual horizons. At least there is now an awareness of how imminent the upheaval must be. Out of this, perhaps, will come a growing understanding of how interconnected our problems are, of how population size, poverty, economic stress, and political strife are related. The most aggressive motorist might realise the full price of his car. We might meanwhile work towards a world in which resources were managed for the whole world and conserved until such time as we could—if ever—develop the technologies necessary to give everyone that notional 'standard of living' that the West has deemed so necessary. It is tempting to think in terms of the national interest still, but that concept is dead. The question really should not be 'How long can we last?' but 'When should we change?' And the answer is an exciting one: now.

of course, extends to monetary expenditure: as a correspondent to the New Scientist pointed out a month or so ago, civil research into nuclear power has cost £1200 millions so far, but this figure never appears in the calculations of generating costs for any future nuclear programme). A less generalised treatment of energy inputs for the car industry was produced 18 months ago in a report to the Illinois Institute for Environmental Quality. In it, R Stephen Berry and Margaret Fulton Fels, both of the University of Chicago's Department of Chemistry, broke down the total energy costs for the manufacture, discard, and subsequent re-use of a typical American automobile.

In a series of impressive sum-and-difference analyses, they worked out the cost of the average (US) car at 37 MWh, or roughly equal to the annual free-energy consumption of each vehicle in normal use. They do not include in their calculations the energy costs required to sustain the labour forces involved. In the long chain of mining, refining, processing, fabricating, scrapping, reclaiming, and reprocessing, these must be large and should, in any future analysis, be included—since a shortage of energy sources, as we have seen in Britain these last two months, affects directly their freedom to take part in the whole process. But Fulton and Fels do indicate the colossal savings that might be made by thriftier use of the thermodynamic potential in each car. Maximum recycling, they suggest, could save almost 30percent of the energy costs; a tripling of the vehicle life, their report declares, can save *roughly 60 percent*.

The conundrum is apparent, for however technically plausible the efficiency equations, fuel saved is invariably paid for by unemployment or reduced income—whether in a supplier country or within the industry itself. In many cases, the efficiency of production of the essential materials for a modern car—iron, steel, aluminium, copper and zinc—is scarcely better than 10per-cent: a large part of the gap between ideal and actual energy efficiencies is directly attributable to the intensity of labour employed. Fulton and Fels take no account of this; nor, disappointingly, do they mention water in all their otherwise fine-tooth combing

continued on page 68

continued from page 23

of the manufacturing processes and their energy costs. More seriously, they imply but do not address themselves to the consequences of energy conservation in the car industry. If we can save 60percent by tripling the life of any given automobile and assume a steady economic/ social state, then the inevitable pressure would be to treble output! I rarely use exclamation marks: in this instance it seems necessary to bring home the full force of our dilemma. Environmentally, it is inconceivable that we should treble car output. Economically it would represent a diminishing return, since the price of imported materials would continue to rise faster than the car-producing countries' economies could bear. The only factor remaining that we can change in our equations is the social one.

If we accept, as the motor industry tells us we must, that the internal combustion piston-engined car will not be amenable to replacement this decade and plan for none but temporary falls in demand, then our future takes on a darker tinge. Much of the present debate about the West's economy as affected by raw material shortage has been informed by the presupposition that we *must* return to a state regarded as 'normal'. But if the economists' traditional reliance on a substitute appearing at fortuitous intervals for threatened materials no longer holds any comfort, then last-resort tactics become more likely. Three months ago, the director of a major oil company told me privately that he considered the possibility of military intervention to secure oil for the West and particularly the US 'a very, very real one'. At about the same time, unknown to him or me, the US moved men into New Mexico for desert-war manoeuvres—the first such exercises to be conducted for years. In the great and continuing play-war it may have looked to the Arabs and the USSR as no more than a piece of sabre-rattling, but it reinforced the desperateness with which America views the oil-supply situation.

A cooler reading of the scene now suggests that the immediate conflict will be resolved at diplomatic levels and that any military adventure would be a clumsy and counter-productive affair. That said, it is not idle to reflect on the number of wars in the past 20 years that have been fought directly or indirectly, partially or wholly, on the basis of securing for international buyers a supply of raw materials at an acceptable price. Surprisingly little has been written about the part played by resource-demand in wars: it has been assumed as having played infinitely less of a part than political, strategic or pure territorial factors, which looks odd when set against Malaya, Portuguese Africa, the Middle East in the '50s, or even Vietnam—where the resources of Cambodia and Thailand are at stake. But there is a very high correlation between rates of population growth, rising Gross National Product, and expanding industrial economies—and military budgets and involvement in wars. Will we go to war to keep our cars on the roads? It is a question we may not be given the opportunity to answer. ●

IS DUMPISM DOOMED?

continued from page 27

other than those on official business, ie, dumping a car. It is Saturday morning and many of us are casually patrolling surrounding roads in cars, feigning interest in mushrooms. Others are nestled in the bush waiting, like Vietcong. The local police make their scheduled 11.45 round. At this moment no true Dumpists are to be seen. Amateurs and kids, yes, and they're chased out. But moments later a score of cars converge, tyres slide, doors slam. Dumpists hiding in the bush spring forth and there's a communal dash for the goodies! First come, first served. A rule.

The electrical fuses go first, along with the seat belts, windscreen wipers, rearvision mirrors and anything else of value that's easily detachable. But if a man has found a sound tranny that he wants he wastes no time in slipping in the timbers, calling for help to flip the beast over (we always help, another rule), and digging in the tender underside with spanners like a voracious beetle. The remainder of us are busily searching and dismantling. We all know it's harvest time. The dump is nearly full, and within days a yellow bulldozer with an evil metal finger will enter and mash flat and stack the wrecks like so many gigantic sandwiches. Huge flatbed lorries will then haul them off, thus clearing the way for a fresh crop.

We're in luck. We find two excellent 7.00-15 snow tyres and relieve them from a Chev hearse. We're intensely pleased.

Then greater luck: a pimply youth in purple overalls arrives in a running Renault R4 with a blown silencer. We Dumpists step back (still another rule) and smile knowingly. The lad tromps the throttle and hurls the machine, demolition-derby style, through the wrecks, carooming off some, smashing into others. His run finished, he slams on the brakes, rams the shift lever into reverse, pops the clutch and he's off again, engine screaming, bashing his way backwards to the other far end where he whams hard into a grey DS21. The boy is good! Six runs. And on the final one he leaves his foot down and slams broadside into a Fiat 850 with a huge metallic clang! He then rekindles the engine, holds the throttle open wide till pistons are ricocheting around, denting up the inside of the bonnet. He then steps out, kicks in all the windows, and sets the whole mess on fire! (By God, we muse. This kid's *really* got style! If *only* it could have been a Bond 875!) We applaud.

Three forty-five meant another round by the police. By then we'd all waved adieu and returned with our booty to our respective garages and cellars. Like human squirrels we were all smugly aware that our 300 semi-usable silencers or that extra differential housing or those 4000 electrical fuses packed away in psychic chestnut trees would see us through many a cold—real and psychological—winter.

But *is* Dumpism doomed? If times get worse you can rest assured that no sane individual is going to be idly throwing away a sound car, especially if a bit of handiwork can keep it going, and it doesn't drink much petrol. But if the immediate future of Dumpism looks dim, we must let it be known that we have a certain intangible faith that motor car production will again, some day, get totally out of control, parts and repair prices will skyrocket out of the Universe and *surely* a new generation of Dumpists will scuttle forth to do their good work.

Thus, we can only say to them, while sitting here comfortably with our 4000 electrical fuses: go to it, lads! God speed and keep your spanners dry! ●

Aqua Manda now for men

The distinctive fragrance of mandarin, coriander and aromatic herbs.

TURNING ON
TO THE TURBO
turbo
PORSCHE

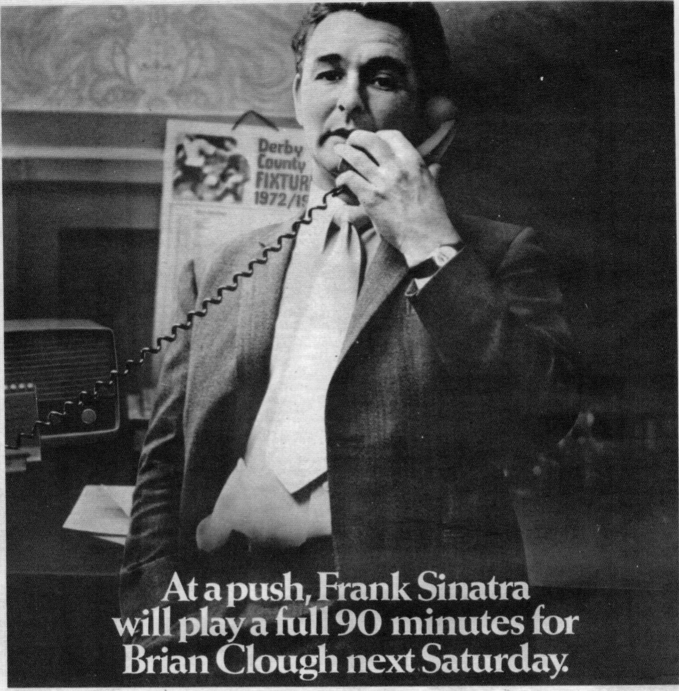

At a push, Frank Sinatra will play a full 90 minutes for Brian Clough next Saturday.

As long as he remembers to push a Sinatra tape into the Radiomobile stereo in his new Mercedes.

And he will. He finds that, whether Derby County win or lose, the soothing voice of Francis Albert always manages to relax his tensions.

Of course, he could always turn on his Radiomobile car radio instead. But how often do you get a full 90 minutes of Sinatra? And as Brian Clough says, "When I want to hear 'My Way,' I want to hear it my way."

Why Radiomobile? Rolls-Royce fit Radiomobile stereo to their Grand Corniche as standard equipment. But then Brian Clough never has been averse to buying in somebody else's brilliant discovery.

Radiomobile Fact File.

Specialist fitting at Radiomobile centres. Model illustrated: No. 102S Stereo 8. 3½ watt output per channel. Speaker impedance 4 ohms. Supplied with 12 volt negative earth, positive earth available. Complete with two speakers. Price: £38.40.*

Send for coloured brochure to: Radiomobile Ltd., Dept. C, Goodwood Works, North Circular Rd., London N.W.2. * Recommended retail price.

By Appointment to H M The Queen Manufacturers of car radio equipment Radiomobile

Radiomobile

THE STEREO ROLLS-ROYCE FIT.

TURNING ON TO THE TURBO

LET ME TELL YOU ABOUT THE PORSCHE Turbo, the 3-litre car that blasts to 100mph in 12.8 seconds and has so much power its makers considered a five-speed gearbox superfluous; a hindrance. Let me tell you about this six-cylinder wonder that tops 160mph on two-star fuel and takes 2+2 motoring into a realm previously attained by only the most exotic two seaters. Should I mention also that it comes with a 20,000-mile warranty, requires servicing but once a year and can apparently return 22mpg?

Comprehending the Turbo's acceleration—it is to the 'ordinary' Carrera what that car is to the 911—is taxing enough. The supplementary knowledge that, on the other hand, your wife could drive the kids to school in it because the flexibility is such that it will pull from 500rpm in top gear calls for another round of bemused headshaking and a second stiff brandy. But then, turbocharging is the magic word at present, isn't it? The thought of a road car appearing with the devilish little blower attached causes people to suck in their breath in anticipation, and it's mostly a result of the giant-killing successes turbocharged cars have achieved in series like the Can-Am races these past few years. Helped by the mystique born of invincibility, the build-up of turbocharging's aura has been complete.

Now, of course, it is with us on the roads. It has transformed a number of Capris, Granadas and Opel Mantas turned out by Ralph Broad, it has turned BMW's 2-litre 2002—the first production turbocharged car—into a bombshell. It has made Porsche's 911 into a supercar of almost unbelievable proportions, bringing eager clients from the Aga Khan downwards knocking impatiently at Stuttgart's door. Naturally, the turbo looks the part. Its body is essentially the Carrera shell, but the wheel arches are wider and there is a different spoiler system edged in foam rubber at the nose. The rear spoiler is the big flat one, also tipped in soft rubber, from the Carrera 3-litre. Because this spoiler is so large, because the wheels and the arches are so obese, because the car hunches down so low over its tyres, it looks like a racer that's escaped to the road. It is mean and aggressive and declares its intention with almost brutal efficiency. When people's eyes are hauled to it they're stunned; and they can't get out of its way quickly enough.

The impact bumpers, fitted with recoil shock absorbers so that after a 5mph impact they'll spring back out as if nothing happened, are standard. Hella's new high-power washers jut up from the front bumper to clean the lights, and the familiar wiper is there on the rear window. Chassis changes are what one might expect: spacers widen the front track 2in over the standard 911 and almost 6in at the rear. The front forged alloy wheels are 1in wider at 7 x 15 and the rear ones are up by 2in to 8 x 15. Front tyres are 185/70VR and the back ones 215/60VR. The torsion bars providing the springing have been uprated, the shockers are gas-filled Bilsteins and the anti-roll bars are stiffer . . . much stiffer. Peer through the black wheel spokes and you'll see that the four disc brakes are drilled axially as well as being vented; they're taken from the racing Martini-Porsche. Weight of the Turbo, at 2514lb, is 144lb up on the standard 911 and Carrera . . . but the power-to-weight ratio is still a mean 9.6lb/bhp.

The six-cylinder horizontally-opposed air-cooled engine uses the same 70.4mm stroke as the 2.7 unit, but a bigger 95mm bore takes its capacity up to 2992cc. Onto this SOHC (per bank) six goes a KKK turbocharger, used in conjunction with the Bosch K-Jetronic fuel injection system—the first time a turbocharger and continuous injection have been mated in a road car. The new Bosch contactless electronic distributor is also used. Compression ratio of the engine is 6.5 to one, but since the turbo pumps air in at almost 12psi the end result is an effectively much higher ratio.

The output from it all is 260DINbhp at 5500rpm with 253lb/ft of torque from 4000 to 5000rpm. Yes, the torque curve is *that* flat; and that is what makes the Turbo, on the road, such a remarkable car. At just 1000rpm there is a hefty 130lb/ft and at 2000rpm that's risen to 174. At 2300rpm you've got more torque than the 2.7 Carrera develops *at its peak*, and it stays that way until the 6500rpm redline. The curve then climbs rapidly until it flattens out completely at 4000rpm, developing that walloping 253lb/ft and holding it until five grand. And it doesn't drop off after that either: at the maximum 6500rpm there is almost 200lb/ft! Meanwhile the bhp curve has been climbing like a rocket ship: the two curves' characteristics could not be better. With such oomph, and a very wide power band despite the relatively low redline, it is obvious that a five-speed gearbox would not be necessary. As it is, the internal gearbox ratios are very tall—third is grossly overdrive at 0.89 and top is 0.65 to one—with compensation coming from a low 4.222 to one differential. The end result is still a long-legged 25.8mph/1000rpm. As for strength, the turbocharged racing cars of just 2140cc develop 500bhp and it would seem that more power might be had from the 3-litre just by turning up the boost screw. Importantly, the low turbo emissions and crash construction mean that the Porsche is the only one of the ultimate supercars that can be sold in America. For that fact alone, it is a very significant car.

The Turbo fires easily, and it fires not with the normal sound of a Porsche but with the deep burble usually found only with V8s. The sound is aggressive, but it is not loud. Relative quiet, as well as very low emissions, are a side benefit of turbocharging. The idle is even, there is no fuss; the injection looks after it all. Nick Faure, who drives the AFN Carrera 3-litre race car, is in the driver's seat. I'm beside him, and we've come to a country where we can drive this car properly. It is the Turbo shown at Earls Court, the only RHD prototype (production does not begin until February) and so far as we know this is probably the first time a Turbo has been taken on the road by outsiders to be driven to its full potential.

We move off; the solid torque is noticeable, the engine's incredible willingness to rev unmistakable. But Nick obviously isn't using more than a modest pressure on the throttle and we're still talking cheerily and we don't seem to be accelerating hard; only moving at a pace that feels briskly natural in the car. But glance at the speedo, my friend, and see that already, as we drift easily into mid-range in third, we're doing well over 90mph. It is unintended, we have merely moved away just as one might do in a suburban street in a family car, using the available torque to bring smooth, steady and sustained performance but certainly not wringing the engine out. That is what the Turbo is like.

Have I become blasé about such power? Do I adjust too quickly to this sort of performance after experiencing the Countach and the BB? I don't know, but it most certainly isn't frightening performance, quick and all as it is. You can feel the quick thrust of the power, but it is so smooth and so progressive; not at all like the BMW Turbo which goes tamely until it reaches 4000rpm when the turbo comes in to thrust the car forward as if a second engine has cut in. There's none of that in the Porsche, no peakiness although you can detect that the pull comes steadily faster after 3000rpm. There are, however, certain things that must be learnt. From 3000rpm onwards the turbocharger keeps boosting (roughly speaking) so that even without increased pressure on the throttle the car accelerates. It isn't strong acceleration within the Turbo's capabilities, but it's potent by normal standards. Understanding this self-acceleration and knowing how to adjust to it is the secret of driving the Turbo. You're constantly backing off.

Hard acceleration? The car dips its rounded tail low over its wheels and you're pressed hard back into the seat, moulding into it. And then, if you look not out the windscreen but out the side windows at the guide posts or other traffic, then you really do know that you're reaching 60mph in five seconds and 100mph in a staggering 12.8sec. At 6500rpm, Porsche's recommended maximum (there is an electric cut-out hidden among the red), the gears give 49mph, 85 and 124. Porsche say only that the top speed is 'above 155mph'. Later I am to learn that they are not wrong.

But for the moment we're caught in a village and Nick is checking that 'self-acceleration' characteristic again, still learning about it. 'Say you put it into second,' he explains, 'and drop back to 2000rpm. You then stroke the throttle very quietly and the thing builds up to 3500rpm without any further pressure, and then it *goes* of its own

TURNING ON TO THE TURBO

accord! See, I'm not putting any pressure on it at the moment, and it's just going faster and faster . . .

'It's surprising how quickly you adapt to this, though, and I think the only time it would really catch you out is on a very twisty road. Even a very good driver could be tricked then—say you're at 2500rpm in second, halfway through a bend with the revs building up. You hit 3500rpm and the power *really* comes on fiercely and you're caught in bloody big oversteer. You have to develop a technique where you back off at the right moment, instead of powering on, to achieve the same cornering balance as in an ordinary car.' He grins: 'I learnt last night that on a greasy road the tail can come around frighteningly fast. Mind you, it comes back very nicely. But you have to be bloody quick—and that's by race standards! I drove it over a road where I regularly drive the 3-litre Carrera hard. It's so much quicker than even that one, and very much more demanding because of the intricacies of the throttle control.'

We're on an Autobahn now, unrestricted by any speed limit, and we're running at a tame 130mph. He can't resist a gentle squeeze on the throttle. The car responds instantly, surging silkily forward, letting us feel the power in the small of the back. Is this how a champion race horse feels when you slacken the reins? It wants to keep on going, and a concerted lift-off is needed. But then, stuff it, we go all the way, the Turbo *hurling* itself forward, speeding on to 160mph before traffic blocks our path. Even Faure is staggered; the top gear acceleration is equal to third gear in his racing Carrera 3-litre, and that has a five-speed gearbox. From 100mph to 130mph, the acceleration is incredibly strong because that corresponds to the peak point of the torque curve. But right now, our 160mph is just a shade over 6000rpm, and there is undoubtedly more to come. From the feel of it the 6500rpm redline should be obtainable, and that's 168mph. I wouldn't be surprised if owners find such figures registering on their dials.

And, when circumstances permit, why on earth shouldn't they do it? The car is rock-steady, moving not an inch from its path. Faure backs off totally and even then it doesn't budge. You can't get better than that (but anything less would be unacceptable, of course). To reach this speed, you've been through a range of noises—the faint whine of the turbocharger as the power comes on strong in the lower gears, the burble you'd swear was coming from a V8 on a light throttle at around 3500 rpm, and the low, sustained sort of rumble which increases steadily in intensity as the throttle goes down. It never intrudes, mind you, merely serves as a pleasing background. There is, however, windnoise around the window edges. It could become tiring on a very long trip at high speed, but isn't loud enough to prevent easy conversation.

The motorway ride is exemplary; even at town speeds it is excellent, feeling little firmer than in the standard 911, and never, never making a sound as it soaks up the bumps. Off the autobahn now and in towards a village. Faure doesn't bother to change down, simply backs off from 140mph and comes down a 25-mph trickle in top with only 1000 rpm showing. We go up a hill like that; the car grumbles not. It makes only a very low, exaggerated sort of Porsche noise up through the gearstick. Next stop and we move a few feet in first and then it's straight into top at 500rpm up. Again, no complaints. It pulls away cleanly.

But then it's the real road we've been seeking, the equivalent of a good British A-road, and in a moment the Porsche is pressing through its curling bends at a steady 140mph. There is no body roll, no effort from the driver other than moving the wheel very slightly and adjusting the throttle minutely to guide the car gently onto the precise line, straight-lining them. I casually continue making notes. An Alfetta, I should think, would have felt similarly unfussed along here at about 90; one of the big front-engined V12s at around 120mph. Only a Countach, BB or Bora would do it like this.

We try the brakes, and end up backing off from a full crash stop in case it is too much for the tyres. The perforated, vented discs do not fade. Then the bends come quicker and tighter, and sometimes there are crests. Over one of them, in the middle of a kink that has become an S-bend at our speed, the car rises, sinks low on its suspension as it touches down and soaks up the impact as if nothing has happened and without any sound. It is at times like this that you know how much quality is in the damping, how much stability the thing has, for it does not deviate from its line.

Nick Faure is really into this car now, almost at peace with the power, and he sights beautifully through a right-hander. The power goes on hard in second, the opposite lock is cranked on early to counteract it; to negate it. Balance it out. It's precisely right and we exit in strong, full-blooded oversteer, tyres yowling and exhaust grumbling.

I hopped out to take an outside look a while later. Nick accelerated away hard after dropping me, and all I could do was to stand on the grass verge and say Christ! over and over again as I witnessed the car's pace and I heard its unique bellow from just a few feet away. It's a sound that stops you dead in your tracks, dramatic and startling rather than beautiful. From the outside, watching it sweep fully sideways through the bends, was breathtaking and educational: it was just as flat as it had felt from inside.

We continued on for two more hours, driving the car hard but not to its limits, for even Nick Faure, who owns two Porsches and races a factory car and who is a superb road driver, could not yet extend it that far. We both learnt certain home truths though: the Dunlop tyres ride well and aren't noisy, but they can be a little untidy in their actions; there is about one 10th of a second lag in throttle response (an astute driver can just detect it) so that overtaking and full power application in bends need slight anticipation. The seats prove to be perfect, never letting you move even when taking bends at what felt to me to be well over 1g.

Back in London, we had a drink and tried to tell friends what it had been like. We weren't really conscious that we'd blasted along by-roads at 140mph, that we'd seen 160mph on the autobahn. The speeds were all in perspective, worthy of note only for comparison's sake. We knew only that we'd enjoyed many hundreds of miles of exquisite motoring; supercar motoring that only two other cars can achieve at this point in time. And still the Porsche had more to give.

In February, the first production Turbos should start arriving. It is probable, if taxation and exchange values remain stable, that they will cost £14,000. Already Porsche GB are holding 12 fully deposited orders with eight more probables. The car will come as a complete package with automatic interior heating sensors to maintain temperature at a pre-set level, leather interior with special tartan inlays, special carpet, electronic speedometer, stereo radio/cassette deck with four speakers, headlight washers, rear window wiper, heated windscreen, two-stage heating for the rear window, electric windows and tinted glass all-round. Fog lamps will be standard, there'll be an electric sunroof and a plug-in pump for the emergency blow-up spare wheel.

The buyer will want for nothing. He will get a 20,000-mile/12-month warranty, his car will require nothing more than the normal 12,000-mile Porsche servicing. He should return from 18 to 22mpg in everyday driving. And even if the Stuttgart engineers merely see the Turbo as the latest in their technology being made available to customers, Porsche GB, conscious that they're stepping up into a new market where the purchase price is very steep, are considering offering customers some special facilities. An advanced driving course could be one example. Whatever they decide upon, the idea is to make the owners feel that they're getting something special for their £14,000.

But I don't know that Porsche GB need to do that: one ride, a real ride, like mine, in this superlative machine and no owner could fail to know that he has something special; something *very* special. ●

YOUR MOTHER WOULDN'T LIKE IT.

From British Leyland
Makers of the best selling cars in Britain

94·5 bhp. 109 mph. 0-50 in 8·0 seconds.* £1393·06†

† Including car tax and V.A.T. Number plates, seat belts and delivery charges extra. *Source Motor

MGB

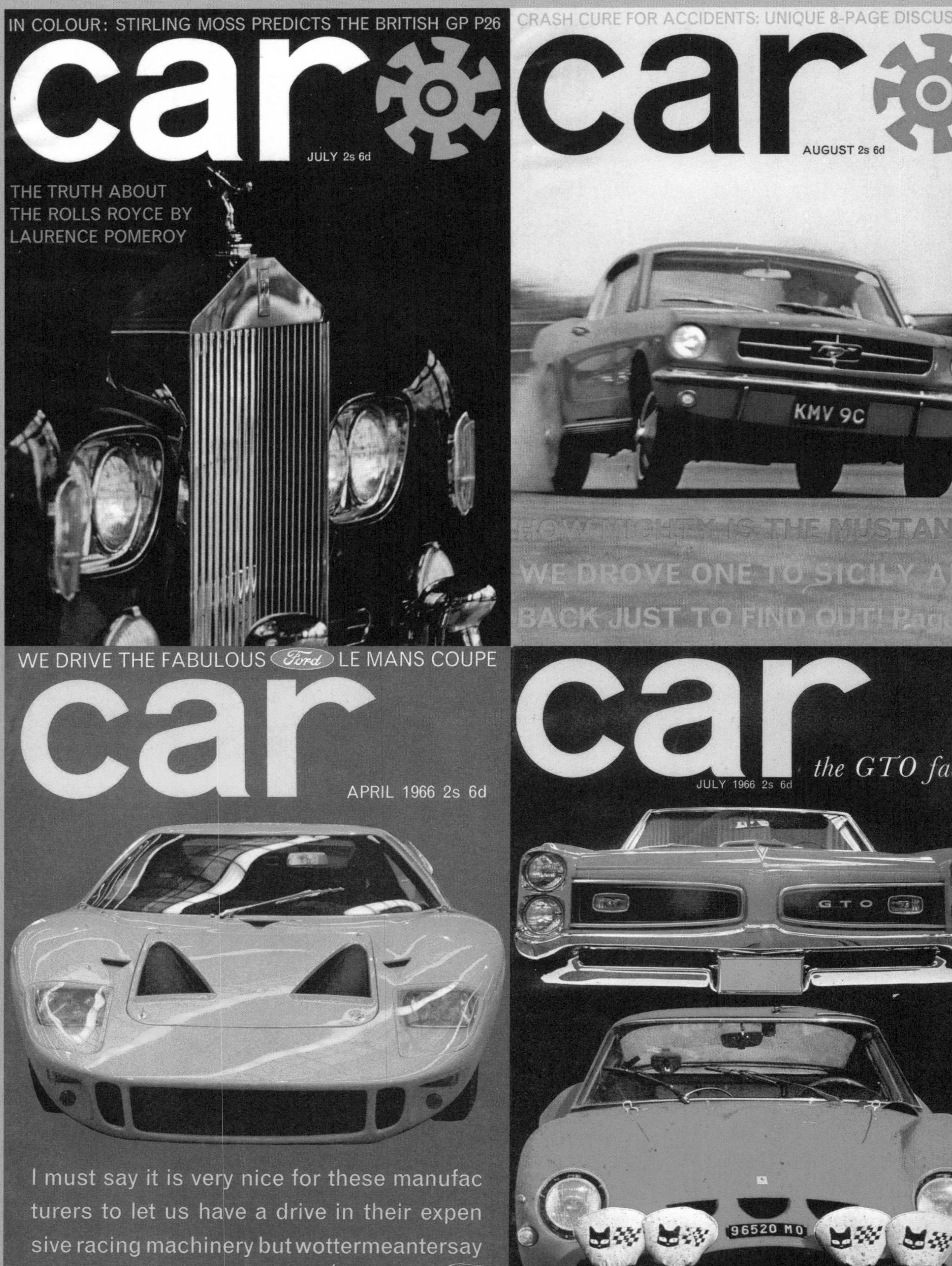
IN COLOUR: STIRLING MOSS PREDICTS THE BRITISH GP P26
car
JULY 2s 6d
THE TRUTH ABOUT
THE ROLLS ROYCE BY
LAURENCE POMEROY
CRASH CURE FOR ACCIDENTS: UNIQUE 8-PAGE DISCUSSI
car
AUGUST 2s 6d
KMV 9C
HOW MIGHTY IS THE MUSTANG
WE DROVE ONE TO SICILY AN
BACK JUST TO FIND OUT! Page
WE DRIVE THE FABULOUS Ford LE MANS COUPE
car
APRIL 1966 2s 6d
I must say it is very nice for these manufac
turers to let us have a drive in their expen
sive racing machinery but wottermeantersay
is that it is all part of some / PAGE 27
car
the GTO fact
JULY 1966 2s 6d
GTO
96520 MO